Building the Interfaith
Youth Movement

Building the Interfaith Youth Movement

Beyond Dialogue to Action

EDITED BY EBOO PATEL AND PATRICE BRODEUR

ROWMAN & LITTLEFIELD PUBLISHERS, INC.
Lanham • Boulder • New York • Toronto • Oxford

ROWMAN & LITTLEFIELD PUBLISHERS, INC.

Published in the United States of America
by Rowman & Littlefield Publishers, Inc.
A wholly owned subsidiary of The Rowman & Littlefield Publishing Group, Inc.
4501 Forbes Boulevard, Suite 200, Lanham, Maryland 20706
www.rowmanlittlefield.com

P.O. Box 317, Oxford OX2 9RU, UK

British Library Cataloguing in Publication Information Available

Library of Congress Cataloging-in-Publication Data

Building the interfaith youth movement : beyond dialogue to action / edited by Eboo
    Patel and Patrice Brodeur.
        p. cm.
    Includes bibliographical references and index.
    ISBN-13: 978-0-7425-5066-7 (cloth : alk. paper)
    ISBN-10: 0-7425-5066-4 (cloth : alk. paper)
    ISBN-13: 978-0-7425-5067-4 (pbk. : alk. paper)
    ISBN-10: 0-7425-5067-2 (pbk. : alk. paper)
    1. Religions—Relations. 2. Youth—Religious life. I. Patel, Eboo, 1975– II. Brodeur,
Patrice, 1962–

BL410.B85 2006
201'.50835—dc22

                                                                    2005057437

Printed in the United States of America

♾™ The paper used in this publication meets the minimum requirements of American
National Standard for Information Sciences—Permanence of Paper for Printed Library
Materials, ANSI/NISO Z39.48-1992.

Contents

Acknowledgments   vii

Preface   *Diana L. Eck*   ix

Introduction   *Patrice Brodeur and*   1
                                 Eboo Patel

Section I: Contexts of Interfaith Youth Work

1   Affirming Identity, Achieving Pluralism   *Eboo Patel*   15

2   Young Adult Development, Religious   *James P. Keen*   25
     Identity, and Interreligious Solidarity
     in an Interfaith Learning Community

3   Theologies of Interreligious Encounters   *J. Nathan Kline*   43
     and Their Relevance to Youth

Section II: International Interfaith Organizations

4   Towards a Transnational Interfaith   *Patrice Brodeur*   51
     Youth Network in Higher Education

5   The Gujarat Young Adult Project of   *Zulfikhar Akram and*   65
     the International Association for   *Ramola Sundram*
     Religious Freedom (IARF)

6   Youth Leadership   *Sarah Talcott*   75

7   The Next Generation   *Josh Borkin*   83

Section III: Higher Education

8   Youth and the Pluralism Project   *Grove Harris*   91

9   Seminarians Interacting   *Karen Wood*   101

10   Towards a Multifaith Community   *Victor H. Kazanjian, Jr.* 109
     at Wellesley College

11   Bringing Interfaith to   *Savva Amusin, Sarah Bier,* 125
     the University of Illinois   *Arielle Hertzberg, Rozina*
                                                Kanchwala, Nicholas Price,
                                                and Alison Siegel

12   Articulating What Is at Stake   *Alison L. Boden*   131
     in Interreligous Work

Section IV: Secondary Education

13 Teaching World Religions   *Jane S. Rechtman*   137

14 Secondary School Teacher Training   *David Streight*   147
in Religious Studies

15 Training Teachers in   *Matthew Weiner*   155
American Religious Diversity   *and Timur Yuskaev*

Section V: Community-Based Projects

16 The Interfaith Youth Core   *Eboo Patel*   169
and Mariah Neuroth

17 The Interfaith Youth Leadership Council   *Julie Eberly*   181
of the Interfaith Ministries for
Greater Houston

18 The High School Youth Program   *Michael Goggin*   185
of the InterFaith Conference of
Metropolitan Washington

19 The Sacred Stories Project of   *Joe Hall*   199
the Ghetto Film School   *and Andrew Unger*

Section VI: Immersion Projects

20 Spirit into Action   *Annapurna Astley*   209

21 E Pluribus Unum   *Sidney Schwarz*   219

22 The Chicago Interfaith Service House   *Lori Eisenberg*   225

23 Face to Face/Faith to Faith   *Katharine Henderson*   233
and Melodye Feldman

Section VII: Pastoral Work

24 Ask Pastor Paul   *Paul Raushenbush*   245

Conclusion   *Eboo Patel*   257

Epilogue   *Imam Feisal Abdul Rauf*   263

Index   265

About the Contributors   269

Acknowledgments

We ARE ENORMOUSLY GRATEFUL to everybody who helped make this book happen. First and foremost, we would like to thank all the contributors to this book. They are not only fellow pioneers in the interfaith youth movement, but also close friends. We would also like to thank Erik Hanson at Rowman & Littlefield Publishers, Inc. for working with us to publish this volume, and Brin Stevens for her excellent editing.

This book could not have been compiled without the time and talent of Jeff Clinger, Alex Frell-Levy, and other members of the Interfaith Youth Core staff.

We are grateful for the support of our friends, mentors, and colleagues at various interfaith organizations, including the Council for a Parliament of the World's Religions, the International Interfaith Centre, Religions for Peace, the United Religions Initiative, the Temple of Understanding, the Cordoba Initiative, *CrossCurrents* Magazine, and many others.

We want to thank our teachers at Harvard, Oxford, and the Institute of Ismaili Studies—particularly Diana Eck, Geoffrey Walford and Azim Nanji—who always encouraged us to break new ground and build new institutions.

Finally, we want to thank all the young people we have met around the world who have said *no* to the path of bombings and *yes* to the way of bridges.

Preface

Diana L. Eck

THIS BOOK IS THE FIRST FRUITS of a revolution, the most important and ultimately consequential revolution of our time: the interfaith revolution. Gone are the days when we could imagine that the religious worlds of our various families of faith do not overlap and intersect. The encounter of people of different faiths is the hallmark of our times. It may be a dangerous encounter where difference is wielded as a weapon of conflict. It may be a passive and inattentive encounter where difference is glossed over or avoided. Or it may be an intentional encounter, where people of different faiths set out to get to know one another—to work together, talk together, and serve together in the hard work of bridge-building. Whether we analyze the religious dynamics of the world of the twenty-first century from a global, national, or local standpoint, ours is a world of profound diversity, a world marbled with many ethnic groups, cultural traditions, and families of faith. Immigration has changed the demographics of our societies, including that of the United States and Canada and made us aware of the interfaith challenge as never before.

The generation of young adults whose interfaith initiatives and projects have been gathered into this volume are the leading edge of this revolution. The multiple sources that have given rise to these projects and the converging energy they represent are signals of a broad and significant movement. After all, a movement is not a single organization. In fact, it is not an organization at all. It has no single center, but is constituted by a multiform energy moving in the same direction, producing powerful currents, gradually reshaping the landscape.

This generation of young people is what we might call the first "interfaith generation." Anyone under thirty today in the U.S. and Canada has grown up in a religious and cultural world markedly different from that of their parents. For those of us in the United States, the newest wave of immigration, beginning in 1965 with the Immigration and Naturalization Act, has brought people from every part of the world and every religious tradition to our shores. For all of us, these past decades have meant the re-framing of our "we" as Americans, recognizing in new ways an enlarged and more diverse national community. These decades have also challenged us as never before to live up to our promise of religious freedom and freedom of conscience. These have been both exciting and turbulent times. As our religious landscape has become more complex, interfaith councils, Abrahamic dialogues, interfaith services, and interfaith service projects have become part of that landscape in cities and towns all over America.

For the "interfaith generation," this new multireligious America has been the very sea in which they swim. They have lived it, grown up with it. They have gone to high school with a far more diverse student body than their parents. They have entered college and, by now, entered the workforce with friends, fellow students, and co-workers from many religious traditions. This generation does not need to be convinced of the challenge of religious identity in a multireligious society. It is the clear, everyday challenge of their social and civic world. While their parents and grandparents may not be as alert to the full impact of our increasingly multireligious society, students and young adults have known this reality from their schooldays on.

Over the past two decades, I have taught a course at Harvard University called "World Religions, Diversity, and Dialogue." We study the ways in which people in each tradition articulate and interpret their faith in the fast-paced and fast-changing world in which we now live. And we ask how people in each tradition think about the "religious other." How do Christians or Muslims, Jews or Hindus, address religious difference? Is religious difference a problem to be solved? Does the religious "other" represent an opportunity for mission? An opportunity for engagement and learning? An opportunity to "compete in righteousness," as some Muslims would say? At the beginning of the course, I ask each student to write an essay about the most significant encounter he or she has had with a person of another faith. What was the nature of the encounter? Why was it significant? For those who are not religious, I ask them to write about an encounter with someone who is.

The range of responses, which I have collected over the years, gives us a glimpse of just how deep in this generation the interfaith encounter goes. In the mid-1980s, there were Baptists who wrote of their encounter with Catholics, Jews who wrote of their friends who were Lutheran. There was the Methodist boy who had traveled to India and was stopped in his tracks by his encounter with Hindu ritual traditions in Banaras. By the mid-1990s, however, the encounter essays were becoming as complex as our society. "My mother is half-Filipino, half-Mexican, and a strict Catholic. My father is Chinese and his family members are devout Buddhists. This has been my life. While my parents agreed to raise us in the Catholic Church when they married, still my father could not forget the Buddhist practice that had long been part of his childhood and family. He taught us the ways of meditation, and I recall family trips to Buddhist temples, even as I was going to Sunday school and preparing for my first Holy Communion."

Another young woman wrote, "I didn't know about the Hindu temple in Pittsburgh until last summer, when my boyfriend, Vinay, a first-generation Indian-American took me to visit. He had attended Hindu summer camps in western Pennsylvania. I had attended Mass in my Roman Catholic Church every Sunday of my life. I had never been to a Hindu temple."

A Catholic student from Houston wrote about her best friend in high school, a Muslim girl, a brilliant soccer player, who sat out the end of the season on the bench because she was observing the Ramadan fast. Not eating or drinking from sunrise to sunset, she could not run up and down the field in the hot sun. Even so, her presence encouraged everyone—and so did the witness to her faith.

A Mormon sophomore wrote, "There we were in the dorm room—a Muslim, a Christian Scientist, a Catholic agnostic, and me. We sat eating pizza and planning our joint project on the Oslo Accords and Jerusalem." A Methodist student described his junior year rooming group: "We include a Pakistani Muslim, a non-practicing Hindu American, a Chinese with leanings toward Confucianism, a devout Evangelical Christian from South Africa, and me, a Methodist from Minnesota. We have, in a sense, formed an experiment in acceptance, understanding, and dialogue."

The diversity of cultural and faith backgrounds is noted by these students with some self-consciousness as they reflect on and write about their own experience. At the same time, this very diversity is taken for granted in the working environment of students today. Every meeting is, in one sense, an interfaith meeting—even if it is not explicitly named as such. Every class is, demographically, an interfaith class—even if it is a class in English literature.

The interfaith youth movement springs from this new reality and steers into it with all the energy, the questioning, the curiosity, and the commitment that comes with young adulthood. As this generation comes to leadership in religious and civic life, we might well expect that the interfaith movement will expand from a budding revolution to a widespread cultural consensus.

Introduction:
Building the Interfaith Youth Movement

Patrice Brodeur and Eboo Patel

FORTY YEARS AGO, in a book titled *Where Do We Go From Here: Chaos or Community*, Martin Luther King, Jr. introduced an image called "the world house":

> This is the great new problem of mankind. We have inherited a large house, a great "world house" in which we have to live together—black and white, Easterner and Westerner, Gentile and Jew, Catholic and Protestant, Moslem and Hindu—a family unduly separated in ideas, culture and interest, who, because we can never again live apart, we must somehow learn to live with each other in peace.[1]

Americans living at the time of King's writing, in the mid-1960s, were probably surprised by this statement. In the first place, King was traditionally associated with inter-racial bridge-building in the United States. His emphasis on global interfaith cooperation must have struck them as somewhere between incomprehensible and irrelevant. Moreover, this was an era where prominent Western academics, star struck by the promise of science and impressed by the penetration of secular ideologies, arrogantly prophesied that religion would soon disappear from the face of the earth. In the United States, the religious conflicts that characterized the turn of the twentieth century had subsided, and tolerance between Catholics, Protestants and Jews became normative. Race was the dominant domestic conflict, and the Vietnam War, fought over secular ideologies, divided Americans on their role in the world.

Today, King's words seem prescient. At the dawn of the twentieth century, the United States is the world's most religiously diverse nation playing a central role in a global era characterized by religious conflict.

This book is based in America with the understanding that its editors, authors, and topics are part of "the world house." Patrice Brodeur's notion of the "glocal"[2] provides a conceptual lens through which this dynamic can be understood. The local is where the global happens. For example, a medium-sized Montreal high school discovered that thirty of its students had either been child soldiers themselves or had witnessed warfare firsthand. Though they now dress and behave like other young people, their experiences of organized violence shape their understanding of everything from video games to high school cliques. Glocal describes the dynamics of our respective local contexts and the impact of our behaviors globally, wherever we happen to be in the world. Glocal also characterizes both the context of this book, a new religious America, and its content. Both will be explained in turn.

"A New Religious America"

This book seeks to understand the emergence of a global interfaith youth movement through the unique lenses of a rapidly changing U.S. religious landscape, what Diana Eck has called "A New Religious America."[3] The 1965 Immigration and Naturalization Act resulted, a generation later, in a radically new religious landscape: in addition to a more ethnically diverse Christian population and stronger evangelical churches, there are now perhaps six million Muslims, four million Buddhists, one million Hindus, a quarter million Sikhs, and probably a few million adherents to a variety of Caribbean religious and spiritual practices that have not been so easily countable; there are also countless new religious movements. While many of the immigrants from this post-1965 era fashioned social lives outside of the American mainstream, their U.S.-born and raised children study algebra in public schools, play basketball at YMCAs, major in sociology at Ivy League institutions, kick rhymes in urban hip hop ciphers, walk police beats in leafy suburbs, join medical staffs in small-town hospitals, and participate in American life in every other conceivable way. The United States is faced with the challenge that Wilfred Cantwell Smith raised when he lived during the 1940s in the religiously diverse city of Lahore, located in present-day Pakistan: "to learn to live together with our seriously different traditions not only in peace but in some sort of mutual trust and mutual loyalty."[4]

In the past several decades, a number of social responses to this challenge have emerged. One response is that of the extremist movements characterized by bigotry and bias. They are telling new Americans, often in violent ways, "We don't want to live together with you." A second response is to assume that people do not bring their faith identities into social situations, and therefore religion need not be a part of public discourse. A third response is to view religion as one more element in an individualistic, laissez-faire culture, and watch with detached interest as people mix and match religious identities. A fourth response is to recognize that people's religious identities impact everything from their private lives to their community institutions to our public square, and understand that a religiously plural society, if it wishes to have harmony amongst its various religious communities, must be proactive about dealing with matters of religious diversity.

We, of the emerging interfaith youth movement, not only hold the fourth position, we act from it. Our basic premise is that not only the United States but the whole world has plenty of "faith," and a healthy amount of "inter," but not enough "interfaith."[5] Regarding "faith," there are many spaces where people from particular religious backgrounds gather to discuss their respective faiths: synagogues, mosques, churches, temples, gurdwaras, etc. Increasingly, many of them understand the importance of also teaching something about other religions, what Eck and others call "developing religious literacy." But if members of other religions are not present, as in the example of a Christian pastor giving a talk on Islam to his Church's youth group, such activity cannot be considered "interfaith," even though it is certainly a step in the right direction.

Regarding "inter," while religiously diverse young people interact in classrooms, playgrounds, and shopping malls every day, unless those interactions intentionally deal with matters of religion, they also cannot be considered truly interfaith. Too often, in our everyday encounters in spaces that bring together people of diverse backgrounds, perhaps felt most acutely in schools, the religious dimensions in the lives of our younger generation remain, at best, silent, and at worst, rejected.

Learning to talk about the variety of religious identities, among many other kinds of overlapping identities, requires active and self-reflective interfaith activities. These activities must be integrated into a wide set of both formal and informal programs. They can result in the promotion of pluralism, that is, a philosophy that seeks deliberate and positive engagement between people of different backgrounds.

The challenge of how to manage these diverse identities so as to promote a healthy pluralism is being faced in all countries that have a high degree of ethnic and religious diversity. This challenge may be more acute, however, in societies with high immigration levels. For example, like the United States, Canada and Australia have also experienced a high degree of demographic transformation in a combination of ethnic and religious terms. However, in comparison, three characteristics make the new religious America stand out. First, the immigration numbers are much greater in the U.S. than anywhere else in the world. Second, because of its weight in international politics and global neo-liberal economics, the impact of new hyphenated religious-American identities is being felt worldwide. Third, the rapid transformation in the American religious landscape post-1965 coincided with an already strong intra-Christian ecumenical and bilateral Christian-Jewish dialogue, resulting in a full-fledged multilateral dialogue, with a subset of many bilateral and sometimes trilateral (i.e., Jewish-Christian-Muslim) dialogues. This trend culminated with the 1993 centennial celebrations of the first Parliament of the World's Religions held in Chicago, with more than 8,000 participants.

The reactions to the terrible events of September 11 only strengthened the interfaith movement in the U.S. In fact, the interfaith movement moved from periphery to center three days later, when following the call by President Bush for a national day of mourning on Friday, September 14, most major urban centers throughout the U.S. responded with interfaith mourning ceremonies. Their organizers aimed to be as inclusive as possible not only because of their own growingly diverse populations, but also to respect the fact that people of many different religious and non-religious perspectives perished on that day.

In the U.S., the early 1990s saw the emergence of a number of projects that brought young people from different religious communities together to engage religion in intentional and positive ways. Over the past several years, the founders and leaders of these programs found one another, began sharing best practices and common frustrations, and started viewing themselves as a movement. A national organization, the Interfaith Youth Core, emerged to network these various interfaith youth projects, as well as to encourage new projects and strengthen the collective movement.

All of the above elements demonstrate how the U.S. landscape has fostered internally the growth of the interfaith movement. As no country is an island on its own, especially with the growth in the degree of interdependence that the information technology revolution has created in recent years, this new U.S. religious landscape has also affected the interfaith movement externally. Both the impact of the U.S. discourse on democracy worldwide, whatever may be the specifics of its supporters and detractors recently, as well as its unique set of approaches to secularism philosophically and ideologically, represent key elements that explain in part how the interfaith movement has been able to grow exponentially in the late twentieth and early twenty-first centuries. In other words, many American citizens—and in this respect Canadians and the British can be included too—have also exported their understanding of interfaith work and what place it can play in promoting the common good around the world.

These elements are often implicit in the intended meaning of many authors' contributions. Our role as editors is to make them explicit, so that the readers may understand that our selection is indeed limited and biased toward this new U.S. religious landscape. This book is a starting point in gathering a set of voices that have developed creative interfaith activities and curricula. It serves as one example of how to strengthen international networks of interfaith youth activists. We hope that this set can be greatly expanded in a second book, so as to reflect the true global nature of the interfaith movement whose history still awaits writing.

Definitions

The questions surrounding the definition of key terms abound in any academic discipline. The central concept of "youth" and its related "young adult" is no exception. While it is possible to distinguish both as we have done above, most people in general and our authors in particular do not. In order to minimize the desire to impose a systematic definition through editorial policy, each author's voice remains unchanged. The result is a juxtaposition of implicit and explicit definitions. For heuristic purposes only, we loosely define youth as people between the ages of fourteen and twenty-five years.

In the academic study of religion, no definition of the concepts "religion" or "faith" is agreed upon either, even less so "inter-religious" and "interfaith." There is a tendency to find the word "interfaith" in more Protestant circles and the word "inter-religious" in Roman Catholic ones. In this book, we follow the definition of "interfaith" offered earlier, bringing together people from diverse religious backgrounds to intentionally engage religion.

Finally, if we are to talk about "an interfaith youth movement," it is also important to address the definition of the concept "movement." A movement is a group of people committed to making an idea a reality. The idea of the interfaith youth movement is that young people from different backgrounds can come together to build better understanding and cooperation for the common good of humanity as a whole. In a world where too many young people are on the front lines of conflicts that are often partially characterized by competing religious identities, our work is of the utmost importance.

Content

Building the Interfaith Youth Movement is the first attempt at collecting the experiences of a range of interfaith youth projects into a book. We recognize from the outset that our choice of articles is heavily influenced by our personal context as scholars living in the U.S. While both of us have traveled worldwide and experienced firsthand interfaith activities outside North America, our network is stronger in this region of the world. The selection of most articles has emerged from a first U.S. national gathering of interfaith youth activists organized by the Interfaith Youth Core at the University of Chicago Divinity School in May 2003. In addition, both of us have been influenced by the work of the Pluralism Project at Harvard University, directed by Diana Eck.

The goal of this book is to begin building a knowledge base in the field of interfaith youth work. Unlike most academically oriented books, there is a distinctly personal flavor to many of the articles included herein. The reason is simple: those of us in the interfaith youth movement take this work to heart. Many of us are people of faith acutely aware that we are living in a religiously diverse society that cuts to the core of our identities. Therefore, the following articles share not only the model of our respective interfaith youth projects, but also our inspiration for starting them. Our faith traditions provide guidance not only for why we are involved in interfaith work; they guide us as to how we conduct this work. Mike Goggin, in his article on the Interfaith Conference of Metropolitan Washington, D.C., describes how his calling to be a Catholic youth minister led him to interfaith youth work. Grove Harris writes about how imagery in her Wiccan faith contributes to how she manages the most important research project on religious diversity in the U.S., and the Pluralism Project at Harvard University.

Most of the articles gathered here were first delivered as papers at the first National Interfaith Youth Work Conference organized by the Interfaith Youth Core at the University of Chicago Divinity School in May 2003. It was supported by grants from the Ford Foundation and the Pluralism Project at Harvard University and many participants also contributed toward their own travel expenses. This conference was conceived to juxtapose academic and activist tracks to reflect the way of the broader interfaith youth movement. By combining knowledge production with concrete program and curricula development, as well as networking opportunities, we can transform the burgeoning interfaith youth movement into an important social force for the common good of humanity.

This book is situated at the intersection of six academic disciplines and their respective applied fields: religious studies, sociology, education, youth studies, community studies, and leadership studies. It includes articles that contain a combination of personal, methodological, descriptive, and analytical reflections on interfaith youth projects. These articles represent a wealth of empirical data on the interfaith youth movement and the beginnings of its theorization. Authors were selected not only for the role they have played in building interfaith youth work projects, but also because they represent a new generation of scholar-practitioners in the emerging academic field of interfaith studies.

One of our goals in this movement is to empower each other to pioneer new cooperative and transformative learning paths at the same time as we make room for critical self-reflection through which scholarship can be produced as another tool for empowerment. Our hope is that this book will serve both as a guide to those who want to organize interfaith youth work in their own local contexts as well as an invitation to join the community of people building this movement.

The introduction and conclusion, combined with the first section, provide a contextual and theoretical understanding of the interfaith youth movement. In the introduction, we locate our movement within the current social reality of religious diversity in the United States of America and the various academic fields with which we interact. In the conclusion, we highlight some of the stickiest theoretical, theological, and political issues in interfaith youth work. We also look to where our movement is heading and offer our thoughts on what we need to do now to get there. We also suggest providing adequate space within our movement so these issues can be appropriately engaged. The introduction and conclusion provide the theoretical and intentional bookends for this book.

The first section, contexts, includes three theoretical chapters that examine the field of interfaith youth studies through a specific academic discipline. Eboo Patel's chapter contextualizes interfaith youth work within sociological theory. The chapter by Jim Keen provides a crucial psychological perspective into the age group known as "youth." His chapter uses empirical data from the E Pluribus Unum project (described more fully in a later article by Sidney Schwartz) and articulates the changes that religious adolescents experienced in the course of this intensive interfaith program. Finally, the chapter by Nathan Kline provides a theological framework for understanding interfaith youth work. Kline relies largely on Christian models. We hope that this is the beginning of the discussion of theology and interfaith youth work and expect Kline's chapter to be responded to by people of other religious traditions. By juxtaposing these three chapter in the first section and recognizing that this selection is by no means exhaustive, our methodological intention becomes clear: multi- and inter-disciplinarity are a sine qua non for understanding and engaging the theoretical conversation around this new field of study and action.

We have organized the rest of the chapters into six categories: International Interfaith Organizations, Higher Education, Secondary Education, Community-Based Projects, Immersion Projects, and Pastoral Work. We expect most people who read this book to turn first to the section most relevant to them. We hope that when the reader has finished that section, he or she will be attracted to other sections too. A high school instructor teaching a "World Religions" course in a religiously diverse classroom will naturally turn her attention immediately to the section on secondary education. But high school students take part in community programs, often go on to college, join international organizations, get involved in immersion projects, and occasionally need pastoral attention too!

Section two includes four chapters written by the youth directors of international interfaith organizations. In the first chapter, Patrice Brodeur describes the youth network of the World Conference on Religion and Peace, paying particular attention both to its transnational nature and the local project that he nurtured at Harvard University. Ramola Sundram and Zulfikar Akram focus on a project of the International Association for Religious Freedom in India. This chapter is particularly important because it articulates how interfaith youth work can play a role in preventing conflict during times of communal tensions. It is also the only chapter in this collection that represents an organization based outside of the United States. Sarah Talcott presents how the United Religions Initiative has used the appreciative inquiry methodology to effectively organize intergenerational, international, and interfaith programs. Josh Borkin's chapter discusses the "Next Generation" program of the Parliament of the World's Religions. Together, these four chapters demonstrate how important the role of youth has become in major international interfaith organizations and what variety of methodologies have emerged to begin mobilizing religious youth worldwide.

The next three sections all focus on various aspects of education. The new public face of multi-religious America is accompanied by a new awareness of the urgency to foster tolerance and respect of diverse worldviews in all educational institutions, including religious ones. If education, whether in private or public schools, does not help make sense of this diversity of worldviews, the next generation will be even more easily manipulated, with great negative social impact in the long term. Paying attention in all of our educational institutions to youth and young adults in terms of these central questions of meaning, especially at an age when their worldviews are being shaped for decades to come, is a challenge addressed in different ways by most of the authors included in this book. A number of interfaith organizations embarked on developing interfaith education conferences and activities, many of which are mentioned in this book's articles. Both educators (in public and private settings) and interfaith activists have participated in this on-going explosion of attention to the educational dimensions of our respective and often overlapping faith and interfaith activities.

Section three focuses on five examples of interfaith student projects that have emerged on American campuses of higher education. Although these articles represent a range of possibilities for doing interfaith work on college campuses, they are only the tip of the iceberg. The explosion of interfaith activities witnessed on university campuses in the 1990s continues to expand in the first decade of the twenty-first century. Still, there is a clear need to do more. College students are at a point in their lives where they are negotiating complex identity issues. This identity development is occurring in a politically charged hothouse environment where different religious communities are in frequent and intense contact with religious conflict unfolding elsewhere, the Middle

East being only one case in point. Campuses need to provide opportunities for religiously diverse students to interact in a constructive manner, characterized by civil discourse.

In this third section, the first chapter by Grove Harris describes the Pluralism Project at Harvard University, founded by Diana Eck. The majority of the researchers in this project have been religiously diverse undergraduate and graduate students. Harris's article explores the culture created by the interaction of these researchers, the work they produced, and the trajectories of their lives as they continued their commitment to religious pluralism in the academy, nonprofit sector, and faith institutions. Karen Wood's chapter on the Seminarians Interacting program describes how Jewish and Christian (and later Muslim) seminary students explored similarities and differences they had with each other during a formative time in their religious education. Seminarians Interacting has trained a generation of American religious leaders in interfaith dialogue, thus promoting actively the practice of pluralism. The third chapter is by Victor Kazanjian, the pioneer of the paradigm shift from the Christian-dominated college chaplaincy model to interfaith ministry. Kazanjian describes the Multifaith Student Council at Wellesley College, its history, challenges, and successes. In the fourth chapter, Alison Boden, Dean of the Rockefeller Chapel at the University of Chicago, shares her insights on the ingredients of successful interfaith work on college campuses. She describes how, amidst an atmosphere of negative feeling and mutual suspicion, a small number of Jews and Muslims built a dialogue group that grew and lasted because it responded to their own ideas of what was important. The final chapter is by a group of students from the University of Illinois who were concerned about inter-religious tensions on their campus. They started a number of interfaith projects that sought to reduce those tensions and build solidarity. They describe how their initial attempts at interfaith work lost steam, inspiring them to research more effective models of building religious pluralism and start campus organizations that garnered broader and deeper support.

Section four focuses on secondary education. High schools are also rapidly growing in religious diversity. They are spaces where there is a palpable need to increase our understanding about the world's diverse religious systems and communities. This section includes three articles by high school teachers and teacher trainers who have focused their attention on this age group. They are practical examples of what has come to be known as the new consensus in secondary education: the need to teach about religion, rather than teach religion. The former seeks to provide information about a variety of religious traditions while the latter tends to be confessional in orientation.

The first chapter by Jane Rechtman describes the World Religions course that she teaches at the Masters School, a private institution north of New York City. Rechtman highlights what her students gain from the readings, site visits, and assignments on religious diversity that her course requires them to complete. The second chapter by David Streight describes the history and approach of Religious Studies in Secondary Schools (RSISS). Streight and his colleagues noticed that school leaders were frequently asking teachers to increase their understanding about religious diversity, but these teachers were ill-equipped to do so. RSISS provides training and resources to these teachers, and special opportunities for students interested in the academic field of Religious Studies. The third chapter by Matthew Weiner and Timur Yuskaev also describes a teacher training initiative organized by the Interfaith Center of New York. This initiative is unique because it attempts to bring the lived experience of religious communities to life by having religious leaders from different communities interact directly with teachers, with a special emphasis on the internal diversity within religious communities.

These three chapters are part of interfaith youth work for two reasons: they provide us with teachers' perspectives on how best to foster religious literacy among teenagers who live for the most part in religiously diverse high schools and neighborhoods. By providing better education about different religions, they are de facto turning the classroom into a dialogue space, even though that is not the central goal of these courses. In short, they play a pioneering role in creating a space where transformational learning happens in and outside the classroom, nurturing both healthier spiritual quests for each student and healthier social communication collectively. Awakened to and managing the diversity of worldviews in and outside the classroom is certainly one of the greatest challenges any educational system must address today anywhere in the world.

Section five presents four chapters by community-based leaders who know that promoting interfaith youth work only through the formal classroom spaces in the secondary school and higher education systems is not enough. What characterizes all of these community-based projects is their local dimensions. They allow students to experience dialogue in very different ways, but always from the security of returning home every day. The chapter by Patel and Mariah Neuroth describes how the theory and methodology developed at the Interfaith Youth Core are put into practice to make Chicago a "model interfaith youth city." The second chapter by Julie Eberly describes the methodology, activities, and participants of the youth program of the Interfaith Ministries of Greater Houston. Goggin describes the evolving youth program of the Interfaith Youth Conference of Metropolitan Washington, D.C., and articulates how interfaith work became an expression of his calling as a Catholic youth minister. The final chapter is by Joe Hall and Andrew Unger on the Ghetto Film School, a project Hall founded in 1999 in the South Bronx of New York City. Its main purpose is to encourage minority students in urban areas to tell their stories through film. In the summer of 2002, Hall and Unger gave the mostly Pentecostal and Catholic students in their summer program the assignment of translating a religious parable into a contemporary film. Their article not only describes the resulting films, but also their encounters with stories (and storytellers) from a wide range of religious traditions.

Section six provides four examples of immersion projects, that is, when youth participants leave home and spend weekends, weeks, or months together. There is an intensity unique to the 24/7 close-quarter experience that differs from the projects included in the previous sections. These immersion projects also raise challenges in terms of gender dynamic at an age of heightened sexual development, a challenge many religious communities sometimes view as an insurmountable problem. The first chapter by Annapurna Astley describes a weekend-retreat model called "Spirit into Action" that took place in South Florida. She emphasizes the importance of directly inviting people to participate in interfaith youth programs. She tells powerful stories about the contributions made by the youngest participants, breaking the stereotype about how old is "old enough" to participate in interfaith youth projects. The second chapter by Sidney Schwarz describes and analyzes the E Pluribus Unum project which he founded. This three-week immersion program in Washington, D.C., brought together sixty Jewish and Christian high school seniors for an intensive program of interfaith dialogue, social action, and the arts. The program ran for three years, involving a small number of Muslims as an exploratory group in the third year, and hosted a highly successful conference to study its model in the fourth year. The project profiled in the next article, the Interfaith Service House, was conceived by a graduate of the E Pluribus Unum. Lori Eisenberg asks herself a simple question: if a three-week EPU program could be so transformative, how much more so could be a year-long interfaith house fostering community service? In partnership with E Pluribus Unum and the Council for a Parliament of the World's Religions, she founded the Interfaith Service House in Chicago and directed it for its first two years of operation. The fourth chapter by Katharine Henderson and Melodye Feldman describes an intensive interfaith youth summer camp outside New York City that draws its participants from areas of religious tension such as Northern Ireland, the Middle East, and South Africa. The humanizing process that is central to the Face to Face methodology is characteristic of what is needed on a large scale if any solution is to work out in the long term in areas of religious conflicts.

Section seven focuses on a new pastoral approach to young people growing up amid religious diversity. "Ask Pastor Paul" is an Internet column that Paul Raushenbush wrote for Beliefnet.com. He beautifully describes the identity issues that young people question him about, everything from "I don't believe in my parents' religion" to "I'm in love with someone from a different tradition." The range and intensity of these questions underscores the importance of developing pastoral approaches to young people growing up in a world of religious diversity. The chapter is all the more interesting because the interaction took place over the Internet, a place where more and more people are turning for spiritual guidance, information, and companionship. The guidelines that Pastor Paul states in offering pastoral advice are relevant in both cyberspace and in the world of face-to-face interaction. We hope families and faith communities will make use of them.

Common Themes

Two common themes emerge from this collection of work. The first theme is the web nature of the interfaith youth movement. Many of us are interconnected through many interfaith organizations and experiences. Our religious identities may be clear and single, for most of us. Yet, our interfaith organizational identities are fluid. For example, Patel participated in the programs of the United Religions Initiatives, the Parliament of the World's Religions, and the Interfaith Center of New York before founding the Interfaith Youth Core. Astley and the student leaders of the University of Illinois worked with the Interfaith Youth Core before founding their own groups. As a graduate student at Harvard University, Brodeur was not only the founder of its World Conference on Religions for Peace graduate student chapter but also worked in the early developments of the Pluralism Project. He later served as mentor to the Interfaith Youth Core and the Interfaith Service House. These three stories illustrate the generative nature of the interfaith youth movement. People who participate in interfaith programs get the "bug" and acquire the skills to take the lead in developing more interfaith projects. The growth of the interfaith youth movement depends on how well its current leaders continue to identify and nurture new talent.

The second common theme is the range of methodologies used across interfaith youth projects. Not surprisingly, many interfaith youth leaders independently discovered the power of particular methodologies adapted to their respective contexts. Schwarz, Hall, Astley, and others noticed that the arts are an excellent medium for interfaith exchange, especially among young people. In other cases, project leaders deliberately chose different, even contradictory, methodologies. On the one hand, Henderson and Feldman directly address conflicting issues between religiously diverse youth. On the other, the Interfaith Youth Core assiduously avoids these "hot" topics, considering them the "private space" of families and faith communities.

Hope

Our hope is threefold: that leaders in the interfaith youth movement debate the merits of their respective methodologies; that they commit to improving their projects by enhancing their existing methodologies and making use of new ones; that they exhibit a willingness to teach newcomers to the movement the ins and outs of their methodologies, so that no one needs to reinvent the wheel.

Conclusion

In closing, we would like to issue a series of invitations:

To the Catholic Sunday school teacher who has tried to explain Buddhism to her students, let this book serve you as a guide;

to the advisor of a Jewish youth group who passes a mosque on her way to synagogue and wonders if their Muslim youth group asks the same questions as her teenagers, let this book encourage you to find out together with your students;

to the college chaplain endeavoring to minister to a religiously diverse campus, let this book inspire you to adapt for your own needs the models that have worked elsewhere;

to the religious young person who seeks ways to discuss faith with her friends from different backgrounds, let this book provide you with a language to embark on this great exploration;

to anyone who dreams of a day when religious people use their hands, heads, and hearts to build a new world of equity for all human beings, let this book be your accomplice and our movement be your home.

Notes

1. Martin L. King, Jr., *Where Do We Go From Here: Chaos or Community* (New York: Harper & Row, 1967).

2. Patrice Brodeur, "From Postmodernism to 'Glocalism': Towards an Integrated Theoretical Understanding of Contemporary Arab Muslim Constructions of Religious Others," in *Globalization and the Muslim World*, ed. by Birgit Schaebler and Leif Stenberg, (Syracuse: Syracuse University Press, 2004), 188–205, esp. 197 for a detailed definition.

3. Diana Eck, *A New Religious America* (San Francisco: HarperCollins, 2001).

4. W. C. Smith, *The Faith of Other Men* (New York: Harper & Row, 1962).

5. For a broader discussion of the term "interfaith," see Eboo Patel, "Affirming Identity, Achieving Pluralism," later in this volume.

1.

Affirming Identity, Achieving Pluralism: Sociological Insights from a Practitioner of Interfaith Youth Work

Eboo Patel

THIS CHAPTER AIMS TO DEVELOP A PRACTICAL SOCIOLOGY of interfaith youth work. I begin by highlighting the significance that faith communities place on maintaining religious identity and the challenges that the pluralist modern world poses to religious identity. I go on to articulate a vision of a pluralist civil society that is respectful of different religious identities and encourages understanding and cooperation between diverse religious communities. I draw from my personal life as a Muslim in America, my professional experience as Executive Director of the Interfaith Youth Core and my academic training as a sociologist of religion to analyze the contextual issues surrounding interfaith youth work. I hope to provide a roadmap that helps interfaith youth-work practitioners navigate those issues effectively.[1]

Maintaining Religious Identity in the Modern World

A leader in the Catholic Archdiocese of Chicago responded to my invitation to involve Catholic youth in Interfaith Youth Core programs with the following statement:

> My primary concern is that Catholic kids become better Catholics. I want them to
> know more about the Catholic tradition and to be more active in Catholic practices

> and institutions. . . . I think my religion has the banquet. I agree that all religions are
> holy and have something to offer, but I think Catholicism has the feast.

This way of thinking is not unique to Catholic leaders. It is common to people of all religions, at all levels of leadership who have a stake in their own salvation, to want the success of the institutions that preserve their tradition and the religious identity of their community's youth. Tariq Ramadan expresses a sentiment similar to the Catholic leader quoted above in his book *Western Muslims and the Future of Islam*: "How can the flame of faith, the light of the spiritual life, and faithfulness to the teachings of Islam be preserved in environments that no longer refer to God and in educational systems that have little to say about religion?" Any attempt to work with youth in religious communities must begin with the understanding that the preservation of religious identity is perhaps the single most important concern of faith communities.

But, to extend the metaphor of the Catholic leader quoted above, we no longer live in a world of separate banquet halls, each exclusively holding the "feast" of our religious tradition and protecting against the intrusion of other types of "food." Our world has always been diverse, but never before have so many people from so many different backgrounds been in such frequent and intense contact. As Diana Eck writes, "The encounter of worlds and worldviews is the shared experience of our times" (1993).

Sociological theories of modernity illuminate the impact that this intense interaction has on religious identity. The sociologist Peter Berger explains the socialization process:

> Worlds are socially constructed and socially maintained. Their continuing reality
> depends on specific social processes, namely those processes that ongoingly recon-
> struct and maintain the particular worlds in question . . . each world requires a social
> "base" for its continuing existence. This "base" may be called its plausibility struc-
> ture. (1969)

In previous eras, what Berger called "the pre-modern situation," a community's plausibility structures (otherwise known as institutions) tended to fully encapsulate its members and could therefore direct their lives.

> This is how things are done, and not in any other way. This is how one marries (and
> whom); this is how one raises children, makes one's livelihood, exercises power,
> goes to war—and not in any other way . . . this is who one is—and one could not be
> anyone or anything else. (1979)

But the modern situation, Berger explained, is dramatically different:

> *Modernity pluralizes.* Where there used to be one or two institutions, there now are
> fifty. Institutions, however, can best be understood as programs for human activity.
> Thus, what happens is that where there used to be one or two programs in a partic-
> ular area of human life, there now are fifty. (1979)

Today, people spend less time encapsulated by the institutions of their traditional communities and more time in spaces where there are frequent interactions between people of diverse backgrounds. This leads to constant exposure to lifestyles and perspectives different from those encouraged by the traditional community. In previous eras,
an individual received the same basic message about her identity from her family, peer
group, house of worship, and school. In the modern situation, an individual can
receive dramatically different messages about how she should live and what she
should believe from the family and the school, the house of worship and the peer
group. Berger claims that in the pre-modern situation, individuals experienced their
identities as fate. In the modern situation, characterized by a plethora of alternatives,
they view their identities as a matter of choice (1979).

The move from fate to choice means that, as Giddens writes, "the self has become
a *reflexive project*" (1991). Faced with a variety of ways of being, believing and
belonging, individuals are required to reflect upon the identity they want and justify
the choices they make. Giddens states: "In a cosmopolitan world, more people than
ever are regularly in contact with others who think differently from them. They are
required to justify their beliefs, in an implicit way at least, both to themselves and others."

Modernity, then, presents a whole new set of challenges for a community committed to passing on its tradition to the next generation. Today's grandparents, who
might not have had any significant contact with people from other traditions or certainly not the same broad range of exposure, were more likely to accept uncritically
the practices and worldview of their community. This is in sharp contrast to the
younger generations, who have a whole range of choices. From the perspective of the
leader of a religious community, Chief Rabbi of Britain Jonathan Sacks writes:

> Long gone are the days when our identities, beliefs and life chances were narrowly
> circumscribed by where and to whom we happened to be born. We are no longer
> actors in a play written by tradition and directed by community, in which roles are
> allocated by accidents of birth. Instead, careers, relationships and lifestyles have
> become things we freely choose from a superstore of alternatives. (2005)

This social dynamic is vividly illustrated by the plot in Chaim Potok's novel *The Chosen*. The book opens with the following lines: "For the first fifteen years of our lives, Danny and I lived within five blocks of each other and neither of us knew of the other's existence." It goes on to describe how the various Jewish communities in Brooklyn lived in what amounted to cocoons, "each with its own rabbi, its own little synagogue, its own customs, its own fierce loyalties." The book is set in the World War II era, a time when some Jewish leaders felt it necessary to prove their community's "Americanness." So a baseball league was formed as a way to demonstrate that Jews were connected to American culture. It is here that the son of a charismatic Hasidic rabbi, Danny, meets the son of a more acculturated Jewish scholar, Reuven. Danny and Reuven develop a friendship that challenges each of their received identities. While Reuven acquires a respect for the harsh and foreign ways of the Hasids, Danny decides to pursue a career in psychology, an interest he developed through secret meetings with Reuven's father in the public library. Encounters on the baseball diamond and in the public library shaped the life choices and perspectives of two teenagers who would otherwise have lived out the script provided by their birth and directed by their community.

Danny and Reuven's lives, however fictional, demonstrate the shift from fate to choice in the modern process of identity formation. Their modern choices challenge faith communities that seek to pass down their tradition in a world where their children are free to adopt other practices and worldviews.

Thus far, I have discussed the challenges that modern interactional diversity poses to faith communities. But, the question of how Christians, Muslims, Jews, Buddhists, Hindus, Sikhs and others interact with one another, as they live, study, and work in increasingly close quarters, has significant implications for the future of our broader society as well.

Pluralism, Religious Identity and Interfaith Youth Work

Political philosopher Michael Walzer writes that the challenge of a diverse society is to embrace its diversity while maintaining a common life. This suggests the need for all communities within a diverse society to take responsibility for embracing a common life while maintaining their uniqueness. It is this dynamic that leads to the ideal of the pluralist society as a "community of communities" envisioned by scholars like Martin Marty, John Rawls and Robert Bellah. Martin Luther King Jr., infusing this political philosophy with his own Christian spirituality, called this "the beloved community."

Diana Eck suggests that this ideal is only achieved by the intentional and positive engagement of differences. Mere diversity, Eck maintains, is simply the fact of people from different backgrounds living in proximity to each other. *Pluralism*, on the other hand, is when people from different backgrounds seek mutual understanding and positive cooperation with one another.

There are very real dangers to not following the path of pluralism. A chasm of ignorance between different religious communities can too easily be filled by bigotry, often turning into violence. In *The Clash of Civilizations*, Samuel Huntington states that the dominant characteristic of the post–Cold War global order is violence between different ethnic and religious groups. While I agree with Huntington's critics, who point out that his thesis is misguided when it suggests that the world's traditions are inherently and inevitably in conflict with each other, the news headlines make clear that far too much violence in our world is somehow related to ethnic and religious difference.

Ashutosh Varshney's work on Hindu-Muslim conflict in India provides empirical evidence regarding the role that strong cooperative relationships between diverse communities can play in preventing conflict. In *Ethnic Conflict and Civic Life*, he writes:

> What accounts for the difference between communal peace and violence? . . . The pre-existing local networks of civic engagement between the two communities stand out as the single most important proximate cause. Where such networks of engagement exist, tensions and conflicts were regulated and managed; where they are missing, communal identities led to endemic and ghastly violence. (2003)

In the United States, the most religiously diverse country in the world, we have dangerously thin relationships between religious communities. At the 2003 American Academy of Religion Annual Meeting in Atlanta, sociologist of religion Robert Wuthnow was asked how he thought faith communities were adapting to the reality of religious diversity in close quarters. He used the metaphor of an elevator: Christians, Muslims, Jews and the rest of America's religious diversity are all riding in it together, we are increasingly aware of the other people around us, but we are doing just about everything we can to avoid real interaction.

I think one of the reasons for this situation is the division between "inter" and "faith" in American life. There are increasing numbers of spaces where people from diverse religious communities gather: schools, shopping malls, universities, YMCAs, corporations, etc. These can be understood as spaces of "inter." There are many places in our society where people from particular religious communities come together to talk about religion. They are called synagogues, churches, mosques, temples, etc. These are spaces of "faith." But there are precious few spaces where people from diverse religions come together and are intentional about matters of religion.

One personal example of this division between "inter" and "faith," which I believe is common in American life, took place in the cafeteria of my middle-class suburban high school in the early 1990s. The group I ate lunch with included a Jew, a Mormon, a Hindu and a Lutheran. We were all religious to a degree, but we almost never talked about our religion with each other. Often, somebody would announce at the table that they couldn't eat a certain kind of food, or any food at all for a certain period of time. Or somebody would say that they could not play basketball over the weekend because "of some prayer thing" that they were being forced to go to by their parents. We all knew religion hovered behind these behaviors, but nobody ever offered any deeper explanation than "my mom said" and nobody ever asked for one.

As Bellah et al. observed in *Habits of the Heart*, one of the primary characteristics of religious life in contemporary America is that it has become "privatized." This is precisely what happened to my friends and me. The reason for this was we had not been taught a "language" that would allow us to explain our faith convictions to people outside of our faith communities. In my case, my religious education consisted of learning the private language of the Ismaili Muslim faith—the prayers, the devotional songs, the rites and ceremonies. It was a language which served me well within the Ismaili Muslim community but felt irrelevant in other situations. I felt I had to leave the Ismaili Muslim part of myself behind when I entered the diversity of the public square.

Jonathan Sacks developed a notion of "languages" to address the challenge of nurturing commitments in both parochial communities, characterized by race, religion and ethnicity, and in the broader society. To achieve this, Sacks claims that we have to learn two languages. He writes: "There is a public language of citizenship that we have to learn if we are to learn to live together. And there is a variety of second languages which connect us to our local framework of relationships." (2005)

Building on Sacks's notion of dual languages, I propose that, in addition to knowing one's private language of faith, there is an urgent need to learn also one's "public language of faith," which I define as a language that emphasizes how one's commitment to a particular faith tradition enriches the broader society. In other words, the "public language of faith" articulates how what makes you a more faithful Jew, Christian or Muslim also makes you a better citizen. For example, the command to minister to the poor and marginalized found in Deuteronomy 24 of the Hebrew Bible, Matthew 25 of the Gospels, and Sura 93 of the Qur'an, is one way a religious commitment clearly encourages the faithful Jew, Christian and Muslim to be of service to the broader society. Becoming familiar with these dimensions of one's religious tradition and developing fluency in articulating them in diverse settings beyond one's own religious community is the goal of learning one's own respective public language of faith.

The importance of learning a public language of faith was brought home to me in a conversation with one of my best friends from high school, a Jew. There was a group of kids in my high school who took up scrawling anti-semitic slurs on classroom desks and shouting similar obscene comments in the hallways. A few years after we graduated from high school, my Jewish friend shared with me how deeply those comments cut him, and worse, how he felt betrayed by the silence of the people he thought were his close friends. I apologized for my complicity in his suffering. He accepted this apology, and then stated, "I wonder if any of you even realized I was Jewish. None of us ever talked about religion."

This revelation does not excuse our inaction in those days, but it does highlight the dangers of diversity without pluralism. Our religious identities remained private because we had no language with which to express our faith to the world of diversity beyond our parochial communities. And without that public language, we had no ability to combat even the most heinous abuse. Had the high school bullies chosen to go after Muslims, I think I would have suffered alone, like my Jewish friend.

Creating and expanding the spaces where religiously diverse people gather to work on matters of religious diversity, and thus develop a public language of faith, is the task of interfaith organizations. The goal of interfaith work is intimated by the term itself: "inter" means our relationships with other people, especially those from different traditions, as was the case at my high school lunch table; "faith" means, in the W. C. Smith sense, the relationship individuals have with their cumulative historical religious tradition. As I suggested earlier, there is plenty of "inter" in our society, and a good bit of "faith," but not enough "interfaith." "Interfaith" is when our experience of the diversity of modern life and our connections to our religious traditions cohere in such a way that we develop faith identities that encourage us to interact with others in intentional and appreciative ways. It is the goal of being rooted in our own traditions and in relationship with others. It is accomplished through the development and use of a public language of faith that connects us to our parochial community while allowing us to be citizens of a diverse society.

This public language of faith allows us not only to prevent conflict but also to bridge and multiply the social capital that exists in diverse faith communities, social capital that would otherwise be isolated. For example, the Reverend Mark Farr, Senior Director for Interfaith Programs at the Points of Light Foundation, often states that over 50 percent of youth volunteers in the United States received their start in doing service through their religious community. A public language of faith would allow us to connect youth volunteers across different religious communities in massive service projects, and also bring their parents, active parishioners and religious leaders into positive relationship with one another.

Affirming Identity, Achieving Pluralism

If religious identity is to be sustained in the modern world, it will have to be affirmed and articulated amidst religious diversity. Religious communities developed their approaches to faith formation for a perceived world of isolated banquet halls. They are searching for strategies to affirm religious identity in a world of high-velocity interaction. Interfaith youth work can help create partnerships between youth and faith communities in fostering this goal. Interfaith youth work can help young people develop a language of faith that is relevant to the world of diversity, where they spend most of their time, thus encouraging them to affirm their faith identity. And because this language of faith encourages positive relations between diverse religious youth and communities, we are helping achieve pluralism.

I will end with the story of a woman I know who runs a large community development program in the heart of Brooklyn. Against the advice of her skeptical boss, she started an interfaith youth initiative. She justified the move by pointing out that religion is the world's greatest motivator of service, and also its most potent force of division. "If this neighborhood can harness the energies of its religiously diverse youth, it has a chance at transformation. But if we continue to ignore the fact that faith is a central part of people's lives, then the petty bickering between communities could snowball and balkanize us."

"Why do you think religion is so important?" I asked her.

"My father was a friend of Dorothy Day. He was part of her Catholic Worker movement from its beginnings. When I was a kid, he would take me to St. Joseph's House on the Lower East Side and we would cut carrots and celery for the soup kitchen. 'God wants us to do this work,' he would tell me, citing the example of Catholic saints and quoting from the Gospels.

"My father got sick when I was still young, and Dorothy often visited him in the hospital. She made it a point to spend a few minutes with me every time she visited, and she noticed that I was always reading. The next time she came, she brought a copy of her autobiography, *The Long Loneliness* and signed it for me. My father told me that I would cherish that book my whole life."

"So you combined religion and service early in your life," I said.

She smiled. "I lost that focus when I was a teenager. But in my twenties, I went to Egypt and lived with sufi Muslims. Their focus on submitting to the will of God through prayer and service reminded me of my father's commitment, and the example that Dorothy Day set. It was my Muslim friends in the Middle East who encouraged me to explore my Catholic roots."

My friend's experience in an informal interfaith encounter strengthened her faith and called her into a life of service. And it inspired her to organize formal interfaith programs so that the diverse religious communities in her neighborhood could affirm their distinctive identities, and working together, achieve pluralism.

Notes

1. For readers who want to learn more about how the organization I lead mobilizes these ideas in a practical program, please refer to the Interfaith Youth Core chapter later in this book.

Bibliography

Bellah, Robert N. (with Madsen, Richard; Sullivan, William M.; Swidler, Ann; and Tipton, Steven, M.) 1985/1996. *Habits of the Heart: Individualism and Commitment in American Life*. London: University of California, Ltd.

Berger, Peter. 1979. *The Heretical Imperative*. Garden City, NJ: Anchor/Doubleday.

———. 1969/1990. *A Rumor of Angels*. New York: Anchor/Doubleday.

———. 1967/1969. *The Social Reality of Religion*. London: Faber and Faber.

Eck, Diana L. *Encountering God: A Spiritual Journey from Bozeman to Banaras*. Boston: Beacon Press.

Giddens, Anthony. 1991. *Modernity and Self-Identity: Self and Society in the Late Modern Age*. Cambridge: Polity.

———. 2002. *Runaway World*. London: Profile.

Huntington, Samuel P. 1998. *The Clash of Civilizations and the Remaking of World Order*. New York: Touchstone.

Potok, Chaim. 1967. *The Chosen*. Greenwich, CT: Fawcett.

Ramadan, Tariq. 2003. *Western Muslims and the Future of Islam*. New York: Oxford.

Sacks, Jonathan. 2005. *The Persistence of Faith: Religion, Morality and Society in a Secular Age*. London: Weidenfeld and Nicolson.

Smith, Wilfred Cantwell. 1963. *The Faith of Other Men*. New York: Harper & Row Publishers.

Varshney, Ashutosh. 2003. *Ethnic Conflict and Civic Life*. New Haven: Yale University Press.

Walzer, Michael. 1996. *What it Means to Be an American*. New York: Marsilio.

Wuthnow, Robert. 2003. American Academy of Religion "Martin Marty" Lecture.

2.

Young Adult Development, Religious Identity, and Interreligious Solidarity in an Interfaith Learning Community

James P. Keen

THIS STUDY FRAMES AN INTERPRETATION of the E Pluribus Unum (EPU) program which is described elsewhere in this volume in an article by its founder, Rabbi Sid Schwarz. After exploring characteristics of EPU participants, the analysis will turn to how the program's purposes, structure, processes, and content meet the interests and developmental needs of this age group.

The paper incorporates material and insights from two yearly evaluations of EPU completed by the author, the second of which is part of a more in-depth research project supported by a grant from the Ford Foundation. This work builds upon previous study of precursor programs by the author completed in 1994 with support from the Lilly Endowment.[1] In pursuing this work, the author has been present during most of the three EPU conferences as a participant observer. Additionally, he has administered several surveys, completed and analyzed more than forty interviews with participants and alumni as well as eight focus groups with participants, alumni and staff.[2]

E Pluribus Unum Participants: A General Profile

Framing an interpretation of the design, functioning and impact of any learning environment ought to include a description of the learners it serves. In the cases of EPU, almost all participants were either seventeen or eighteen years old and were in the transitional summer between high school and college. The 1999 group consisted of thirty-four females and twenty-four males, reflecting a consistent pattern of a higher percentage of females in the applicant pool, a dynamic which has been characteristic of other intensive programs focusing on topics such as public issues, religious issues and community service. Six participants identified themselves as Black, four as Hispanic. Many had previous experience with pre-college enrichment programs, most often focusing on leadership development or on religious formation, but the diverse religious composition of the group (one-third Catholic, one-third Jewish and one-third Protestant) was the outstanding characteristic. EPU participants confirmed their eagerness to engage this diversity when, on a pre-conference survey, they expressed their strongest preference for "learning more about other faith traditions," "exploring how my faith tradition relates to the other traditions" and "meeting and working with young adults from other faith traditions" as opportunities that drew them to apply to EPU.

Responses to other survey questions revealed five frequently recurring interests among the incoming participants: 1) they were seeking to frame a meaningful philosophy of life; 2) they desired to collaborate with others to "make the world a better place"; 3) they wanted to learn more about social justice issues at EPU; 4) they believed "that people of good will could create community and collaborate on the common good, even if their beliefs differ"; and they were experienced at, and eager to engage in, community service.

Community service turned out to be a highly valued aspect of the past experience and future plans of this group. In 1999, fifty-six out of fifty-seven participants reported engaging in community service projects during their senior year in high school. At the conclusion of the conference, fifty-three out of fifty-six thought they would be involved in community service in the following year while a fifty-fourth participant said it would depend on time constraints. These are very high numbers, especially since prior community service was not a requirement for admission to the program.

Developmental Characteristics

Research conducted on the 1999 program aimed at gauging in greater depth the developmental characteristics of the group with an eye toward clarifying ways in which the EPU program design dovetails with the developmental dynamics of its participants. Selected survey and interview questions were directed towards illuminating aspects of intellectual, identity, and faith development. It should be noted that, due to a compressed schedule, there was not sufficient time to conduct formal developmental interviews in any one of these areas. Instead, queries aimed at eliciting several developmental dimensions, along with questions directed towards generating other insights, were integrated into two protocols: one used to interview twelve participants during the first two days of the conference, and a second employed with the same twelve participants at the end of the conference. A firmer foundation for the developmental interpretation of the participant group was built through the use of an essay form, paper-pencil tool, the Measure of Intellectual

Development (MID), using standard essay prompts provided by the Center for the Study of Intellectual Development (CSID) in Olympia, Washington.

Within hours of their arrival at the EPU conference, each participant composed a written essay in response to MID essay prompt "A," which invited them to describe their preferred learning environment. Similarly, on Friday of the third week (the final full day of activities) each participant wrote again, this time in response to MID essay prompt "B," which invited them to reflect on EPU as a learning environment. These essays were then shipped to CSID for analysis by teams of raters, experts in interpretation of where participants stood in reference to Perry's scheme of intellectual and ethical development, the developmental dimension the MID is designed to measure.[3]

Contracting with CSID for this work permitted us to generate data on the entire group in a highly efficient manner, employing a developmental lens widely recognized in higher education, with ratings provided by bona fide expert readers with no particular prior knowledge of EPU. Administering these essays before the first program activity had begun and at the latest possible moment within the three-week span of the program opened the possibility of detecting developmental gains that might be attributable to the impact of EPU on the participants.

The MID results place all fifty-eight EPU participants within a fairly narrow range on the nine-position sequence presented by William Perry in his 1970 book *Forms of Intellectual and Ethical Development in the College Years: A Scheme.* Perry and his team spent a number of years discovering, documenting, and interpreting an odyssey in which male undergraduates begin with dualistic thinking (seeing things in binary, right-wrong terms), move to multiplistic thinking (the truth is no longer understood as absolute and singular but is reframed as multiple, infinite and probably not knowable, except in personal terms), and advance to thinking (the truth is related to context and can be mediated by commitments to particular intellectual and ethical points of view, which may be shared by others). Perry's scheme begins with "dualism" in position one and proceeds to traverse seven intermediate positions and eight transitions, culminating in position nine, "commitment in relativism," characterized by an achieved capacity to embrace tentative, yet whole-hearted, commitments in an uncertain and complex world.

The MID results indicate that all fifty-eight EPU 1999 participants displayed intellectual and ethical development that fell within the range which Perry terms multiplistic thinking. Before delving further into the implications of the MID results for interpreting the dynamics within the EPU learning environment, a closer look at the MID data will be useful because of the robust developmental growth that it reveals within the three-week span of the EPU conference.

On the first essay, administered on the first day of the conference but prior to the beginning of the conference program, fifteen participants displayed the Perry two-thirds transition, seventeen participants displayed Perry position three, and twenty-six participants displayed Perry position three and twenty-six participants displayed Perry three-fourths transition. Less than three weeks later, on the second essay, the same set of CSID raters found only three participants displaying the Perry two-thirds transition (two were repeaters and one moved down from Perry three). Perry position three included twenty-three participants (nine moved up from two-thirds transition, twelve had remained at three, two had moved down to position three, after having been rated at the three-fourths transition on the first essay) and, once again, the largest group (this time thirty participants, up from twenty-six) rated at the Perry three-fourths transition (including twenty-three who remained there and seven who progressed there, including four who moved from Perry two-thirds to Perry three-fourths in just nineteen days). One participant, who rated at Perry three-fourths at the outset, did not complete the conference.

A pattern of development in which about 30 percent of participants moved forward in so short a span of time adds weight to findings from other areas of the research on EPU. In-depth interviews, focus groups, evaluators' observations, and the reflections of program alumni all point to the dynamic nature of the EPU learning environment. But the primary purpose of administering the MID was not to demonstrate that the program is conducive to intellectual and ethical development, however gratifying this evidence might be. Rather, as stated earlier, the MID results permit us to gauge more confidently the developmental level of the participants, while providing outside validation for findings from other areas of the research that point in the same direction. One advantage of the Perry approach is that it reorganizes the transitional nature of much of the developmental odyssey. Between every position, Perry describes a transition. This provides an organic account of growth, with movement away from a position also interpretable as movement toward the next position. By analogy, it helps us see development as a moving picture rather than a snapshot. The MID results, for example, capture the fluidity of transition as participants negotiate gradations within the developmental phase Perry calls multiplicity.

In 1986, the team of Mary Field Belenky, Blythe McVicker Clinchy, Nancy Rule Goldberger and Jill Mattuck Tarule (henceforth referred to as Belenky and associates) published their study, *Women's Ways of Knowing*, in which they set forth a developmental model, which, while consistent with Perry's, goes far beyond his more limited sample of male undergraduates by depicting the intellectual development of young women of a full range of social and economic classes, including those who show up in higher education and those who do not.

Belenky and associates acknowledge a close parallel with Perry's work, especially at the general stage of development displayed on the MID by EPU participants. "We chose the term subjectivism as a more apt description of women's experiences of inner knowing than 'multiplicity' however in most cases the terms are interchangeable. . . . The basic dilemma for the dualist moving into multiplicity, as Perry sees it, is how to position the self vis-à-vis defrocked authority. With the progression to multiplicity, the individual develops the capacity to carve out a domain in which all opinions are equally valid; everyone, including the self, has the capacity and right to hold his or her own opinions."[4] Whether one terms this movement and the developmental phase it traverses multiplist or subjectivist, it is quintessentially one in which the individual moves away from externally derived to internally constructed voice.

Based on evidence provided by the MID and buttressed by in-depth interviews, focus groups and observations within the learning environment, it is possible to identify the internal construction of one's voice as the key developmental task for EPU participants. This is true not only from the perspective of intellectual development, it also makes sense from the vantage points of other related developmental frames such as identity and faith. Due to constraints of time and budget, we did not conduct formal interviews to assess each participant's faith development in James Fowler's framework, presented in his study, *Stages of Faith*. Nevertheless, the research did incorporate several interview questions that helped gauge faith development stages of participants.

The research found that participants were in transition between, in Fowler's terms, "synthetic-conventional faith," a stage that emphasizes interpersonal relationships and a conventional orientation to authority, and "individuative-reflective faith," a stage that features the critical distance of the individual from the matrix of social relations and from conventional forms of authority. EPU participants, in the process of moving away from high school, from family, from home congregations, appeared to be establishing a more internalized locus of control consistent with the subjectivist project of developing internally constructed voice, seeking more of a place to establish themselves in relation to their own religious tradition and in relation to the traditions other than their own. Yet, they clearly had not arrived at the point of consolidating "individuative reflective faith," as Fowler describes it. Rather, they appeared to be experiencing at EPU a kind of precipitating "encounter with groups or persons other than those which had supported them in 'synthetic conventional faith,'"[5] That most participants indicated they came to EPU seeking a deeper understanding of their own tradition and an opening to understand faith traditions other than their own would seem to indicate a willingness to move beyond conventional faith into framing a relationship more authentically one's own within one's faith tradition.

One way we can look at the developmental trajectory of EPU participants is that they are in the process of establishing a more autonomous identity. The developmental movement seen on the MID could indicate significant progress towards this growth in the EPU context. Elsewhere we will talk about ways in which EPU supports a deepening and refining of existing loyalties in tandem with the initiative of new loyalties that incorporate solidarity across boundaries of religious difference. This kind of maturation appears to mesh well with the movement towards individuative-reflective faith. One indication that participants have not yet arrived at Fowler's individuative-reflective faith is that the forms of logic and reasoning described by Fowler for this level are consistent with those Belenky and associates frame as "procedural knowing," a stage that comes immediately after "subjectivist knowing." Subjectivist knowers are certainly capable of self-reflection, to the point of becoming self-referential and at risk of becoming excessively self-focused. Yet, they are not quite capable of fully approaching either systemic thinking or critical analysis, although they can apprehend aspects of these as they move through a developmental trajectory towards these positions. The internal voice that the subjective knower is constructing is not yet strong and supple enough to support procedural knowing.

From one angle, the subjectivist knower can be seen as involved in a rather long transition between the received knowing that fits with the instructional and content methods of high school and with adolescent confirmation in religious institutions and the frameworks of procedural knowing that are initiated by the instructional and content orientations of higher education. It is reasonable to speculate that attending college, as most EPU proceed to do, will provide an appropriate environment for moving into procedural knowing and, relatedly, for consolidating individuative-reflective faith.

The Development of Identity

Another related perspective from which we can view the developmental trajectory of EPU participants—one which includes the development of voice as well as transition from conventional to post-conventional faith—is the perspective of identity development. We can view EPU participants as working on the adolescent challenge of establishing a consistent sense of oneself and yet beginning the process of developing a more durable young adult identity capable of establishing, in Perry's terms, "commitments in an uncertain world." Developmental psychologist and theologian James Loder locates transitions from adolescence to young adulthood in seventeen- to eighteen-year-olds, the very age group of EPU participants.[6]

On the adolescent side of transition, Loder builds on Erikson's definition: "Identity is a consistent sense of oneself. That is, identity establishes self-consistency from one social and cultural context to the next, and allows for a balance between resistance to adult conformity, on the one hand, and subjective self-absorption, on the other."[7] Following Loder's helpful definition of identity, we can frame the adolescent project as a growing capacity to mediate among multiple aspects and contexts of identity. This image is congruent with Perry's multiplicity (a phase through which EPU participants are traversing), which entails an increasing apprehension of multiple aspects of one's own world along with varying contexts of the worlds of others. Moreover, we can regard subjectivism, as framed by Belenky and associates, as congruent with establishing a sense of self, a reliable sense of one's own voice, as a means of meeting the challenges posed by multiple aspects and contexts of identity. Of course, we ought to distinguish between subjectivism, as described by Belenky and associates, and Loder's subjective self-absorption, which is a pitfall common to subjectivism and multiplicity.

On the young-adult side of transition, Loder points to Sharon Daloz Parks's description of the college-age young adult as moving out of adolescence through a dialectic between authority-determined judgment and unqualified relativism, which she frames as the emergence of contextual relativism, combining idealism and relativism. Parks's account of this consolidation of young adulthood includes the search for a meaningful philosophy of life and the framing of a young-adult dream,[8] which is congruent with what Perry describes as a newfound ability to come to commitment in an uncertain world.

One important way in which young adult identity differs from adolescent identity is in regard to the capacity to link intersubjectively with others in the common pursuit of meaning and purpose in ways that are mutualistic. One's identity begins to stabilize around basic commitments that are made as one works out issues of vocation and profession and of the deeper intersubjective sharing of intimacy. Establishing a reliable stance and sense of orientation towards a more enduring adult identity and foreseeing a life of commitment and responsibility become key aspects of identity. In a sense, one learns to mediate among a multiplicity of identity aspects and contexts by framing a sense of self which is defined by the emerging adult's commitments and vision.

For EPU participants, who are in transition between adolescence and young adulthood, the characteristics of adolescent identity are manifest even as they stand on the threshold of young-adult identity.

The Learning Community Model

One of the direct influences in the design of EPU is the "learning community model" developed in the early 1980s (at institutions such as Stony Brook University, LaGuardia Community College and Lesley College—following from experimental college innovations of the late 1960s and the 1970s at vanguard institutions such as Antioch University and Goddard College). While examples vary, learning communities constitute small—to moderate—size groupings of students who pursue a common curriculum with a core seminar facilitated by one or more faculty who also serve as advisors and participate in other ways in the curriculum. The core seminar offers an opportunity to draw connections among various strands of the curriculum and the questions framed by the participants. Learning communities were developed largely to reduce alienation among students by addressing the impersonal culture and fragmented curriculum that often characterize higher education.

A Short-Term Intensive Learning Community

Another direct influence in the design of EPU is the model of the short-term intensive learning environment, which is, of course, a generic educational form. As we define it, a short-term intensive learning environment is one which sufficiently insulates a group of learners from the flow of concerns of their everyday lives as students, workers, professionals, family members, and the like, so that they are able to bring themselves as persons (including their broader cognitive and affective potentials) to the task at hand, more fully and deeply than is usually the case in the typical class of three-quarters of an hour to three hours. The spatial and temporal framework of such a learning environment must be sufficiently removed from the flow of things, so that it is experienced as set apart from the flow and bulk of the forms, activities and other contents that are routine with that flow. The place of a short-term intensive learning environment is usually somewhat apart—in the same sense that one usually goes away somewhere to retreat or vacation—so that one can get away from one's usual preoccupations and distractions. The time is sufficiently long that one can achieve a sense of "being away" from the normal flow and, therefore, find oneself less caught up in attention to its demands. But in neither the case of space or time is the normal flow forsaken (the return will come shortly) so that one is not sacrificing one's attachments, responsibilities, interests and commitments—one is just leaving them for a brief time—a few days at a minimum, a few weeks at the most.

What happens within the time and space framework of a short-term intensive learning community is somewhat like what takes place in a gripping movie or novel. Take Bertalucci's movie, *The Last Emperor*, during which viewers are drawn into the presentation of a life that covers many years. As we view the movie, most of us have the sense of being drawn into the temporal and spatial landscape of the story and we experience virtual years of time in another place while sitting in our seats for several hours. I refer to this aesthetic time, which is a commonplace of narratives, as the "virtual" time within the art form in contrast to the "actual" time, say, of three hours or so that we are sitting there watching the film. In an aesthetic sense, a short-term intensive learning environment offers an opportunity of "virtual" time in which participants can pay attention to subject matter, self and other in ways that are usually constrained in the everyday flow of events. This relative freedom from familiar constraints is balanced by the structure of the intensive learning community so that participants are more open to trying out new ideas and concepts regarding subject matter, self and the other, and are supported in doing so by the structure, process and content of the learning community. This balance of concerted attention, freedom from a number of usual constraints, and support from an intentional design of structure, process and content, offers a myriad of possibilities for developing innovative approaches to learning and teaching, most of which will be useful as a counterpoint to the usual flow of learning and teaching experienced elsewhere.

Many residential summer pre-college programs would qualify as short-term intensive learning environments. Some may also be designed as integrative learning communities, but most, even those which may refer to themselves as communities, do not feature explicitly integrative structures for the support of multiple dimensions of learning. A key feature of the EPU model is that each aspect of the learning community is intended to feed back into every other aspect, yielding an integrative program design.

Not all learning communities, as defined above, are short-term intensive learning environments. Often they are set within the regular flow of college together, sharing meals, recreational activities and moments of relaxation. But when these two models are brought together, they reinforce each other by intensifying the experience of connectedness among the participants and between the participants and what is being learned. Hence, they become integrative both at the level of design and at the level of the experience of participants.

The Covenant Group

The key to this integration in EPU, the covenant group, mediates the intersection of formal and informal learning by promoting conversations focused on these questions: "Who am I? What is my experience of the world? What am I currently learning? and What does this mean for me?" There is an emphasis on reflection and dialogue which aims at the construction of more "connected" levels of meaning and at the development of a stronger sense of voice which integrates student's affective experience with their growing intellectual understanding of what they are studying. In these sessions (which meet four or five times a week) students and counselors (called mentors in EPU) work together to clarify connections among the formal subject matter of the program, the life of the community and their own experiences, feelings, and perspectives. Students are asked to assume a routine of stopping once a day to reflect on these matters and to write one-page "integrative journals" in preparation for each seminar meeting. While these are collected and read by the covenant group leader, the session does not focus on them, but rather on the questions or issues that various participants bring to the group on any given day. That is to say, the purpose of the journal is to prepare for dialogue through a routine of reflection outside the covenant group, but the seminar itself operates in a reflective dialogical frame of here and now. The mentors facilitate, holding the group to an agenda of serious dialogue and intervening with occasional probing and clarification, but it is the students who decide upon the topics and, for the most part, direct the conversation.

The informal conversations of, say, the dorm are sometimes very trenchant, but they are often confined to others with whom one feels a strong affinity. In contrast, covenant group conversations mirror the more serious of the informal conversations but they occur within a group that is diverse by design, and in a context in which active listening and civility are mandated guidelines. By encouraging students to bring the voices they use to articulate what they care about in formal conversations into the quasi-formal, intermediate context of the covenant group, the program nurtures the development, within each student, of a voice that connects the personal with the societal—a key element in the development of religious, moral and political agency. For the mentors, the challenge is to foster a dialogue that is authentic and not frivolous. This task requires a person who is both interested in what young people think and have to say and one who can model excellent practices of listening, reflection, and dialogue.

Common among intensive pre-college summer programs is the energy participants generate in intensive conversations that take place in the informal learning environment, for example, in the dorms and over meals. At EPU, incoming participants are often surprised by adults conceding to them that these conversations may turn out to be as important to what they learn about themselves, about others and about the world they coinhabit, as what they may encounter in the formal areas of the program. But there is method in this concession as it opens the door to a multidimensional approach in which loops of formal and informal learning feed into each other, and, in effect, reinforce each other. And, as this reinforcement takes place, it creates a context in which participants become more powerfully self-reflective as learners.

We have already noted the way in which the short-term intensive program supports participants in bringing themselves more fully to the task of learning. The reinforcing integration of formal and informal learning through the intermediating structure of the covenant group capitalizes on this fuller measure of involvement by facilitating participants in making multidimensional connections within themselves, bringing together intellect and feeling, societal concerns, the analytic and aesthetic, and most of all, opening the possibility of seeing each other as multidimensionally as they are experiencing themselves. And this experience of seeing themselves and each other multidimensionally works congruently with the characteristic of EPU participants as subjectivist knowers. Each participant can learn to listen with greater fidelity to the particularity and "truth" of the other, in part because she or he is in an environment in which her or his own "truth" will in turn be honored as it is revealed. Because the subjectivist is capable, indeed, inclined to allow each person's truth as "right for them" just as one's own is "right for me," and because the status of the individual as knower is given great weight in the subjectivist's view of things, it is possible to initiate a practice of interreligious dialogue that builds on intersubjective honoring of the truth claims of others.[9] EPU takes full advantage of this possibility.

Covenant groups, thus, act as a key platform for learning the art of interreligious encounter in the safety of a mentor-mediated context. While a great deal of the interreligious dialogue at EPU takes place informally, such conversations can sometimes lead to misunderstandings and antagonisms among participants that can be more fully and fruitfully clarified in a mediated context like a covenant group. Likewise, issues raised in plenary sessions often prove very challenging to participants, causing some of them considerable discomfort. While faith-alike groups often process issues raised in plenaries, they do so with an eye to relating these to religious teachings, and they process them in the relative homogeneity of faith-alike groups. Covenant groups, by contrast, work on such issues in a more open-ended manner, without the authority of one tradition or the other as arbiter, and therefore, they take full advantage of EPU's explicit religious diversity.

Functioning as microcosms of the larger program, covenant groups are small enough (hardly ever more than ten people including the mentor) that an intimate level of group trust sufficient to process significant tensions can be achieved. Participants report challenging each other in these contexts at the same time as that they report developing a strong sense of caring support for one another. It is through these counterpoints of revealing oneself, while learning to listen to the other, and challenging while caring and supporting that EPU participants begin to come to terms with and to mediate the irreducible differences among their religious traditions and among their experiences. This is of utmost significance because it is in this very process of learning to recognize irreducible differences that participants may begin to discover a deeper, more authentic sense of common ground.

Religious Identity and Interreligious Solidarity

Faith communities often struggle with fostering in their young people knowledge, understanding, and affinity for their respective faith traditions. Reports from directors of EPU as well as from the founding director of the precursor program, the Youth Theology Institute, indicate that concerns are sometimes voiced by religious leaders and parents that intense interfaith dialogue might weaken commitments of young people to their particular faith traditions. Yet, interviews with interfaith participants and alumni indicate that the EPU experience tends to refine one's identification with one's own religious tradition while concurrently initiating a strong sense of solidarity among this group of religious young people that appears to transcend boundaries of religious difference. Multiple loyalty theory offers a useful lens for clarifying how this works. According to social psychologist Herbert Kelman, building on earlier work by Harold Guetzgow, human beings are capable of multiple loyalties "as long as the groups to which (these loyalties) are directed serve different functions and apply to different domains of behavior."[10]

By devoting a significant amount of prime program time to formal instruction and exploration in faith-alike groups, the EPU design provides a context conducive to the maintenance and development of self identification with, and loyalty to, one's own faith tradition. In this design, faith-alike groups function as confirmational contexts in each of which a talented teacher, representing that tradition, provides instruction and clarification while inviting participants' deep questions and concerns. That these directed conversations among circles of Catholics, circles of Jews, circles of Protestants are set within a larger learning environment of interreligious dialogue and collaboration, offers an opportunity for participants to act from a heightened sense of particular religious identity (nurtured by the faith-alike groups) in the interreligious interactions that take place within the larger learning environment. Consistent with this analysis, participants report that the interreligious nature of the learning environment as a whole stimulates their reflection and exploration of their own traditions as they seek firmer ground on which to stand as interreligious collaborators.

In their interviews, participants indicated that it was important for them to be responsible agents and representatives of their traditions in the interreligious dialogue and collaboration of EPU. Hence, the engagement in the interreligious work appeared to enhance identification with their own tradition while adding a sense of purpose and immediate urgency to the work of faith-alike groups. In this sense, the interreligious work itself appeared to have a reinforcing effect on refinement of identity with one's faith tradition. Moreover, the increased skills they report in listening across boundaries of religious difference appear to function in their conversations within their own traditions where they discover and clarify significant areas of difference. This counterpoint—this going back and forth between faith-alike conversation and interreligious dialogue and collaboration—appears to be the central identity enhancing aspect of the program, stimulating the development of identity at both levels simultaneously. Hence one is confirmed as Catholic, as a Jew, as a Protestant, who can also identify with interreligious engagement and work in solidarity across lines of religious difference.

This counterpoint between faith-alike conversation and interreligious dialogue is key to facilitating the challenge that EPU puts to its participants: to create community in the full recognition of diversity. All three faith-alike groups explore how their respective traditions support engagement with issues of social justice, community service and the common good. Each group gains an understanding of how traditions themselves support engagement across lines of religious difference towards these goals. The conversations in the faith-alike groups balance inward with outward focus with the effect of helping students to mediate levels of identity clearly by distinguishing between in-faith exploration and interreligious engagement in ways that are supportive of both particular religious identity and interreligious engagement. Thus, these young people develop a sense of self in which loyalties at both levels are consistent and mutually reinforcing rather than contradictory.

A key guideline for interreligious dialogue at EPU is that participants are entitled to and encouraged to witness to their faith while they are also obligated to respect each other and their respective religious differences. Simply speaking, a proscription against attempting to convert others is necessary to set up an environment of sufficient trust and obligation for participants to learn how to know others as they are known by others, to listen carefully across thresholds of difference and to risk sharing themselves across the thresholds.

One reason that such proscriptions, whether explicit or tacit, are common to most interreligious engagement is the necessity of achieving an atmosphere that balances trust and risk. Religious differences sometimes come down to contradictions that are irreducible and that cause discomfort. Learning how to own and act on one's discomfort even to the point of feeling entitled to withdraw or decline to participate at certain moments, is as important to the integrity of identity as learning how to appreciate and learn from that which is different.

The Centrality of Dialogue

Given the dialogical nature of EPU and the characterization of participants as subjectivist, it is not suprising that one of the key things interviewees valued in the program was a context to work on themselves as listeners in dialogue. As one participant put it, toward the end of the third week: "I think I've become a better listener, because that's part of respecting another person when they're telling you about their faith and their differences. You have to respect that person to let them get their point across without interrupting and saying, 'But what about this?' I think you should let them finish and then say, 'I was wondering about this.' So [EPU] has helped me develop my listening skills."

Closely related to the increased skill and attention participants reported in the ways they listen to each other is their apparent commitment, registered at the end of three weeks, to engaging in further interreligious dialogue.

As one Protestant participant put it: "I'm definitely into interfaith dialogue. Actually where I go to school I thought of sitting in on Hillel meetings, the Jewish activist group. Letting other people know I care. I know when I went to the first Shabbat service (at EPU) the Jewish students were just so alive and they were like 'You came! You're an honorary Jew now!' They were like, 'You didn't have to come but you came anyway. You came on your own accord so we really appreciate it.' And I like them saying that so I think I will keep it up."

Another student linked interfaith dialogue directly with community service: "What I'd like to do is get together or join a club at my college that talks about the religious motivation for doing community service. If there is a club, I want to join it. If there isn't a club, I want to found it, start it on campus. I already know Hillel is fairly active and maybe they would sponsor something like that."

Crossing Thresholds of Difference

In 1996, my spouse, Cheryl Keen, and I joined our co-authors Laurent Parks Daloz and Sharon Daloz Parks in publishing *Common Fire: Leading Lives of Commitment in a Complex World*, the result of more than a decade of research into how people develop and sustain commitments to working on behalf of the common good, defined to include the whole human family. The most salient pattern we found, in this intensive interview-based study of one hundred people who sustain this kind of commitment, was what we termed "a constructive engagement with otherness." All of our respondents recalled having experienced formative, enlarging encounters across thresholds of difference, in which someone who had previously been seen as "they" became part of a wider, reconstructed sense of "we."

In fact, I was originally drawn to the vision of EPU because its bold and straightforward attempt to connect interreligious collaboration with community service and the common good described the kind of environment that I felt would nurture enlarging encounter with difference. Indeed, my observation of and research on EPU has confirmed that the program elements of EPU promote in participants the same quality of commitment described in *Common Fire*. But nothing has been so confirming of this as several focus groups I conducted in the summer of 1998 with alumni of the 1997 EPU cohort.

In my conversations with this group, I found substantial evidence that EPU had fostered for them a substantial and constructive engagement with diversity that they connected directly with the pursuit of the common good. As one group put it: "We feel like it has a lot to do with expanding how many people you include in your circle and when you get to talk to people of other faiths we personally feel like you begin to realize that even though you have different practices of worship and different rituals, and different names for things, you all have an abiding faith. And when you expand your definition of people you have something in common with, then you feel much more committed to the common good."

In focus sessions I conducted with this group, participants told of how, as a result of EPU, they better understood "how to listen across difference"; they are "more self-reflective in the process of listening and talking"; they react "less defensively when encountering difference"; they are "more analytical around difference"; and they "ask better and deeper questions" in the face of difference.

Four and a half hours of group interviews ran consistently in the same direction. The following quotation is representative of these conversations and of EPU: "What we discovered last summer was when you bring together people who believe in their faiths and find that the three different faith traditions each teach that you should go out and do community service and social justice, that working for social justice and the common good is something we definitely had in common—and could all work together for—and that's a major thing that actually happened after we started having all the interreligious dialogues—that we all discovered that the idea of working for the community and the common good and going out and making a difference is something that's common in all our religions and that's where it started."[11]

Lessons from EPU

That EPU succeeds so well at fostering interreligious dialogue and connecting it to the common good makes it, to my mind, an exemplary program from which others who share similar visions can learn several important lessons.

First, EPU demonstrates that it is possible to structure learning environments in which participants are likely to have enlarging encounters with difference. The integrative design of the program supported such encounters through various aspects of the program. The faith-alike, covenant group counterpoint picked up the energy from the informal interactions in the dorm and elsewhere, yielding an approach that neither over-directed interreligious dialogue nor left it to chance. In particular, the reflective, dialogical nature of the covenant groups supported participants in initiating new aspects of their voices suited to, and reflective of, interreligious dialogue and collaboration.

Second, the covenant group design is one that could potentially be incorporated into any learning environment in which participants are strongly invested in their learning and share a real interest in dialogue and reflection. In the integrative learning community design that is common to EPU and its antecedent programs, the covenant group integrates the program by mediating in a reflective dialogical manner between the formal and informal dimensions of a learning environment. But the form can be used in other ways as well. For example, something like a covenant group can be employed for non-residential students as a base community on a residential campus. The form can also be adapted to mediation between experiential learning that takes place off campus in community service or internships and formal aspects of the learning environment. Research that Cheryl Keen and I are currently pursuing for the Bonner Foundation indicates that students value the group reflection and dialogue frameworks that are a part of Bonner Scholar programs on twenty-four American college campuses and that these groups play an important role in sustaining Bonner Scholars' ongoing commitment to service.

Third, by placing covenant groups in a framework that also incorporates faith-alike exploration of one's own religious tradition and introduction to the religious traditions of others, EPU supports a practice of interreligious dialogue in which participants can come to grips with irreducible difference, and therefore, find a more authentic sense of common ground and the basis for interreligious solidarity in a pluralist approach to common good.

Those interested in supporting the development of robust practices of interreligious dialogue will do well to take notice of both the faith-alike, covenant group dialectic, with its potential of deepening identity with one's own tradition while creating solidarity among traditions. Interested parties will also notice that superordinating challenges to build community in the face of explicit diversity, to care together for the world in solidarity across lines of particular difference, and to enact that caring through performing community service, can function to bring purpose to interreligious work beyond its value as an end in itself.

By flipping this coin, we can see that those interested in recruiting young people to a concern for social justice and community service can both usefully ground such concerns in the exploration of their religious traditions and, without contradicting this aim, can foster a sense of solidarity in which this religious grounding can support interreligious collaboration towards a pluralist concept of the common good.

While lessons from the E Pluribus Unum Project cited above can be applied in a variety of settings, the program stands as testimony to the value of short-term intensive learning communities as vehicles for integrative and multidimensional learning. Earlier in this paper I described how such environments can act to permit participants to bring themselves more fully to the learning task at hand. Our survey and interview results indicate the intensity of EPU was for many participants a defining characteristic. That results from the MID point to recognizable developmental movement in the course of three weeks speaks to the potential of such a "hot house" environment to nurture growth, particularly among participants who are experiencing developmental transitions.

Notes

1. James P. Keen, *Pre-College Programs as Communities of Imagination, Exploration and Foresight.* A report to the Lilly endowment, 1994.

2. For additional insight into the author's methodological practices, see L. Daloz, et al., *Common Fire: Leading Lives of Commitment in a Complex World*, (Boston: Beacon Press, 1996). James P. Keen is co-author of the book and the methodological notes can be found pp. 243–247.

3. W. G. Perry, *Forms of Intellectual and Ethical Development in the College Years: A Scheme*, (New York: Holt, Rinehart and Winston, 1970).

4. M. Belenky, et al., *Women's Ways of Knowing: The Development of Self, Voice and Mind*, (New York: Basic Books, 1986), pp. 62–63.

5. K. DeNicola, et al., *Manual for Faith Development Research*, (Atlanta: Candler School of Theology, Center of Research in Faith and Moral Development, 1993), p. 52.

6. James E. Loder, *The Logic of the Spirit: Human Development in Theological Perspective*, (San Francisco: Jossey-Bass, 1998).

7. Ibid, p. 207.

8. For an excellent analysis of the young adult development, see S. D. Parks, *Big Questions, Worthy Dreams: Mentoring Young Adults in their Search for Meaning, Purpose, and Faith*, (San Francisco: Jossey-Bass, 2000).

9. For the purpose of establishing a habit of interreligious dialogue this works better than engaging in an academic or philosophical debate aimed at demonstrating the inherent or "objective" superiority of one "truth" or of one tradition over another. In this sense there is something wonderful about the potential for interreligious dialogue among subjectivist knowers that can potentially be eclipsed in the onset in the college years of what Belenky and her associates call the separate mode of procedural knowing, which features what they term, "the doubling game." However, if the procedural knower develops a countervailing "connected" form of procedural knowing or a fully developed capacity for contextual relativism (See Sharon Daloz Parks cited in previous footnote) the eclipse can be weathered and interreligious dialogue can be maintained or renewed.

10. H. Kelman, "Education for the Concept of a Global Society." *Societal Education*, vol. 32, no.7, (1968), p. 661.

11. For a report in greater depth on my conversations with this group of alumni, including a number of additional quotations that I find equally compelling, see my article "Appreciative Engagement of Diversity: E Pluribus Unum and the Education as Transformation Project," in *Education as Transformation*, edited by Peter Lawrence and Victor Kazanjian, (New York: Peter Lang, 2002).

3.

Theologies of Interreligious Encounters and Their Relevance to Youth

J. Nathan Kline

A PRINCIPLE OF INCLUSION—and by extension, exclusion—has its place in every institution, secular and religious. No religious institution has succeeded in being everything for everyone. To varying degrees, each one establishes its boundaries and seeks to maintain them. Even the most open and accepting community or organization finds it necessary to define itself and inevitably functions by some principle of inclusion/exclusion. Some religious communities and organizations derive a sense of identity by whom they include and/or exclude; others are much less concerned or conscious that such a principle is at work. A clearer understanding of how a principle of inclusion/exclusion informs a religious institution or organization can contribute significantly to its effectiveness in executing its mission.

This article is specifically concerned with the inclusion/exclusion related to interreligious ministry. The aim of my research has been to search for answers to the following questions: What are the terms or grounds on which religious communities can cooperate for larger social issues? What unites them? Are they simply looking for some type of common denominator? If, for example, justice and the common good serve as these grounds, do religious communities cooperating with one another need to buy into a particular understanding of justice or what constitutes the common good? For interreligious cooperation to take place do participants have to believe religious differences are irrelevant to cooperation? Or are identifying and discussing differences essential? Is there anything about the terms/grounds for cooperation that are inherently Christian or Western? How do they serve the sectarian and the "conservative" who, historically, have been suspicious of interreligious activity?

An awareness of the plurality of religions inspires a variety of theological questions: Why are there so many religions? Are they really different? Or are the religions related in such a way that one could understand them as individual aspects of a whole? From a theistic perspective, if God is one, should there not be one religion? How should my religious tradition relate to other traditions? Is there anything I can learn from them? Might I learn more from them than I learn from my own? How do I account for the good I encounter in other traditions?

In this cosmopolitan age of heightened telecommunications and international travel one can only expect that the frequency and specificity of questions like these will increase.[1] It is assumed that all religious communities have something at stake in these questions, some more than others. Religious youth in particular are confronted with this unprecedented degree of exposure to the growing religious diversity of most societies worldwide. It is therefore crucial to develop a better understanding of the various theologies behind the different models of interreligious encounters that have emerged in the last few decades and analyze how relevant they are to young people in particular. This article focuses on Christian theological efforts in this direction.

A Continuum of Four Models of Interreligious Activity

Interreligious encounters often begin with casual relationships; analyzing and evaluating the activities defining the relationship may not result until much later, if at all. Further, guidelines for interreligious activity likely reflect a particular theological position that one may not have articulated yet. It is assumed that interreligious encounters cannot be postponed until one has fully articulated the theological grounds supporting it, since the position is best worked out in the encountering process. However, it may also be problematic to find oneself, one's community, or one's organization deeply involved in interreligious encounters without considering the justifications for such involvement. Organizations, especially, will benefit from a fuller articulation of the theological/philosophical grounds for interreligious activity, even those who claim a secular status. To enable such articulation to proceed, a continuum will be provided on which to plot the general theological positions for interacting with the religious other.

In *Introducing Theologies of Religions*,[2] Paul F. Knitter surveys Christian theologies of religions that have developed in response to the awareness of the plurality of religions. Knitter's introduction categorizes the varieties or models of Christian theologies of religions that have formed over time in various contexts. I suspect Knitter's categorization of models will make some contribution to every tradition, even though the models are admittedly Christian—or formed in response to Christian questions. These models will provide structure for thinking about the grounds for interreligious activity. The four models have sometimes been referred to as exclusivist, inclusivist, pluralist, and relativist. It is more common for one to discover affinities with several of these models than to simply position oneself fully in just one. A brief summary of Knitter's four models follows. To varying degrees, each of the four models is a response to the Christian soteriological concern, that is, how is one saved?

The Replacement Model

The first of these models is the replacement model. It has been the dominant model throughout most of Christian history. According to this model, Christianity is ultimately meant to replace all other religions. If the other religions have any value at all, it is only provisional. God's love is universal, extending to all—but that love is realized through the particular and singular community of Jesus Christ. Those currently working from this model are largely conservative, Evangelical Protestants. Those functioning from this model share, to a large extent, four basic beliefs: 1) The Bible is the standard by which one judges truth. 2) Believers exhibit a lifestyle of commitment and talk of being "born again." 3) Jesus is savior of humanity. 4) This good news must be shared with everyone in the world, in an effort to convert them.

The theology of Karl Barth is instrumental in informing the total replacement model. For Evangelical Christians who function out of this model, the fundamental theological question is soteriological, and the answer is four-fold: humans are saved by grace *alone*, by faith *alone*, by Christ *alone*, and by scripture *alone*. There is little for Christians to relate to in other religions; there is no revelation, no saving grace, because there is no Jesus. Interaction with the religious other is justified by the possibility of convincing him or her that Jesus is savior; unless knowledge of other religious traditions serves this end, it is useless, even harmful. What the total replacement model advocates is a holy, evangelizing competition between the many religions and their respective truth claims.

The Fulfillment Model

Those functioning from within this model, a perspective sometimes referred to as inclusivist, see Christianity as the fulfillment of other religions. The general view is informed by theologies that give equal weight to the convictions that God's love is *universal*, extending to all peoples, but that it is also *particular*, made real in Jesus Christ. Karl Rahner reasoned that because "God is love" (1 John 4:8b), and God "desires everyone to be saved and to come to the knowledge of the truth" (1 Timothy 2:4), God makes salvation possible for all people. As such, people can truly experience God and find salvation *outside* the church. God's grace is active in and through other religious beliefs, practices, and rituals; God is drawing people to God's self in and through other religions. Therefore, other religious traditions may be "ways of salvation."[3] Those graced in and through their own religions are also oriented toward the Christian church. They are, in a sense, already Christians and are directed toward what Christians have in Jesus; they simply do not realize it; they are *anonymous* Christians.[4]

The Mutuality Model

Knitter's third model, the mutuality model, corresponds to ecumenical/interreligious organizations and philosophers of religion, more than it does to particular traditions or denominations. To those of the Mutuality Model, it appears that traditional understandings of Christ and the church throw up *doctrinal* obstacles to the *ethical* obligation to engage in authentic interaction with others. Knitter refers to John Hick as one of the spokespersons for this model. A Christian who believes that the Real is Father and a Buddhist who believes that the Real is Emptiness can both achieve similar lives of peace in themselves and compassion for others. Similarities in ethics suggest, for Hick and other mutualist Christians, that differences in doctrine may not be that important. Raimon Panikkar proposes that to speak of Jesus as "the *only* Son of God" is meant to say something positively of Jesus; it was not meant to say something negatively of the Buddha. Rather than a particular doctrine or philosophy, it is one's own religious experience that enables him or her to recognize and learn from his or her neighbors of other traditions.

The Acceptance Model

Knitter's fourth and final model for interreligious activity—the acceptance model—is the most recent to address theological issues in response to religious pluralism. The acceptance model neither holds one tradition as superior, nor searches for the commonality that makes them all valid; its aim, simply, is to accept religious diversity. The theologies of George Lindbeck, Paul Griffiths, and S. Mark Heim help to illustrate the emerging, but sometimes contrasting, views that inform the acceptance model. Lindbeck argues:

> Adherents of different religions do not diversely thematize the same experience, *rather they have different experiences.* Buddhist compassion, Christian love, and French Revolutionary *fraternité* are not diverse modifications of a single fundamental human awareness, emotion, attitude, or sentiment, but are radically distinct ways of experiencing and being oriented toward self, neighbor, and cosmos.[5]

Griffiths is disappointed that, too often, interreligious dialogue seems to have as its guiding principle that participants be nice to each other and stress similarities over differences. He argues: "Such dialogue is also a practice that ought to cease; it has no discernible benefits, many negative effects, and is based upon a radical misapprehension of the nature and significance of religious commitments."[6] S. Mark Heim's reply to Lindbeck is that religions have different languages because they are different religions to begin with; difference *precedes* language. Heim presents the Christian doctrine of God as Trinity as an explanation of how the real differences among the religious traditions are both a reflection and a perception of this divine manyness. There is plurality among the religions because there is plurality *within* God, and as such, there must be permanently co-existing truths. In dialogue, the main possibility for Heim, and responsibility for Griffiths, is the understanding of dialogue as the embrace and the clash of really different "superior" viewpoints will always preserve the character of competition or apologetics. Each religious tradition, while accepting the validity of others, will seek to convince that its view is, as its adherents believe, *more* superior.[7]

Interfaith Theology and Youth

When asked to speculate on the relevancy of these models for interreligious interaction between youth, several questions come to mind. How are youth different from adults with respect to religious thought and experience? Can youth be expected to have developed a sufficiently thorough theological system that allows them to identify themselves on a continuum such as Knitter's? Would youth participating in interreligious activity be able to identify with a particular model if it were different than the model used by the majority in their group? It quickly becomes apparent that these and similar questions should just as appropriately be asked of adults.

Youth identifying with the fulfillment and mutuality models will necessarily be more interested in ethics and what it means to be one's neighbor than they will be interested in what it means to be "saved" and whether their neighbor is saved or not. Interreligious activities where youth are engaged in service projects or exercises to expose them to the beliefs and practices of the religious other would seem to be the ideal types of activities for those identifying with these two models. Such activities do not seem affected by religious differences. It is common for participants of these activities to be unaware of the differences in religious belief and practice of their counterparts.

Contrary to what one might expect from reading Knitter's description of the total replacement model, I have witnessed participants of interreligious activity from conservative or Evangelical Protestant denominations. Those who have been active voice their religious convictions (which may include an invitation to consider and accept a particular claim), but they also listen to their interlocutors. Whether participating in an interreligious dialogue on the nature of Jesus or cooperating in an interreligious activity to collect money and resources for disaster victims, these Christians have maintained their particularly rigid universal faith claims while being genuinely involved in "loving their neighbor." Some might argue that since these Christians are even bothering to listen to their interlocutors they cannot really identify with the total replacement model. One begins to see that such activity is as descriptive of the type of acceptance model espoused by Griffiths as it is the total replacement model. However, these Christians have told me they listen respectfully, because that is what they believe Jesus would do in their situation. They believe that without genuine listening and understanding on their part, their witness of Jesus as Christ to their non-Christian sisters and brothers is incomplete. Interreligious activity with persons informed by the total replacement model, even when they are interested in listening to others, requires their interlocutors to be especially understanding. I speculate that it is because this type of understanding is uncommon that we find so few Evangelical Christians, Orthodox Jews, and conservative Muslims in dialogue with one another. With so few modeling this behavior for youth, I expect to see very few youth who identify themselves within the total replacement and acceptance models participating in interreligious activity.

Personal Observations

Having worked for four years as the manager of interreligious programs for the Chicago and Northern Illinois Region of the National Conference for Community and Justice (NCCJ), I am well acquainted with the interreligious dynamic of metropolitan Chicago and the issues facing the various religious communities. The majority of my activity has been with religious and political leaders and all of it has been with adults. However, in May 2003, I was hired to serve as the Director of a new interfaith youth initiative: Interfaith Collaboration of Emerging Leaders (ICEL).[8]

ICEL is a September 11 Anti-Bias Project funded by a grant from the Chevron-Texaco Foundation. It is led by the Council of Religious Leaders of Metropolitan Chicago in partnership with the Chicago Board of Rabbis, the Council of Islamic Organizations of Greater Chicago, the Greek Orthodox Metropolis of Chicago, and the Sikh Religious Society of Chicago. These four communities were selected because they were variously affected by the backlash following September 11. In ICEL, high school juniors and seniors from the corresponding communities of these organizations cooperate in an effort to increase their capacity to identify and respond to bias and bigotry. These young people are receiving age appropriate human relations training that will inform project activities such as administering questionnaires in their communities, hosting events in their respective houses of worship for their fellow participants from other religious communities, cooperating to serve the greater community, and showcasing their experiences to the broader, civic community. The responsibility of directing this project has raised questions I have never before considered.

At each ICEL activity, I have asked participants why they believe it is important to interact with young people from other religious communities. Even though they eventually became annoyed with the repetition, answering the question never became easy. The novelty of meeting young people from little-known religious communities, or common curiosity, seemed to be an initial motivation for participation, but no one identified it as that which made interaction *important*. In answering this question, it has been common for participants from all four communities to express an agenda. Muslim participants expressed an interest in helping to correct others' misimpressions of Islam. They also expressed the belief that one cannot be an observant Muslim and avoid contact with others whom God has created, and whose religious traditions God has allowed, even willed into being. Some Muslims expressed belief that interaction was good because it allowed them to witness or exemplify the truth of Islam. Jewish participants expressed a belief that interaction would facilitate a greater harmony in the public sphere, and that misperception and stereotype would eventually give way to information gained from personal experience and exposure to the other. Greek Orthodox participants expressed a concern about the mistreatment of Muslims—and those perceived as such—and believed interaction would allow them the opportunity to reassure the members of these communities that such treatment was wrong and that they might also befriend them; the parable of the Good Samaritan and the command to love one's neighbor were often part of their responses. Sikh participants expressed an interest in raising general, public awareness of their religious tradition. But they also had the greatest difficulty with the question. It is helpful to understand that not only are Sikhs a relatively small religious community in the United States[9], but Sikhism also assumes the various religious traditions are equally true and their adherents capable of peaceful coexistence; therefore, for Sikhs, avoiding interaction with the religious other is both a temporal and an ideological impossibility. This being said, at the beginning of the ICEL project, Sikh participants were no more familiar with others' beliefs and practices than their fellow participants.

As the project moved along and participants had repeated opportunities for interaction, I observed casual friendships developing (participants exchanging phone numbers and email addresses, etc.). On at least on one occasion, there was an incident involving two participants flirting with one another, and drawing the unwelcome attention of their respective religious leaders and fellow participants; needless to say, their plans to meet one another later that evening were foiled. One adult leader saw the incident as an unfortunate occurrence, sure to result in condemnation from parents and other leaders of future projects and activities of this type. Another leader saw the incident as an indication that the participants were moving into real-life relationships beyond superficial niceties common with these types of social settings.

It is worth mentioning a few additional motivators informing some of the participants' decision to be involved in ICEL. Participants preparing for college were not only interested in learning skills for leadership in diverse societies common to so many college and university campuses today, they were also aware of how their participation in ICEL might look on their applications to these schools. Others were motivated by much more immediate factors, such as the encouragement or insistence of a parent or even a religious leader who found him/herself involved as support staff to the project. It was also my observation that although not a *motivator* or even *grounds* for participation, the socio-political ideal of democracy and multiculturalism presupposed by public institutions (such as those they encounter in public schools, athletic organizations, and art societies) seemed to inform participants' sense of justice as much as any strictly religious principle.

Notes

1. Striving for manageability and relevance, I explored these questions by performing a critical case study on the current interreligious activity of metropolitan Chicago. Specifically, I researched and analyzed the interreligious programs of the National Conference for Community and Justice (NCCJ) Chicago and Northern Illinois Region. In its efforts to collaborate with and organize the efforts of specific religious communities, NCCJ Chicago determines the grounds for participation and exercises a principle of inclusion/exclusion. Recognizing the principles of inclusion practiced by NCCJ Chicago directly influence the religious communities participating in its programs, it was assumed one could discover how their participation has helped them advance inclusion while protecting their respective identities. The results of the case study were analyzed in light of NCCJ's mission relating to its interreligious programs. In the interest of space, neither the case study nor the results of its analysis are provided here.

2. Paul F. Knitter, *Introducing Theologies of Religions*, (Maryknoll, NY: Orbis Books, 2002).

3. Karl Rahner, "Christianity and the Non-Christian Religions," in *Theological Investigations* (Baltimore: Helicon Press, 1966), 5:115-34. (See Knitter 68–72).

4. Karl Rahner, *Foundations of Christian Faith* (New York: Cross Road, 1978), 178–203. (See Knitter 72–74).

5. George Lindbeck, *The Nature of Doctrine: Religion and Theology in a Postliberal Age* (Philadelphia: Westminster Press, 1984), 40. (See Knitter 178–82) [Emphasis added].

6. Paul Griffiths, "Why We Need Interreligious Polemics," *First Things* 44 (1994): 32. (See Knitter 187).

7. (See Knitter 197–200).

8. ICEL's website provides more in-depth project information and pictures that document participants' level of activity and involvement: www.interfaithleaders.org.

9. There are approximately 5,000 Sikhs living in metropolitan Chicago. See "Sikhism" in *The NCCJ 2005 Interfaith Calendar.*

4.

Towards a Transnational Interfaith Youth Network in Higher Education: The Harvard/WCRP Model[1]

Patrice Brodeur

Introduction

THIS CHAPTER SEEKS TO DESCRIBE and analyze a successful university campus experience in interfaith youth work which emerged at Harvard University between 1990 and 1998, within the transnational context of the largest interreligious organizations in the world, the World Conference on Religion and Peace (WCRP), recently renamed "Religions for Peace."[2] The methodology which was developed during those years was student-led, with minimum support from existing chaplaincy or other student services. This grassroots approach proved that students can be active promoters of campus interfaith activities whether supportive infrastructures exist or not, even though the work is generally easier if permanent staff and faculty get involved.

In 1989, I was elected chair of the WCRP International Youth Committee at the Fifth WCRP World Assembly in Melbourne, Australia. I inherited a small and loosely organized network of young religious activists who were primarily involved locally, except for the WCRP Japanese National Youth Committee which was able to carry out serious national activities. Under the impetus of the Melbourne Assembly, two dozen energized young adults returned home to strengthen or, for the most part, establish new WCRP youth groups. Several of these efforts were linked to university campuses in Tübingen, Germany; Cambridge, England; and Coimbatore, India for example. As my appointment coincided with the beginning of my doctoral studies at Harvard University, I realized that developing what I now call a transnational interfaith youth network required involvement at universities worldwide. I needed to find out first whether there was anything already in existence in my new home. After spending my first year exploring a variety of student groups, I concluded that there was nothing close to what the other university-based WCRP youth groups were developing within the WCRP International Youth Committee. So in the fall of 1990, under the impetus of the recent invasion of Kuwait by Iraqi forces, a small multi-religious group of like-minded activists founded a Harvard/WCRP student organization at Harvard Divinity School.

The Harvard/WCRP model can best be understood as one node within the fledgling transnational youth network that was emerging out of the growing activities of the WCRP International Youth Committee. By combining my responsibilities as chair of a small international youth organization with my desire to be active locally (in order to avoid the danger of being a jet-set without any local roots), I helped foster the development of a transnational model for the development of a global interfaith youth network.[3] In seeking to balance this local/global tension, I was planting the seeds for what I later called a "glocal" approach to interreligious dialogue as part of a new field within the academic study of religion, that is, the *applied* academic study of religion or, in short, "applied religion."[4]

The centrality of interreligious dialogue in addressing almost every contemporary issue stems from the fact that most of our local and national realities worldwide have grown more diverse exponentially due to increased migration patterns around the world over the last fifty years made possible by the technological revolution in transportation. As access to education is one of the basic rights of the child,[5] the frontline of this new diversity is found in the primary and secondary public school systems around the world. In the last decade, this greatly expanded diversity erupted onto university campuses, especially in larger urban and elite institutions. Compounded with the exponential increase in student exchange internationally,[6] the results are clear: there is an urgent need to provide spaces where students (as well as faculty, staff, and administrators) learn to celebrate their diversity, which implies both the recognition of our common humanity as well as the acknowledgment of important and valuable differences. But this celebration is not enough; educators in particular have the responsibility to nurture skills that help us learn how to manage this diversity so as to ensure that new patterns of social interaction will promote values of inclusivity and justice for all.

The Harvard/WCRP model therefore reflects one small effort at nurturing such a university campus space within the WCRP transnational interfaith youth network. By sharing my undoubtedly biased perspective of this experiment, I hope to demonstrate how a conscious effort at integrating study and activism remains one possible path for students who want to make a difference in the world starting with their respective here and now, however transitional it might be.

Description

The Harvard/WCRP group was formed in the academic year 1990–1991 at Harvard Divinity School. It expanded to include a section with the Graduate School of Arts and Sciences in 1993 in view of the United Nations International Year of the Indigenous Peoples and the Year of Interreligious Understanding and Cooperation.[7] It lasted until 1999 when its leadership fell to be renewed precisely at a time when the need for interreligious dialogue was increasing on campus. A variety of interreligious activities did take place during that time, but none with the same transnational vision initially developed within the Harvard/WCRP student group.

The Harvard/WCRP aims were to:

1) Develop and participate in a university-wide student network for the promotion of interreligious cooperation for peace and justice with both undergraduates and graduate individual participation as well as representatives from various religious and related student organizations;

2) Provide a campus-wide forum where local and global issues can be debated from different faith perspectives;

3) Expand the concept of multi-culturalism to include the various spiritual/religious dimensions of our diverse cultural identities (for example: cooperate with the Harvard Cultural Foundation);

4) Broaden the awareness of the university community on global, international, and local issues of injustice in which religious people are part of the problem, the solution, or both;

5) Provide a forum for inter-personal exchanges on matters of religion and peace, including, where and when suitable, possibilities for learning about each other's personal faith commitments and faith communities, especially in light of their respective contemporary spiritual expressions and social struggles;

6) Develop among its members skills as interreligious facilitators, whether within each one's own faith community, across different ones, or as third party mediators;

7) Cooperate with the United Ministry to coordinate students' increased awareness of religious diversity and concerns on campus.

These aims reflect three salient features. First, there was a growing awareness that multi-culturalism in the 1990s could no longer reduce religion to a "culture" or, even worse, leave religion outside of the realm of celebrating diversity of identities on campus. Second, the activities of the group aimed consciously to integrate the local and global dimensions in our lives. Third, younger religious people can learn to be both self-critical and proactive so as to discover experientially how intertwined the inner life of prayer and contemplation and the outer life of social action for justice truly are.

This close relationship was expressed through a simple concept, the three H's (Head, Heart, and Hands), symbolizing the interconnection between intellectual life (Head), compassion (Heart), and action (Hands). I developed this simple language early in my tenure as chair of the WCRP international youth committee because it proved to be easily understood by the many youth not fluent in English and easily translatable, literally and figuratively, into many languages and religious traditions. Yet behind its simplicity lies a challenging process of carefully integrating these three different dimensions in our lives. We sought to achieve this by consciously balancing the kinds of activities that would ensure that all three areas would be present at every meeting. Of course, that balance varied tremendously from one meeting to another, in part because different meetings and activities had their own emphasis. For example, activities that brought in outside lecturers were primarily intellectual while those related to the week of prayers for world peace were primarily spiritual.

A more precise examination of the Harvard/WCRP activities[8] reveals a six-fold categorization: lectures, training, activism, fundraising, excursions, and spiritual growth. The choice of activities in all areas relied completely on the interests of the group members. If someone felt strongly about a particular topic, he or she took the lead in organizing an activity around it, which others would support to the best of their abilities and time. This approach ensured that every member became an active participant, both receiving and giving. It did not matter what multiple identity configuration we were each made up of (i.e., majority or minority): everyone had a chance to exercise leadership on some aspect of the group activities. Whatever one's nationality or religion, to take but two identities, there was a place for everyone interested in promoting dialogue, peace, and justice from an interreligious perspective. As in any student group, the composition and size of the group fluctuated from year to year. At its core, the number varied from half to a full dozen, while activities gathered anywhere from a dozen to over a hundred participants.

Each one of these six kinds of activities was bi-directional: sometimes the group members received from outside sources and at other times shared their own expertise with outsiders. In terms of lectures, on the one hand, many guest speakers were brought in to speak on a variety of contemporary topics; on the other, many group members also lectured themselves either to the rest of the group or to broader audiences within larger contexts. For example, Manny Belino was an active Filipino member who helped organize a number of activities related to the Philippines; Raphael Abiem, a refugee from Southern Sudan, did the same with matters related to the civil war in Sudan; and Anita raised our awareness about the civil war in Sri Lanka. The beauty of graduate student groups in particular is that many of their members already have rich experiences to share with each other as well as with the broader university community and beyond. Capitalizing on these internal group resources ensures that the group creates and sustains its own transformational space.

The training activities were also bi-directional. For example, one year we all attended a training workshop on nonviolence; we also led workshops in interreligious dialogue both in the U.S. (workshop on interreligious dialogue, on the Convention on the Rights of the Child, on Global Ethics) and abroad (Belorussia, India, etc.) as well as helped organize training workshops for youth interested in developing interreligious dialogue skills at two UN International Conferences: on Population and Development in Cairo (1994) and on Social Development in Copenhagen (1995).

The activism also took the form of participation at public demonstrations (anti-Gulf War, vigil for Bosnian war victims), letter campaigns, especially related to Amnesty International but not exclusively, fasting (Oxfam/Bread for the World), and awareness raising in many contexts.

The fundraising activities helped us respond to both sudden humanitarian crises (refugees from the Pinatubo volcano in the Philippines in 1991, the victims of the L.A. riots, and the war in Yugoslavia in 1992, the victims of the floods in Nepal in 1993, etc.) as well as the many needs related to structural injustice (food drives for homeless shelters, etc.). We decided that it was important to use our privileged position at Harvard to organize one fundraising activity per semester, alternating local and global issues. We came to realize that we could also combine purposes, such as sell the beautiful Interfaith Calendar published in Vancouver, Canada, as a fundraiser for any cause we chose, while educating its user about the variety of religious celebrations in the world. Another example was fundraising for the "Adopt-a-Room" program of the Interfaith Assembly on Homelessness and Housing, where we were able to meet recently housed people and learn more with them about the structural and human problems of homelessness in our own backyard.

The excursion category only contains two examples: a local trip to the Peace Abbey in the distant suburbs of Boston, and a week-long spring break interfaith trip to Montreal, Canada. The excursions proved more difficult to organize in part because of competing demands on the members' free time and the financial resources necessary to carry them out. Yet, the trip to Montreal proved important to consolidate our group dynamic and learn the significant differences between Canada and the U.S. in regard to social justice.

The activities directly related to the category of spiritual growth include the dimension of praying linked to our letter writing campaigns (explained below), learning about each other's personal religious practices, such as fasting in Judaism and Baha'ism, and playing a role as consultants for the Boston Theological Institute's Ecumenical Worship Service which we of course attended as well. The most significant and sustained effort, however, was our organizing the Week of Prayers for World Peace (WPWP) for seven consecutive years. This easy-to-plan event can be as simple as reading the provided leaflet which contains a set of readings for each day of the week or as complex as involving the various religious groups on campus to take charge of one day a week or one dimension of the program for a whole week. I hope that this activity in particular can one day be a standard event on campuses throughout the world.

Finally, the Harvard/WCRP group hosted for a few years the publishing of the WCRP International Youth Committee newsletter under the editorship of Luis Girón Negrón. This bi-annual activity also helped foster a sense of transnational identity among many of the local Harvard members. It was also another way of sharing our resources with the rest of this youth network.

Analysis of Methodology

The Harvard/WCRP model is based on a methodology that, locally, combines the common characteristics of grassroots and student club activism in higher education. A global dimension was added by virtue of the fact that, as coordinator of the WCRP International Youth Committee, much input into our local activities came from the WCRP network, both youth and otherwise. The reverse was equally true: the activities and model developed at Harvard were shared with the rest of this growing transnational network of interreligious youth activities, much of which took place in university campuses on four continents. This approach was self-consciously transnational, that is, it crossed and in some ways transcended national boundaries; it coincided with the advent of the Internet. But it was also glocal, that is, it built on the reality that all human beings can only be at one place in time, thereby being always physically local while our physical, intellectual, and spiritual movements can indeed be global to various degrees.

I thought about the idea of "glocal" three weeks before I read about it online in 1997. I believed, and still do, that this contraction of "local" and "global" was a simple way to reflect the reality of this new philosophy that reflected my efforts to think anew the limited paradigm "think globally, act locally." For example, our Harvard/WCRP fundraising took part one semester for a local cause and the next semester for a global cause, understood as going to a cause "abroad." Yet we knew that this division, while practical, did not convey the many ways by which our group's reflections and social justice actions were transformative for each one of us precisely because we also received a great deal from other WCRP youth around the world who participated in the same or similar kinds of activities. For example, we may have been the first multi-religious youth group to develop a regular cooperation with Amnesty International specifically based on identifying cases of religious discrimination. Our cooperation, followed up with countless letters, was based on three arguments.

First, the juxtaposition of letters written by a multi-religious group of individuals who openly identified as religious in one way or another, with one particular religious tradition or another, was a much more powerful way of requesting government and military officials to abide by several different UN conventions, including the United Nations Declaration on the Elimination of Discrimination based on Religion or Belief.

Second, depending on the faith of the prisoner, we could collectively sign greeting cards on the occasion of their respective major annual religious holidays. We knew that such collective cards would resonate powerfully with prisoners who may share cells with people of various faith backgrounds, whether they would be practicing or not.

Third, our multi-religious group also prayed for all prisoners to whom we wrote. Sustaining this careful walk on a relatively unexplored path was our shared belief that praying for prisoners, in whatever way we felt called to do so, was a powerful tool we young religious people had at our disposal to make a difference. Of course, the question of interfaith prayers is extremely delicate, which allowed each one of us to discover the boundaries of our respective limits when praying as a group. But given that prayer was an important spiritual dimension of all the members of the Harvard/WCRP group at that time, it made sense to explore how far we could go together while respecting the uniqueness of our respective religious perspectives and practices.

Finally, this one activity became a powerful means of enhancing our group cohesion, even when we simply decided that each one of us would pray in silence together because we could not always agree on the wording suggested by one group member or how to word a collective prayer together. Rather than waste too much time crafting this prayer together, we sometimes chose silence as a powerful means of being in communion with each other in the room as well as with the far distant prisoners we were carrying in our minds and hearts.[9]

These experiences helped us grow in our personal faith as well as in our understanding that there is a deep interrelation and interdependence of the local and global. In fact, the two are so intertwined that their boundaries blend into each other to a point of disappearance. What has become more important for many of us is the search for the integration of the less and less clearly defined local and global dimensions in our daily lives. The power dynamic that emerged from this understanding necessitates further study and praxis, for many of our activities and our learning have come out of discovering this glocal reality.

Conclusion

The question of how to assess such student campus groups as the Harvard/WCRP model remains open. Using Ken Wilber's model of transpersonal spiritual growth, it would be possible to measure the impact of this kind of interfaith campus activities on the educational development of its members by comparing the spiritual growth of its participants with those who either remain within their own religious group or are not involved in any. A similar assessment survey to the one developed and integrated into the E Pluribus Unum project, for example, could be adapted to measure the importance (or not) of such interfaith campus activities in our understanding of self-development in the post-teenage years or young adult years. For example, it could help answer such a question as how does the integration of what the WCRP youth model has called the three H's (Head, Heart, and Hands) happen for individual group members and, more important, how does it become self-reflective? This integrative process, key to spiritual development, when purposely engaged in a religiously (and otherwise) diverse group, can be a powerful force in transforming individuals and their worldviews, resulting in the discovery of not only their unique set of life-long commitments but also their responsibility to develop sustainable living patterns that correspond to their feelings of living a common humanity on one shared planet.

The results of the Harvard/WCRP model can achieve much more than educating for citizenship understood too often within narrow national boundaries; they can transform young adults into global citizens who learn to navigate their manifold responsibilities, from their ever-widening civic levels in the street, town, state, country, and planetary neighborhoods, to the ever-deepening layers of our spiritual relations with each other and the Divine.

The particular experience of the Harvard/WCRP model, despite its present defunct status, can still help us in the process of finding out what can become the best practices in the field of Interfaith Youth Work. While its weakness may have come from its leadership not being interconnected sufficiently with on-going institutional structures, thereby relying primarily on the steam of individual students rather than sharing the organizational burdens with existing and paid staff, the Harvard/WCRP model still demonstrates many powerful examples of successful practices that can easily be emulated on campuses worldwide.

The development of an effective transnational interreligious youth network on campuses worldwide is a crucial component for enhancing peace with justice because it helps promote global awareness at a crucial age. Without such a network, I am afraid the growing migration trends will only exacerbate tensions in the face of increased competition over resources claimed by selfish group identity dynamics. The various levels and long-term needs that are required to ensure true pluralistic societies require the existence of an effective transnational interreligious youth network. The alternative is stark, as the post-9/11 world has already demonstrated: a retrenchment into exclusivistic ghettos that fuel greater violence.

Harvard/WCRP: List of Past Activities

1990

Oct. 21:	Co-sponsored Matthew Fox Program
Oct. 21-28:	Week of Prayer for World Peace (at Harvard Divinity School Chapel)
Oct. 27:	German Reunification Discussion and Dinner
Nov.:	Participated in Oxfam/Bread for the World Week
Nov. 18:	Workshop on Non-Violent Action and Social Responsibility
Dec.:	Two presentations on South Africa
Dec.:	Participation in Boston rally against war in the Gulf

1991

March 6:	Letter campaign on behalf of innocent victims of the Gulf War
April 24:	Co-sponsored visit of Christopher Titmuss, MP in the U.K.
May-June:	Furnished 6 rooms in the "Adopt-a-Room" program of the Interfaith Assembly on Homelessness and Housing
Oct. 7:	Presentation on: "The Aftermath of the Pinatubo Eruption"
Oct. 20-27:	Week of Prayer for World Peace (HDS Chapel)
Nov. 4:	Presentation on: "Rebirth of Faith/Religion in Russia"
Nov. 10:	Lecture by Dr. Aram, Gandhian Activist and Moderator, WCRP/International on: "Multi-religious Cooperation"
Nov. 18:	Presentation on Christian Women Initiative in El Salvador
Nov. 25-26:	Co-sponsored fundraising drive for victims of the Pinatubo eruption in the Philippines: raised $260 for the American Red Cross efforts there
Dec. 8:	Workshop on the Convention on the Rights of the Child
Dec. 16:	Presentation on the Sri Lankan civil war

1992

Feb. 10:	Presentation on the Carter Center, Atlanta
March 3:	Human Rights letters sent to Sri Lanka's Prime Minister
March 23:	Presentation on Fasting in Judaism and Baha'ism
March end:	Spring Break Interfaith Trip to Montreal, Canada

April 13:   Presentation on political developments in South Africa
April-May: Donations to St. Agnes Church in South Central L.A.
Sept. 27:   Consulting for the Boston Theological Institute's
               Ecumenical Worship Service
Oct. 5:   Program on the "World's Religions for the World's
               Children" a UNICEF and WCRP/International cooperation
Oct. 11-18:   Week of Prayer for World Peace (at Dudley House)
Oct. 19:   Documentary video on the Peace Process in the Philippines
Nov.-Dec.:   Interfaith Calendar fundraising: $550 was given to
               Caritas/Austria and to the Harvard Islamic Students Association
               for their respective work for Bosnian refugees
Nov. 30:   Christmas greeting cards were sent to Philippino prisoners
Dec.:   Participation in letter campaign for immediate U.S.
               action in Bosnia-Herzegovina
Dec. 14:   Letter to President Ramos on behalf of Filipino children

1993
Oct. 1:   Participation in Vigil for Bosnians at the Boston City Hall
Oct. 28:   Presentation on the civil war in the Sudan
Nov. 4:   Lecture by UN Youth Diplomat from the Netherlands
Nov. 8:   Lecture on "Human Rights Violations: A Search for Causes"
Nov.-Dec.:   Interfaith Calendar fundraising: $500 to Nepal reconstruction
               project in Katmandu for victims of July 1993 floods
Dec. 6-9:   Week of Prayer for World Peace (at the Harvard Memorial Church)

1994
March 12:   Participation at the Conference on Future Reforms for the
               U.N. with:
               Writing letters on behalf of Greek prisoners of conscience
               and participating at workshop on the Sudan
April 8:   Participating at a workshop on the Sudan as part of a
               Harvard School of Public Health Conference on
               "Violence and Human Rights"
               Also co-sponsored workshop on Global Ethics
April 9:   Writing letters on behalf of China prisoners of conscience
Oct.   Week of Prayer for World Peace (Dudley House)
Nov.   Participation at Sixth World Assembly of WCRP/International
               in Italy

1995
March: Participation at the World Summit on Social Development

March 1:	Presentation on "Peace and Social Justice: An Orthodox Jewish Perspective"
April:	Visit from a representative of the Sri Chinmoy Foundation
Aug:	Participation at the UN Youth Forum in New York City
Oct.	Week of Prayer for World Peace (Dudley House)
Nov.	Participation at the First Belarussian Interconfessional Conference in Minsk

1996

All year:	Early developments of IRYOS project: International Religious Youth organizations Seminars
March:	Visit from three Harvard-Radcliffe Interfaith Forum members (undergraduates)
Autumn	Participation in planning for a multi-university project on "Education as Transformation: Religious Pluralism, Spirituality, Higher Education" (up to summer 1997)
Oct.	Week of Prayer for World Peace (Memorial Church)
Nov.	Middle East discussion

1997

March 24:	Presentation on "Liberation theology in the Andean South"
April 15:	Presentation on Namibia and discussion on possibility of cooperation on IRYOS project
May 8:	Participation in HRIF day of social service
May 27:	Further planning for IRYOS and "Education as Transformation"
June:	Social event

Notes

1. A first version of this paper was presented at the first Education as Transformation Conference at Wellesley College in September 1998; a second, at the first annual National Conference on Interfaith Youth Work, at the University of Chicago Divinity School in May 2003.

2. The World Conference on Religion and Peace (WCRP) started officially in 1970 with, whence its first name, a World Conference on Religion and Peace in Kyoto, Japan. It has since then been renamed "World Conference of Religions for Peace," and recently simply "Religions for Peace." Its initial driving force was the need to seek an international religious response to the Vietnam War within the broader context of the growing Cold War. The organization subsequently developed national chapters in over 30 countries and held quinquennial world assemblies. In 1974, the Japanese National Chapter founded a Youth Wing. Under their impetus, ten years later, WCRP/International established the International Youth Committee at the Fourth

World Assembly in Nairobi, Kenya. Five years later, in January 1989, I was elected chair of the International Youth Committee in Melbourne, Australia. In this capacity, I served on the WCRP/International executive committee until November 1994, when during the Sixth World Assembly in Riva del Garda, Italy, I was replaced by Dr. Vinu Aram, a Hindu from India. She was herself replaced in November 1999 by the current chair Mr. Ziad Moussa, a Greek Orthodox from Lebanon. This five-year rotation ensures that the important leadership skills gained by the responsibilities associated with this position are not controlled by any one person but rather shared across the continents and religious traditions.

3. An earlier international effort in which I played an important role, but in no way as global in scope, was the establishment in 1988 and subsequent development in mostly Europe, North America, and the central region of the Middle East, of the Youth Section of the International Council for Christians and Jews, based in Heppenheim, Germany. These youth developments also included Muslims, especially Palestinians and Egyptians.

4. See Patrice Brodeur, "Pour faire place à l'étude critique appliquée de la religion," in *Religiologique*, Vol. 29 (Spring 2004), "Interreligious Dialogue as the Cornerstone for an Applied Academic Study of Religion," in *Proceedings of the LISOR International Conference on Religious Change in Pluralistic Contexts*, ed. by P. S. Van Koningsveld, H. L. Beck, and G. A. Wiegers (Leiden: Brill, 2005).

5. See UNICEF's *Implementation Handbook for the Convention on the Rights of the Child*, rev. ed. 2004.

6. For comprehensive global statistics and future projections, see Todd M. Davis, *Atlas of Student Mobility*, (New York: Institute of International Education, 2003).

7. While efforts were made initially to include undergraduates, the laws regulating student campus life prohibited such cooperation on the basis that graduate students could exploit undergraduate students or their funding resources. Even if undergraduates were to develop their own parallel interreligious organization, it became clear that fears of any outside organization infiltrating Harvard undergraduate activities would have prevented any form of inter-campus or beyond campus interaction within a WCRP transnational youth network. I hope that this situation has been alleviated in recent years.

8. See list of major activities between 1990 and 1996 in the appendix to this article. The activities following that year continued under the leadership of another graduate student, Mark Farha. Some of them were linked to the "Education as Transformation" project which was launched in September 1998 at Wellesley College, MA, USA. Efforts were made in the preparation to this major national conference to emphasize multi-constituency teams from each participating institution. The Harvard/WCRP group only partially succeeded in assembling such a team. A leaflet written in preparation for the 1997-1998 academic year stated: "At Harvard, four kinds of activities are being planned: 1) a religious open house (early November); 2) a major roundtable discussion on "Religious Pluralism at Harvard: the Historical Context"; 3)

Separate undergraduate house meetings and graduate school meetings; 4) separate religious community meetings. Each of these activities can be further developed to serve the needs of and reach out to every Harvard community member interested in this topic. A final report will be compiled to reflect the results of each one of these activities. Hopefully, a clearer picture of religion at Harvard will emerge from our combined efforts. The Harvard/WCRP group is one of many participating bodies behind this campus wide effort." It is not clear to me how far this project was achieved.

9. The scholar in me is hoping that maybe one day a scientific double-blind experiment can be developed to measure whether or not such a multi-religious advocacy for Amnesty International prisoners, with interfaith prayers, is more effective than a regular AI support group.

5.

The Gujarat Young Adult Project of the International Association for Religious Freedom (IARF)

Zulfikhar Akram and Ramola Sundram

THE WESTERN STATE OF GUJARAT TYPICALLY REFLECTS the multi-religious society of India. As in the rest of the country, Hindus constitute the majority, while Muslims make up about 11 percent of the population. There are small numbers of other faiths— Christianity, Sikhism and Jainism. The state has a reputation and track record of being disturbed and communally unsettled; there have been violent clashes between Muslims and Hindus. Muslims on their part have generally tended to distance themselves from the Hindus by living in separated colonies in some areas and avoiding social interactions with them. The activities of certain Christian missionaries and the issue of conversions have angered some Hindus. Illiteracy, unemployment and widespread negative stereotypes have only contributed to widening the social divide between the different religious communities. Of late, there has been an upsurge in the activities of Hindu fundamentalist and nationalist forces. Both Muslims and Christians have been attacked, as have their places of worship. This has been further fuelled by the exploitation of long-standing religious intolerance, old hatreds and misunderstandings for political ends. Thus, the minority religious groups have been feeling a growing sense of suspicion, insecurity and threat to their lives and religious freedom. Finally, several natural calamities have also hit Gujarat in the recent past. Most devastating of all was the earthquake of January 2001, a humanitarian disaster that cost thousands of lives and homes, cutting across all religious, caste, and economic divisions.

In light of this history and recent events, the challenge became clear: How could an organization working for interfaith harmony and religious freedom make an appropriate contribution to an area ravaged by a long history of interreligious mistrust and recent natural disaster? As a century-old organization working in different countries to promote interfaith understanding, harmony and religious freedom, the International Association for Religious Freedom (IARF) had no prescribed role in the face of such a combined challenge. Yet, IARF sought to answer this challenge by developing a unique methodology of interreligious cooperation in the face of post-conflict reconstruction. This article examines the trajectory of this creative response that reveals lessons for future incorporation of young adults in interreligious peacebuilding initiatives.

Project Description

With the requests and suggestions of affected Gujaratis, the South Asia Co-ordinating Council of IARF proposed an intervention designed to bring the different religious communities together to cooperate in alleviating the suffering. Along with their homes, many people had also lost their places of worship, which had additional significance as people were seeking solace and spiritual support through prayers and worship in the wake of the enormous tragedy. IARF decided to focus on rebuilding a temple and a mosque. As the plan evolved, it became clear that such a project's impact could be increased through the involvement of local, national and international young adults. Four groups were eventually involved: IARF, young adults with the Religious Freedom Young Adult Network (RFYN), the local communities, and external agencies.

The Religious Freedom Young Adult Network

IARF has for many years been encouraging and involving young adults around the world in its religious freedom work. It believes that through their energy, enthusiasm and positive attitude, young adults can be real agents of the change required for the work of promoting interfaith co-operation and religious freedom. It also believes that by starting early, young adults will have ample time and opportunity to experiment, learn, understand, and then contribute effectively to religious freedom on a long-term basis. The RFYN aims to have young adults working actively around the world for the promotion of religious freedom through local initiatives, many assuming leadership roles and networking with each other. The Gujarat project was determined to involve international, national and local youths in a program that would not only help the local communities, but also assist the young adults themselves to learn about each other's religion, culture, beliefs and practices, and related issues of intolerance, discrimination and religious freedom. One of the expected outcomes of the program was to inculcate in the young adults a respect for and an understanding of other religions and to put them on the path of working for the promotion of interfaith co-operation and religious freedom.

IARF

The project was a challenge to IARF for three reasons: First, it was conceived and designed for an area that was known to have witnessed religious intolerance and violence; second, it was an area where Hindu fundamentalist forces were strong and active, and had made it virtually inaccessible and non-conducive for any interfaith work; third, the area had just experienced a terrible natural calamity, and humanitarian initiatives were the immediate priority. There was also the persistent risk of being misconstrued by the different groups. The local people could misunderstand IARF as a relief and rehabilitation agency, or as an agency that builds temples and mosques without being aware of its philosophy and objectives. Then there was the threat of Hindu fundamentalist groups viewing the project with suspicion, and then possibly creating obstacles to its smooth and effective implementation. Against all these and other potentially misleading perceptions of the local communities, the challenge for IARF was not only to present from the beginning its purpose as clearly as possible and sustain it throughout the project; the wider public needed to appreciate its value to avoid any further religious violence.

Local Involvement

Indeed, the local community was the most unstable of all the cooperating elements associated to this project. The different religious communities in the state of Gujarat have a history of mutual mistrust, intolerance, and hatred. Religious harmony, understanding and tolerance were prerequisites for peaceful co-existence and prosperity. In a strange twist of fortune, however, the anguish caused by the earthquake united the locals in their appreciation of IARF's work. They were able to put aside their differences and animosities and unite to work for a common good. A program was created that would encourage a spirit of interfaith understanding and co-operation.

Identification of Project Sites

The villages for the project were identified in the following way: A team consisting of the IARF South Asian Co-ordinating Council Chairman, a civil engineer, and the project administrator surveyed the earthquake-affected parts of Gujarat through extensive travel. They were assisted by some local people and NGOs as they went about meeting and interviewing people in the affected areas. Several damaged temples and mosques were examined closely. Some of the temples and mosques found in the towns needed repair and restoration, but local people wanted them to be restored to their original glory, which was beyond the monetary scope of IARF. Besides, IARF was considering repair and reconstruction of a temple and a mosque only as a symbolic gesture to achieve the broader objective of interfaith co-operation and religious freedom work. At some places, damaged temples were located, but the population around was mostly Hindu, with no visible Muslim and Christian presence. Similarly, a few mosques were found in places that were predominantly Muslim, Hindus living only in distant parts.

From the towns, the team moved into the rural areas. There were damaged mosques and temples, and the villages deserved our attention; but they were either Hindu or Muslim villages exclusively, and separated by long distances. Finally Nana Dahisara, a Hindu village with about three hundred houses, out of which about fifteen belonged to Muslims, and Kajarada, a 100 percent Muslim village with four hundred houses, were selected. The villages were located not too far from each other and in the same *Taluka* (part of a district) called Maliya, deserving of and ideal for the implementation of the proposed project. They are also close to the town of Morbi near the major city of Rajkot.

The villagers welcomed IARF work in their villages and assured full participation and co-operation. Design and layout for the temple and the mosque were prepared in consultation with the civil engineer, an architect and the villagers. A budget and a time-frame for the completion of the construction were also drawn up. As the entire village of Nana Dahisara was being relocated to adjacent land, building a new temple was agreed upon, whereas in the Kajarada village the badly damaged mosque was taken up for repair and restoration. Work on the mosque and at the temple site began in November 2001 under the supervision of the respective committees and the project administrator. Three to four months were estimated for the completion of both structures.

The Young Adult Program

As construction work on the temple and mosque began, the fourteen-day young adult program that had been built into the project as the main component got underway, from 23 December 2001. There were fifteen local Gujaratis (five each from Nana Dahisara and Kajarada villages and from Morbi town), nine nationals (from Bangalore, Coimbatore, Khasi Hills, Kerala, Mysore, Vizag,) and ten international young adults (from Canada, Hungary, Japan, South Africa, UK and the USA). The thirty-four participants, between ages nineteen and thirty, were from different faith and belief traditions—Bahá'í, Buddhism, Christianity, First Nations spirituality, Hinduism, Islam, Jainism, Unitarian and Unitarian Universalist, and there were also some of no fixed belief. When the international and national participants arrived at their accommodation in Morbi, they were accorded a great welcome by the local youths and elders.

The main activity of the program was the involvement of young adults in the construction of the two places of worship in the villages. The time in the villages was also utilized for meetings and interactions with the villagers. Back at the hostel, there were interfaith prayer services and workshops, group discussions on issues related to interfaith and religious freedom, and cultural presentations. Visits to places of worship also figured in the activities. Although the overall program and activities were designed in advance and were clearly outlined for the fourteen days, most of the youths were getting exposure of this kind for the first time. Flexibility and freedom to decide on the schedule within the framework of the original design was the key to giving them a sense of ownership of the program. Some who had experience of attending other programs prior to this had been identified as the facilitators. The inexperience of the majority notwithstanding, the entire program was a do-it-yourself experiment for them, starting with an innovative way of introducing themselves to each other, getting acquainted with the sites of work and with the local people and their culture, marking out a day-to-day schedule for the fourteen days, and conducting it through the formation of different committees, etc.—all done by the young adults themselves. Seven committees were formed as the young adults volunteered to take on the responsibility of doing a good job: interfaith, intercultural, sports and entertainment, construction work, food, healthcare and safety, as well as transport and sightseeing.

Schedule and Insights

A typical day would start with sunrise worship and meditation (for early risers) followed by a prayer service and workshops, visits to the villages for construction and repair, and meeting with the villagers. Once at the sites, the young adults listed out the tasks with the help of the contractor and the masons. The tasks at the mosque included demolition of the damaged walls, clearing the rubble, removing the old and worn-out floor tiles, carrying sand, water, etc. inside the mosque, chipping the old plaster from the columns and arches, painting the new walls, and watering the plastered walls. The temple work consisted mostly of laying the foundations.

Lunch at the work sites was especially fulfilling, as the young adults cleaned the place and sat together inside the mosque precincts. There were prayers five times a day and on Friday (when the gathering would be much larger); the young adults would suspend all work and watch the villagers offer prayers. Later they would have interactions with them. A participant from Hungary remarked: "When we were working in the Muslim village, we experienced the Friday prayer. It was a very special feeling for me, because in that very moment I really had the feeling that we had done something useful. We stopped working, and were listening to what the Imam was saying (some of us did not understand a word, of course). However, we were part of their life, and they became part of my life at that very hour." At Nana Dahisara the young adults would take lunch in the house of one of the participants, then go around the village and sit with the villagers to discuss matters of religion, culture, and traditions.

The day would end with continuance of workshops and cultural presentations back at the hostel. Sometimes, on topics related to religious freedom, leading questions were set for group discussions, and participants actively voiced their views. Workshops on different religions were held, the young adults making presentations on their own faith traditions and answering questions raised by others. This removed many misconceptions and stereotypes about different religions and their followers. Prayers from different spiritual traditions were a regular feature.

The language barrier posed a major challenge during these workshops, presentations and group discussions. The international young adults used English; the national youths from different parts of the country could communicate in both English and several Indian languages; the local young adults, particularly those from the two villages, knew only Gujarati and Hindi. To solve this problem, which of course had been foreseen, some local and national youths volunteered to do translations. Interestingly, the participants with language problems were seen spending more time with those with whom they faced the barrier. Some participants were more active and knowledgeable than others, but they did not allow the group interactions to be one-sided and dominated by individual views and presentations.

The most engrossing component of the whole program was the construction and repair activity around which everything else revolved. As a participant from the UK noted, "It seems to me that shared physical labor of the most simple, enduring kind is part of the humble spirit that helps break down barriers of culture and religion; and, that particularly in a situation where communication cannot be perfect in the linguistic sense, such physical acts of communal spirit can speak volumes."

Sharing Labor

The work at the temple and mosque sites presented two very different sets of tasks and operations, as the former was for a totally new structure and the latter entailed repair and restoration. In a strategic approach to their tasks, and to ensure a proper division of labor, the project participants decided to form small teams among themselves to take up several tasks simultaneously, and then rotate them among the teams. After the initial adjustment, the teams gained a rhythm and worked in co-ordination and harmony with each other. At times, the different teams would dissolve into a big group to form chains and circles for supply of bricks, sand, concrete, etc. The action at the sites of construction and repair involving young adults belonging to different religious backgrounds and genders, was a testimony to interfaith in action. The young adults excelled in the work while working shoulder to shoulder with the regular construction workers. They proved to be accomplished workers as faith, fun, and fortitude fused in a spirit of interfaith understanding and co-operation. Their effort not only gave foundation and shape to the structures, in the process it transcended barriers of cultural, religious, geographical and linguistic diversities. An Indian young adult said there was "unity in spite of our diversity." A First Nations participant remarked, "We moved sand and painted and destroyed a wall. The falling of that wall was symbolic of the religious barriers that were collapsing. All of us on our knees in the mosque is a memory I will cherish. Then there was the tiring work at the temple. The sun burned hot, beating down on all of us and weakening our backs, but our resolve was strong. We poured concrete, moved dirt and built the foundations. At the same time we were building foundations of interfaith tolerance."

Challenges

There were, however, moments of pain and anxiety as some of the youths were laid low by fatigue and sickness. Some admitted that they had not imagined that construction work would be so tough. On several occasions they differed on issues and approaches, but agreed to respect each other's point of view.

One of the most compelling points of difference that surfaced and refused to settle down easily was about the amount of work at the sites, amount of rest and the time for workshops, discussions and interactions. There were two diverging views: One group was of the view that construction work should occupy most of the program time, as construction for them was like giving themselves—or part of themselves— for a noble cause; giving their physical labor, which is called *shramadhan* in Hindi, was the greatest contribution they could make to the communities who had gone through so much suffering. They felt that *shramadhan* exemplifies and upholds a true spirit of human understanding and interfaith. This view found expression in their keenness to have more work at the sites. They said that they could never come so close to their fellow human beings as they had been able to come through the construction activity. Of course, they also expressed the need to have closer social interactions with each other and with the local communities.

The other group felt that the construction and repair activity should only be symbolic, to underline their participation, and that it should not be stretched to an extent that it becomes painful and leaves them too tired to take part in other activities like workshops, interactions, sightseeing and being with each other at leisure. For these, the construction activity should only be a vehicle to reach out to the local communities, identify with their concerns and needs, and build a strong rapport with them. This, they believed, would create the necessary platform for closer sharing and understanding of their beliefs, practices, culture, likes, dislikes and fears, and convey the purpose and message of the project effectively. Despite the different perceptions, the two groups appreciated and welcomed each other's views as contributing to the greater good and success of the program. They prepared as balanced a schedule as possible, and tried to include all the components. For good measure, each group also started taking an equally active part in the program areas that were proposed, recommended and favoured by the other group. This brought to the fore their preparedness to accommodate, reconcile and adapt to the requirements of a successful team effort.

Preventing Violence

It was very evident that the immediate impact of the program on the young adult participants, the people in the two villages and in Morbi town, was direct and positive. It helped the Muslim and Hindu communities to come together in a spirit of interfaith. The suspicion, hatred and intolerance gave way to understanding and co-operation as they mingled and visited each other's village and homes freely. They had begun to realise the futility and repercussions of distancing themselves from each other only because of their difference in religious affiliations. The completion of the structures and making them ready for use needed some more work and time. The villagers planned to have a joint inauguration program in the two villages and give them wide publicity once the structures were ready.

In February 2002, when the structures were almost ready and the villagers were planning for a ceremony to inaugurate them, unprecedented communal riots broke out in the major cities of Gujarat. Large-scale violence and looting brought the entire State to a standstill. It has been reported that the riots were sparked off by an incident in which about fifty-eight Hindu pilgrims travelling in a train were burnt alive by a group of Muslim extremists. (There have been several versions and counterclaims about this incident and the aftermath). The pent-up hate and anger was ignited. In retaliation, carnage was unleashed. The Muslim community was targeted and attacked. There was terror and curfew in most of the cities including the nearest city, Rajkot. Though Morbi remained by and large peaceful, it was also brought under curfew as a precautionary measure. The Muslims lived in fear and in danger of violence from the Hindu majority all over the state.

The riots proved to be a test of the impact the program had made on the two communities in the villages. The communalist virus was sweeping the state. There were calls to drive out Muslims from the state. In the two villages, however, the program had possibly insulated the communities and immunized them against the frenzy. The Hindu villagers strongly condemned the mindless killings and violence. A few Hindus from Morbi who had active involvement in the program, and some Hindus from Nana Dahisara village, braved the tense situation and visited Kajarada village when the curfew was relaxed in the daytime to give their Muslim friends courage and express solidarity. The IARF project co-ordinator, a Muslim, had stayed throughout the riots in the home of a Hindu and together they helped to facilitate this encounter. The villagers were sad at the terrible events that were unfolding in the state, and expressed deep anguish at the loss of innocent lives. They also felt helpless, as right-thinking and peace-loving people, both Hindus and Muslims, had been reduced to a silent minority. They resolved not to get carried away with the hate rhetoric and propaganda that was going on against the Muslims, and to work towards protecting and maintaining peace and understanding in their villages.

When the temple and mosque were ready in early April 2002, the situation in the state was still volatile. The villagers thought it sensible not to give too much publicity to the inaugural ceremonies, which might invite the attention of the fundamentalists and riot groups, and pose a threat to their villages and the two symbols of interfaith understanding. There were already numerous instances of places of worship being destroyed by the rioters. Instead, they decided to make the whole program a low-key affair and confine it to the two villages and a few friends in the Morbi town. Muslim representatives from Kajarada visited Nana Dahisara for the temple inauguration ceremony, and Hindus from Nana Dahisara village attended the mosque inauguration ceremony at Kajarada. A small group of Hindus and Muslims from Morbi also attended both the ceremonies. As the religious violence was raging in Gujarat, anxious and worried national and international adults made repeated phone calls, sent emails and posted letters to the Gujarati youths, villagers and the project administrator enquiring about their safety and well-being. They sent messages of prayers to their friends for peace and normality to return. Some of the young people based in Gujarat sent emails with updates on the situation, and this was a very moving experience.

Thus the riots proved to be both a test and a hindrance; they tested the impact of the project on the villagers and the concern that the young adults had for their friends and the communities for whom they had worked just a few days back. They also proved to be a hindrance in giving wide publicity to the inaugural ceremonies program within the state. Nevertheless IARF ensured that the news and impact of the project reached its members and others through its website and publications. The temple and mosque are now frequented daily by the villagers of Nana Dahisara and Kajarada respectively. Gujarati young adults, as well as others involved in this specific project, have continued to play an important role in the RFYN.

Conclusion

The collaboration of the IARF Religious Freedom Young Adult Network with religious communities in Gujarat proved that organizations like IARF, through their young adult programs, can indeed work with different religious communities to establish interfaith harmony, tolerance and understanding. This Gujarat Young Adult Project provides a template for programs which could be organized in cities and towns where different religious communities live together with all the undercurrents and explicit expressions of intolerance, hatred, and stereotyping. Furthermore, our project-model could be applied under conditions of peace, as a preventive strategy against intolerant behavior and possible outbreaks of religious conflict. Clearly, the work need not be on such a large scale and different methodologies can be incorporated. Further RFYN projects have since taken place in India and in other countries, such as in the Philippines, where indigenous Muslim and Christian young adults have worked together. The Gujarat project has shown that a meaningful program can succeed even under adverse conditions. Young adults can make it happen not only through their enthusiasm, good intentions, self-conviction, and positive attitude, but also through their complementary skills and dedicated teamwork.

6.

Youth Leadership: A Catalyst for Global Good

Sarah Talcott

We have the vision, the power, and the faith to make our dream a reality. We, as people of faith, can transcend the boundaries that have divided us for so long. I am excited for the future. Let us begin now, celebrating our diversity and, in the face of challenges, offer a bright, bold leadership for all.

A TWENTY-FIVE-YEAR-OLD MUSLIM STUDENT FROM AFGHANISTAN voiced this powerful call at an interfaith youth conference in 1995 to discuss the possibilities for creating a United Religions organization. On the eve of the fiftieth anniversary of the United Nations, more than two hundred young people and adults came to the University of San Francisco to begin this interfaith conversation. They brought to the table the wisdom and practical experience from their diverse faith traditions to explore the potential for rediscovering justice in their faiths and in their lives. They discussed the possibilities for a global forum for religious cooperation and the role it could play in restoring their visions for justice and peace in the world. Young people and elders spoke their truth, discovered common ground, acknowledged their differences, and reached out to "the other." The roots of the United Religions Initiative (URI)—now a global interfaith organization active in forty-seven countries of the world—can be traced back to this history-making conference *Rediscovering Justice* and its conviction that young people have a critical role to play in building a better world.

The images of the gathering are striking: Nobel Peace Prize Laureates Betty Williams from Ireland and Archbishop Desmond Tutu from South Africa issue a call to action and words of inspiration to an audience of young leaders; young people stand up to passionately and respectfully challenge their peers and guest speakers with different points of view; participants—young and old, Sikhs, Buddhists, Christians, Muslims, Hindus, Wiccans and Jews—stand together in concentric circles on a grassy field, arms outstretched, hands interlaced, praying for a return of peace and justice, each in their own tradition. As one conference participant describes, "We found that defining justice and coming up with ways to seek justice depended on our experiences and prejudices. . . . We sought to find the common ground in all of our faiths that deals with justice on a global and humane level."[1]

URI began in such a way—with an intention to include voices from every faith tradition in a conversation to catalyze a dream; with young people bringing their questions to the table to explore a new way of doing things; with people of faith defining a new context in which to live. Through this process, participants came to understand and experience justice as a multi-faceted lens through which to view themselves and their lives. As Diana Eck describes, "Justice is a process and not a definition. It's a process of participation, of involvement with each other, of engagement with one another—on the things that are difficult, on the ethical issues of our time, on the spiritual issues of our time—in the recognition that none of us as human beings can go it alone."[2]

It is not surprising that the catalyst for a United Religions organization came from young people. There are examples throughout history of young people taking heroic stands for what they believe in to make a change in the world. Students protesting in Tiananmen Square, the Student Nonviolent Coordinating Committee and its organizing role during the US Civil Rights movement, Anne Frank, Joan of Arc, Che Guevara—these young leaders challenged the status quo to deliver a higher vision for human engagement. Archbishop Desmond Tutu said, "I think there is something in young people everywhere really—this capacity to *dream* and to say 'We have been made for something better than this' and there are some things that are so important that it is even better to die for them. . . ."[3]

Today, URI continues to engage young people in its mission to mobilize people of faith in response to religiously motivated violence and to utilize faith as a vehicle for transforming communities to bring about peace and justice. URI works with everyday leaders, recognizing that we must empower young people today with the skills and sensitivities necessary to lead the generations of tomorrow. As a guiding call, we take to heart Gandhi's message that "We must be the change we wish to see in the world," for if *we* do not take responsibility for being global citizens, then who will?

URI—An Incubator of Youth-Led Projects and Youth Leaders

One nineteen-year-old's story: I first became familiar with these words of Gandhi when I found my way to the United Religions Initiative in 1999. Through an internship at URI, I was given the extraordinary opportunity to coordinate a global, grassroots project for the new millennium—72 Hours of Peace around the world. I learned first-hand what the "Initiative" in URI really stands for: it is the impulse of leadership that exists in every one of us and is channeled into action as we respond to the call to be that change.

As a Sociology and Cultural Anthropology student at Principia College, I was inspired to take classes and engage in discussions about the rich diversity of the world I was living in—classes that explored "culture" in its broadest ideological framework and through in-depth study of social enclaves, migratory communities and cultural traditions throughout the world. The college I attended was a small, private institution for Christian Scientists. Though I appreciated many aspects of this specialized liberal-arts education, I found myself wanting to know more about religions other than my own. To this end, I designed an independent study outside of the core curriculum to study non-violence practices from three Eastern traditions—Buddhism, Hinduism and Jainism. Through this study, I learned that many (if not all) religions share an ideological and practical commitment to peace. This paved the way for my interest in and exposure to United Religions Initiative. I read the words of its draft charter online and was instantly hooked:

> The purpose of the United Religions Initiative is to promote enduring, daily interfaith cooperation, to end religiously motivated violence and to create cultures of peace, justice and healing for the Earth and all living beings.[4]

In the Spring of 1999, I began my internship to coordinate the "72 Hours Project" —an invitation to people of faith around the world to mobilize their communities in simultaneous commitments of peace for seventy-hours at the turn of the millennium. Though at times overwhelming, the work was so inspiring and rewarding that I was compelled to take on increasing degrees of responsibility and leadership. The project gave me the opportunity to talk with people of many different faith traditions—Buddhist monks, Catholic nuns, Hindu swamis, Jewish rabbis, Muslim imams, indigenous elders, and many others. It also exposed me to the incredible groundswell of grassroots peace initiatives in the world. These experiences filled me with that same feeling of peace and spiritual buoyancy I experience when I pray, in my own tradition, to Father-Mother God. I was seeing One Mind expressed in laughter, in tears, in the human face and voice of people from all walks of life.

My job was to be in continual communication with the project coordinators, and to publicize their stories on the web, in the media, and with other coordinators. Along the way, I learned an important principle for empowering the leadership of others. I noticed that as I shared the stories from different project coordinators—by word of mouth and over the public website—more and more people were inspired to take part and to tell their stories, and the project galvanized increasing support. The most effective leadership, in this case, was leadership that inspired and made visible the leadership of others. In the end, more than two hundred fifty community-based projects were organized in more than sixty countries, with over a million people participating in efforts for peace from December 31, 1999, thru January 2, 2000! It was an honor and privilege to be a part of this inspiring and transformative initiative.

Since this project as a college intern, I have worked in different roles and capacities at URI to connect and bring in new youth leadership to the organization. I know that young people have a vital role to play in the interfaith movement as leaders of present and future generations, and I have seen that the global community of URI honors their voice and perspectives. It is essential to engage young people's talents in making interfaith work an integral component of the networks and initiatives of which they are involved—from campus dialogue to educational workshops and peer-to-peer training to civic and community service projects.

Appreciative Inquiry Methodology: Awakening Shared Leadership

URI works to inspire the leadership potential inherent in every individual, leadership that can be awakened and magnified through dialogue and cooperative action with others. URI brings together grassroots activists, religious leaders, Buddhists and Hindus, rabbis and imams, business leaders and theologians, conflict transformation practitioners and social workers—to engage and empower each others' efforts to build a better future. As a core methodology to evoke shared global vision, explore common ground and awaken leadership, URI utilizes Appreciative Inquiry in one-on-one dialogue, triad discussions, small and large group processes.

Developed by Dr. David Cooperrider from the Weatherhead School of Management out of Case Western Reserve University, Appreciative Inquiry begins with "the unconditional positive question." This mode of inquiry signals a new modus operandi for studying and developing systems of change. "And the metaphor speaking best to our primary task and role—'the child as the agent of inquiry'—is one where wonder, learning, and the dialogical imagination will be modus operandi."[5] The seed and tool of this inquiry is the art of asking positive questions of another person, which is fueled by a sense of wonder and curiosity. Dr. Cooperrider describes this quality of wonder and its conditions, ". . .it is not so much a process of trying romantically to go back to the state of being a child. . . . It begins in ordinary circumstances of discovery, conversation and the deepening relationship. . . . Inquiry itself creates wonder. When I'm really in a mode of inquiry, appreciable worlds are discovered everywhere."[6]

URI Global Assembly in Rio de Janeiro: Focus on Partners in Leadership

URI uses Appreciative Inquiry to bring improbable partners together, to shine light on the values and experiences held in common and to investigate the unique experiences and qualities we can learn from in the other person. One such occasion took place at the URI's tri-annual global conference, the Global Assembly 2002 in Rio de Janeiro, Brazil. As a special focus, we planned to bring young people and spiritual elders together to inquire into the nature of leadership and how it is manifest in their lives. The idea was to jumpstart an action/reflection training program that would equip emerging leaders within the URI to be more effective at organizing in their local areas and extend their learning and expertise to the URI global community. We thought it would be powerful to have cross-generational partners take time to ask questions of each other one-on-one, then share their learnings with the group. As we arranged this informal A.I. study group called "Partners in Leadership," synchronicities emerged, revealing deeper layers of significance for the particular focus we had chosen.

One such synchronicity occurred at a workshop at the Assembly in Rio focused on developing and sustaining leadership in Cooperation Circles—the local grassroots organizing and membership units of URI. An indigenous woman of the Kolla people, a community now based in Northern Argentina, explained to the group her people's vision of community as a model for understanding the concept of shared leadership. To describe the community of her people, she drew a large circle on a piece of paper. Then she drew her finger around it, indicating the four parts of which it is made—the children, the adolescents, parents, and grandparents. These are the constituent bodies as well as being sacred parts of the whole, without which the whole would not function in harmony. Each group and phase of life has its gifts and wisdom to impart. For that reason, in any cooperative system, these areas of life—new beginnings, trials and transformations, stewardship, wisdom-keepers—must be engaged for their integral contributions.

I was thrilled to hear this woman, who carries on the legacy of preserving and imparting the ancestral values of her people, articulate the importance of valuing young people and elders as essential members and contributors in any cooperative body. Margaret Mead has echoed this observation with her hypothesis "that the best societal learning has always occurred when three generations come together in contexts of discovery and valuing—the child, the elder and the middle adult." What better reason to bring cross-generational pairs together to listen to each other, share their learnings and model the leadership needed to sustain this interfaith grassroots movement?

The actual Appreciative Inquiry session on "Partners in Leadership" took place in a small window of time at the Global Assembly after dinner and before the evening activities began. Participants included young people from the Dharma Realm Buddhist

Youth, a rabbi from Chile, a young Hindu organizer from the Gandhi Puri Ashram in Bali, a Muslim woman pursuing her studies in Germany, a Muslim Jordanian, a converted Muslim American teacher, a woman scholar from Pakistan, a Brahma Kumaris sister, a Mahayana Buddhist monk, the Executive Director of the United Muslims of America, a Catholic Orthodox scholar from Israel, the Communications Director from the Interfaith Youth Core and a representative from Habitat for Humanity. We were incredibly blessed by the wealth of knowledge and organizing experience in this room of twenty people from a wide range of religious and spiritual traditions.

We asked people to self-select into cross-generational partners for a half-hour "Appreciative Interview." The questions we had pairs ask of each other were:

> Looking back over your life, think of a time when you felt your leadership strengths and skills were truly being used to their full potential. Please tell me about this experience. What was happening in your life, your community, in the world at this time? How was your leadership encouraged, enhanced or inspired by the environment or people around you? How did your leadership make a difference? How did it bring benefit to you and to others? What shifted for you as a result of this experience?

In coming back into a full circle to share highlights of these interviews, some of the common threads and emerging principles of leadership that were shared included: "best leadership comes from a selfless place; leadership comes from a grounded self —empower others with one's own groundedness; leadership is inspired by seeing a community living into its fullest potential; one's environment creates leadership— wanting to fulfill something that is not yet fulfilled; and leadership is supported by community" (examples given were the City of Ten Thousand Buddhas—a Buddhist monastery in California, and Chicago's diverse interfaith community in Roger's Park).

The second question is highly characteristic of Appreciative Inquiry, in that it prepares the mind of participants for what are called "provocative propositions," or positive visions of the future that one dares to visualize and make audible to at least one other listener. It has been said that "language creates reality," so the idea is to invoke one's dreams by voicing them aloud. The question we used was:

> Imagine you can see the world fifteen years from now. The year is 2017. See yourself standing in your community, surrounded by the people you have come to know and be with every day. What do you see? What is different? What are your dreams for a community living into its fullest potential? What has happened to make these dreams come true? What has happened within yourself to make these dreams come true?

Though we didn't have time to share the details of those visions in the whole circle, some ideas were shared for how to make those visions real. These were: "Community is a space where you can find your dreams; being a leader of yourself is essential; a leader takes initiative to realize his/her dreams; a leader surrounds him/herself with capable people and allows them to do their job."

Another outcome of this focus on Partners in Leadership was that the young people who showed up for the Appreciative Inquiry came looking for ways to further their project ideas. They brought their energy and enthusiasm for action, so that a conversation about leadership became a conversation of leaders learning from each other to take action. Most of these young leaders joined the Global Youth Cooperation Circle, which exists to be a strong youth presence in the URI. Its purpose is to: "develop young people's skills, capacities and confidence so that rooted in our traditions, we can respect each other and serve the world in which we live; and to support communication flowing between young people and exchanging stories, ideas and values as a model of cooperation and how 'to build cultures of peace, justice and healing for the Earth and all living beings.'"

Youth delegates at the Global Assembly also met with each other throughout the week, formulating collaborative plans, and offered their gifts and contributions in a variety of leadership positions. One evening, the youth participants met together for an incredible three hours of consensus-building to organize their youth-led meditation in plenary: reading the purpose statement from the URI Charter in eight languages, chanting together in Sanskrit, and singing in unison the Buddhist transference prayer from the Interfaith Songbook. Their presentation was a vision of URI principles in practice—unity in diversity, respect for different traditions and languages, deepening in one's own faith, and using our combined resources "for nonviolent, compassionate action."

A thirteen-year-old delegate gave special demonstrations and answered questions from peers and elders about the URI Kids' site, an online educational resource that features teachings and information about eight of the major world religions. Two college students participated in the five-day pre-Assembly peacebuilding course to learn and practice "Skills of a Religious/Spiritual Peacebuilder." They are now applying these skills in their current work—one, as a Spanish teacher in Texas, the other, a blue-eyed Muslim who is building bridges between diverse groups on her college campus in San Francisco. The Dharma Realm Buddhist youth acted as Buddhist ambassadors—sharing the stories and principles of their faith at several local places of worship in Rio, including the local Brahma Kumaris temple, Zen Buddhist temple, a Catholic mass, and more.

All of the youth delegates participated together in a field trip to Vigario Geral, a cultural center in the *favelas* (slums) that provides a positive alternative to crime and drugs, where they learned *capoeira* and drumming and got to know other Rio youth—

building bridges across race and class. They also participated in a Yahoo! Live Web broadcast for youth that asked the question, "What from your faith tradition inspires you to serve the world," reaching out to a broad public audience to talk about their faith and life values. And many of them woke up at 5:30 each morning for sunrise meditations on the beach before the activities began, sharing in a first-hand experience of the sacred.

Conclusion

The international interfaith movement is working to build bridges of understanding and respect between people of "difference"—in every culture, on every continent. With their insatiable curiosity, high-minded idealism, and open, receptive hearts, young people are essential contributors and catalysts for carrying out the vision. From my own experience as a young person growing up in one of the most religiously diverse nations in the world, I know that I feel more alive when exposed to new and different ways of being. They are like mirrors that reflect my subconscious assumptions back to me, and I delight in the process of shedding these judgments so I can more clearly appreciate the incredible diversity we live in. In closing, I would like to share a metaphor from the Buddhist tradition for the interconnected, multi-faceted paradigm we are building—"The Net of Indra"—as described in the Avatamsaka Sutra:

> Far away in the heavenly abode of the Great God Indra, there is a wonderful net which has been hung. . .in such a manner that it stretches out indefinitely in all directions. . . . The artificer has hung a single glittering jewel at the net's every node, and since the net itself is infinite in dimension, the jewels are infinite in number. . . . If we select one of these jewels for inspection and look closely at it, we will discover that in its polished surface there are reflected all the other jewels in the net. . . . Not only that, but each of the jewels reflected in this one jewel is also reflecting all the other jewels so that the process of reflection is infinite.[7]

Notes

1. Video: *Rediscovering Justice*, 1995.
2. Ibid.
3. From Archbishop Desmond Tutu's speech at Rediscovering Justice conference, 1995.
4. Purpose statement, URI Charter, 2000.
5. Cooperrider, David L, "Child as the Agent of Inquiry," *OD Practitioner*, p. 6.
6. Ibid.
7. Francis H. Cook, *Hua-Yen Buddhism: The Jewel Net of Indra*, 1977, www.heartspace.org/misc/indranet.

7.

The Next Generation: Training Leaders Under One Big Tent

Josh Borkin

"THE PEOPLE FROM ZIMBABWE *HAVE* TO BE AT THE Parliament of the World's Religions in Barcelona," a young Zimbabwean woman energetically told me over lunch. It was obvious from the passion in her voice that she was going to bring a delegation from Zimbabwe to Barcelona. By the end of our lunch, she had me convinced that I *had* to help her. While I was well aware of the many hardships people are currently facing in Zimbabwe, her reason for wanting to bring people to the Parliament surprised me: "We don't want to feel alone. Zimbabwe is very isolated right now. We need to feel connected to something bigger." At that moment I realized that this woman did not want to attend a Parliament of the World's Religions to present a paper or even tell the rest of the world about the hardships that were happening in her country. She wanted to bring a group to Barcelona so that a group of compatriots could discover or rediscover why interreligious cooperation is essential to our world's survival, including in Zimbabwe.

This young woman is not alone: many young people worldwide need to feel this connection to a wider reality that transcends the limits of their homes, neighborhoods, cities, regions, or countries. They seek a more meaningful world by connecting to a variety of global movements. The Parliament of the World's Religions is one such avenue that enables young people to join into the global interfaith movement.

The Parliaments of the World's Religions are events designed for up to ten thousand people to experience the power of interreligious dialogue and cooperation on a grand scale. More than simply a conference or even a popular gathering, a Parliament is at its best a "happening." A Parliament is a complicated affair with over four hundred fifty different programs, dialogues, discussions, presentations, and performances aimed at reaching an intensely diverse audience. Its participants share a belief that religion should not be a source of violence, discord and strife; it should be part of the various solutions that address the world's problems. A Parliament's power lies within the idea that creating this large space does contribute tangibly to promoting peace on a grassroots level.

The Parliament of the World's Religions ultimately rests on a sense of religious populism. Religious populism is the notion that religion's power does not lie in its leaders, academics, or doctrines. The power of religion lies in its practitioners and their ability to best live out their tradition's ideals in the world. This chapter will illustrate the role religious populism played in defining the modern history of the Parliaments of the World's Religions as well as discuss the challenges and opportunities for organizing young people under this "big tent." As youth coordinator (1998–2004) in the organization that has sponsored these Parliaments, I tell its story not as a distant and impartial observer but as a former employee who dedicated five years of my life to add and integrate youth voices into this organization.

History

The Parliament of the World's Religions intends to be an open, inclusive, and large space for inter- and intra-religious dialogue and relationship building. It creates a safe space for dialogue between religious practitioners at all levels of power within their communities, as well as with individuals not connected to any specific religious or spiritual tradition.

The first Parliament of the World's Religions took place in 1893 as part of the Chicago World's Fair. Known at the time as the Colombian Exposition, the Parliament was largely organized by segments of the Protestant community in the United States as part of a series of expositions showcasing the latest development in business, religion, education, etc. The 1893 Parliament of the World's Religions was the first meeting between eastern and western religions on the United States national stage. A few participants traveled from halfway around the world to take part and give speeches about religion in the upcoming twentieth century. One speaker, Swami Vivekananda, captivated audiences with inspiring talks about the commonalities of religion, the power of young people, and the need for religion to be a source of positive change in the world. At the end of the World's Fair, the Parliament of the World's Religions was praised as the most important component of the fair.

While many existing interfaith religious reform organizations trace their history back to the 1893 Parliament of the World's Religions, the event's formal legacy dissipated early into the twentieth century. After the event, Vivekananda and D. T. Suzuki went on to become major Hindu and Buddhist figures, respectively. Suzuki translated many of the great works of Buddhism into English and Vivekananda became an inspiring religious activist who started Vedanta centers in the United States and around the world.

Within the history of this first Parliament lies a forgotten history of youth participation. This history began with Swami Vivekananda who was twenty-four years old in 1893. A hundred years later, many young adults participated also in the Centennial celebrations, although none emerged as visibly as Vivekananda had. The subsequent parliaments in Cape Town (1999) and Barcelona (2004) actively involved and engaged young adults, who collectively affected the overall results. At each Parliament event, young people have pushed the organization in new directions and have had subsequently an important impact on the interreligious movement. The promise of a world engaged in dialogue, fused with the energy and enthusiasm of young people, has always been a powerful combination. Yet, this power has barely begun to be harnessed worldwide.

The first modern Parliament of the World's Religions started largely as a grassroots endeavor to celebrate the centennial anniversary of the 1893 Parliament. It was initiated in the late 1980s by two Swamis from the Vedanta Center of Chicago who approached other religious communities with this idea. Unlike the 1893 event where many different religious leaders met in Chicago after having traveled from afar, a century later these diverse religious people were now part of the rich religious landscape of Chicago itself. Soon a formal board comprised largely of religious leaders from Chicago was formed. Each religious community took the responsibility to identify potential speakers for the ambitious program containing over 800 lectures, workshops, dialogues, and demonstrations that comprised the seven-day Parliament.

Host committees were essential to the 1993 Parliament for two crucial reasons. First, it took the responsibility of organizing a large event out of the hands of a small number of organizers and placed it squarely on the shoulders of Chicago's religious and spiritual communities. For local Zoroastrian and Sikh communities, for example, the Parliament was an important forum for introducing themselves to the broader city. Second, because organizing a Parliament was a gigantic task, it helped form a network of relationships that have bonded many individual religious people and communities together in this common vision of building a big tent to host others from around the world.

The structure of the 1993 Parliament was extremely broad and inclusive. The abundance of programs allowed for a wide range of diversity both within and across religious and spiritual traditions. It gave a platform to numerous smaller communities. Programs were structured around the themes of identity, dialogue, and critical issues, which featured presentations ranging from "What Is Islam?" to advanced discussions about science and religion. Evenings were capped by large-scale plenaries that celebrated the many gifts that religious and spiritual communities bring to the world. Overall, the Parliament created a safe place for dialogue and discussion where all participants were asked to adhere to basic rules of civilized dialogue.

During the last three days of the event, a group of religious and spiritual leaders met to discuss and eventually to endorse a document authored by religious scholar Hans Küng, "Towards a Global Ethic: An Initial Declaration." The document set forth a set of ethical and moral principles that lay beneath all religious and spiritual traditions. The following excerpt captures a central element of the 1993 Parliament of the World's Religions: "Earth cannot be changed for the better unless the consciousness of individuals is changed."

Participants at the 1993 Parliament described the atmosphere as electric. Organizers refunded four thousand of the twelve thousand registrations because only eight thousand people could fit in the Palmer House Hilton. They estimated that slightly over 40 percent of the participants came from outside the U.S. Many participants left the Parliament feeling that they had attended a life-changing experience. Since then, many of them are still in touch with the Parliament and have mentioned to me how lifelong relationships were built at the 1993 Parliament. Around the world, many new interreligious endeavors were empowered by the energy resulting from connecting global issues to tangible relationships, the core of the Parliament's ethos.

Just as the Parliament's modern history began with a large burst in 1993, so did the Parliament's youth initiative, the Next Generation. Originally the inclusion of young people during the 1993 Parliament of the World's Religions was largely an afterthought. While many young people attended the event independently through schools or their own religious institutions, intentional youth organizing only started three months prior to the event. Thirty young people met weekly to share their religious or spiritual tradition and prepare for a special youth plenary where young people would share their experiences with the broader gathering. Named the "Next Generation," this group brought an extremely powerful and poignant punctuation to the Parliament proceedings. The group adopted unity, justice, and sustainability as its own theme. It drafted its own statement to the world's religious and spiritual leaders. After the plenary, many participants were left feeling that interreligious dialogue was not a marginal concept championed by a majority of graying churchgoers but rather an intergenerational movement with global constituencies.

Ultimately, like its predecessor it was commemorating, the 1993 Centennial Parliament of the World's Religions was a watershed event. Up until this point, interreligious dialogue was, for the most visible part, highly defined. It was formal conversations among official leaders from major religious traditions. The 1993 Parliament, by contrast, attempted to be a truly inclusive "Big Tent" event. It challenged the definition of what is a religious tradition by including numerous religious and spiritual paths. It also attempted to be a space that was open to everyone from religious scholars to casual practitioners and non-religious supporters. As new interreligious groups have begun to act as important intermediaries between religious and spiritual communities, the Parliament now held every five years around the world is seen as a capstone event for the global interfaith movement.

1999—Cape Town, South Africa

Between 1993 and 1999, when the second modern Parliament took place in Cape Town, South Africa, the initial organizing committee had evolved into a formal organization, the Council for a Parliament of the World's Religions (CPWR). Its mission is to foster interreligious dialogue and understanding in Chicago and around the world. The Council chose Cape Town because religious cooperation helped play a role in ending apartheid in South Africa in 1994. The Cape Town Parliament adopted many of the same programmatic elements that defined the 1993 event: over seven hundred fifty programs, six plenaries, and a three-day assembly. The biggest difference was the inclusion of a formal youth program called "The Next Generation."

The Next Generation included seven distinct programs for young people, one per day. Broad and varied in nature, these programs were designed to have young participants take responsibility for educating each other by sharing their experiences and working towards building a better world. One such program was entitled "Youth Reactions to the Call." In preparation for the Parliament, young people had written essays on the Parliament's second signature document, *A Call to Our Guiding Institutions*. In Cape Town, they then led discussions with the larger group on the document and shared how such a document would be implemented in their community. One of the principal framers of the Call explained the basic concepts and rationales for the document and young people shared the benefits and challenges of religious people engaging guiding institutions such as business, media, education, agriculture, government, civil society, etc. Those who wrote essays were then challenged to present the larger group's ideas to the Parliament's Assembly of Religious and Spiritual Leaders in the final three days.

The educational aims of the Next Generation program were best illustrated during a program entitled, "Honoring District Six," a multi-racial neighborhood that was leveled thirty years earlier. This program featured young people whose families were relocated from District Six near downtown Cape Town to further away townships. Participants talked about the ongoing effects of relocation on their families.

During these conversations, a young Navaho woman was moved to speak about the displacement of her family members one hundred years earlier, a dislocation that still affected her life and that of her whole community over more than three generations.

A common concern that young people have at conferences all over the world is that, "It is all talking and no doing." The truth is that at most conferences, especially those focused on interreligious dialogue, there is indeed a great deal of talking. At the 1999 Parliament, it was decided in advance that more doing needed to be included in the Next Generation program. There was a successful service excursion to a local township as well as various visits highlighting local service projects. Like interreligious education, service is an aspect of a young person's life that should not be limited to an overseas event. The Parliament is a place that connects people with service projects experience and ideas, which inspires further projects. While everyone realizes that making sandwiches for the homeless is not going to solve systemic problems facing our world, service remains a valuable window into the harsh realities of our world as well as the myriad ways religious and spiritual communities address the problem concretely and move people to positive action. Service can thus be a powerful tool for building relationships and grounding ongoing action in one's own values and traditions. Concrete interreligious service projects integrated into interreligious conferences can serve as a tangible cooperative approach to social action, thereby also providing a balance between the head (listening to lectures and participating in discussions) and the hands (addressing issues through direct action on the ground).

Because the Parliament is a multi-generational event, all young people are bounded by one essential commonality—they are young. Youth participants were constantly asked to sit on panels at the last minute and, as in 1993, the Next Generation plenary had a moving effect on the broader audience. While each parliament featured a wide variety of talented young performers and inspiring future leaders, the process of letting young people decide what should be said to the larger community and who should say it remained at times challenging. This process in which young people become in charge of what they will say publicly is as important as the message itself. In most environments, young people are rarely given the responsibility of articulating how and why young people are essential to making the world a better place. When charged with such responsibility, a genuine message emerges that reflects the struggle and compromise that naturally goes into creating any performance or statement. Such a message can have a profound effect on the larger audience. Because most religious and spiritual communities want to be relevant to young people in the wake of rapidly changing times, many participants leave feeling reminded that young people are the world's greatest resource for overcoming the challenges that have faced previous generations. In turn, this dynamic creates a sense of empowerment for young people who become more aware of their responsibility for the future.

Creating an autonomous space for young people at an event such as the Parliament is always a balancing act. While young people need a safe space to build relationships with other young people, their voice also needs to be present in the broader conversations. As plans for the next Parliament unfold, more emphasis will be put on multi-generational engagement. Young people will be part of "Base Groups" that will meet daily, giving students the freedom to choose programs that they want to attend. The purpose of base groups is to allow young people to build relationships and contextualize their experience.

The Big Tent

The Parliaments of the World's Religions are events that attempt to create community on the largest and most diverse possible level. This particular methodology is by no means perfect. Creating a truly diverse environment where all voices are heard is challenging to achieve; it is certainly not an exact science! Relationships are being built so that every Parliament can be a place truly hosted by the host community with maximum openness to others from around the world. While there is a recognition that the most long-lasting interreligious work happens in local settings, such as community hall basements and at someone's office after work, at its best the Parliament can be a place that stimulates and magnifies all those local activities, turning them into a voice of hope, peace, and justice that can sing much louder than the voice of complacency, prejudice, misunderstanding, and hate. In brief, the Parliaments are places where human relationships can be the building blocks to making the world a better place.

8.

Youth and the Pluralism Project: An Open, Energized Network

Grove Harris

THE PLURALISM PROJECT AT HARVARD UNIVERSITY has been described as the mother ship for an emerging field of interfaith youth work. Over the past decade, the Pluralism Project has created a wide network of current and former researchers, affiliates, friends, and staff, many of whom began their connection with the Project while in college or graduate school. They have carried the fruits of their Pluralism Project research and experiences into their further work in academic research, teaching, and in many cases, leadership in the growing interfaith youth movement.

Young adults have always been central to the Pluralism Project. They were the primary inspiration for the inception of the Project and currently serve as the project's key knowledge producers. In the early 1990s, an increasing number of students from the full range of the world's religious traditions were enrolling in Diana Eck's courses on world religions at Harvard University. Their presence signaled a new opportunity: to study "world" religions in a specifically American context. Eck shifted her research focus from the religions of India to those same religions in the new and changing religious landscape of the U.S. Her students produced research papers and, with early grant funding, conducted summer research that formed the body of the Pluralism Project's initial research, the best of which was published in 1997 in the CD-ROM, *On Common Ground: World Religions in America.*

This research opportunity was and remains unparalleled. The Pluralism Project has the opportunity to study the world's religions as they interact with a new social context. In tracking unfamiliar forms of sacredness imported to the U.S., Pluralism Project researchers have the opportunity to see ancient rituals performed in new lands

and to consider the challenges of passing on religious tradition to a younger generation born into a dramatically different context. Our research investigates how these
religions may both change and be changed by new circumstances, with an eye on differences and parallels in these changes across the traditions. Through this research, the
Pluralism Project is exploring the challenges and possibilities facing one of the most
religiously diverse countries in the world and serving a vast educational need in the
face of these dramatic changes.

Mission and Methods

The Pluralism Project mission is to assist Americans in engaging with religious
difference through the active dissemination of resources. Our methodological context
includes working with insiders in religious traditions as well as those with exclusively
academic training, in a web that privileges both the centralization of knowledge into a
national picture and the local expertise of affiliates, leveraging resources at every
opportunity and ensuring that our results are accessible to multiple constituencies.

Student Researchers

The Pluralism Project is youthful in many senses of the word; since its inception
in the early 1990s, undergraduate and graduate student researchers have fanned out
across the United States documenting the religious diversity of their hometowns. The
preliminary model was of Harvard students doing "hometown" research in the summer months. The enthusiasm, eagerness, and fresh perspectives brought by youth
enhance their work and effectiveness as researchers. The pride and intensity with
which they dive into their summer projects reflect their passion for the work, as well
as their academic ambitions. Many are members of the religious communities they
study, and thus bring the kind of access to communities, including connections and
trust, that is essential for this research to be successful, particularly when conducted
over a short period of time. Others engage with religious traditions and communities
that are not their own, often reporting "awesome" expansive experiences.

In recent years, the Pluralism Project has continued to fund student research and
to publish this work on the Web. In 2003, the Project funded over thirty-five student
research projects across the United States; in 2004, over forty student researchers went
into the field. From research on the Swami Narayanan Hindu Temple in Atlanta, Geor-
gia, to mapping the religious diversity of Montana, from research on the South Asian
religious communities of Los Angeles, to exploring the organization of Sufi communities in Boston and New York, from documenting the religious diversity of Austin,
Texas, to studying the service work of Ismaili communities in Texas, Pluralism Project

researchers continue to document and assess the complexities of the changing religious landscape of America.

The Pluralism Project is now intensifying its work on the burgeoning interfaith movement, adding film projects, and increasing research on Muslim communities in the U.S. The network of researchers now extends far beyond Harvard University, drawing on students from across the nation. The call for grant proposals goes out far and wide over an open e-list. The responses indicate a vibrant and growing interest in this field of research among the nation's youth. Our network of affiliates and other colleagues in related fields have supported this interest, and they serve as faculty sponsors for projects, thus expanding the network while maintaining high standards.

Opportunities for Growth:
From Student Researcher to Managing Director

My own work with the Pluralism Project began in 1994 with research on Paganism in the U.S. I was inspired to improve upon the research presented at the research conference the prior year. In order to provide a more accurate representation, one that was guided with an insider's access knowledge and graduate training, I approached Dr. Eck about research and writing for the Project. Now, as managing director, I welcome critique from members of religious communities of the representation of their religious center or tradition. We work in a dialogic relationship with practitioners, in consultation with our academic advisors in each tradition. Recently, researchers in Kansas and Montana have inspired leaders of local religious communities to write additional text for us to better nuance our presentation. Currently, I am working on exploring the history, issues, and contexts of Pagan involvement in interfaith work. My own integrity requires that I do this, to bring all of myself to the table rather than avoiding discussing my own religious specificity while encouraging others to share theirs. In the past I have been very careful not to let my own religious affiliation negatively affect the Project and so have often described my own tradition in very general terms, aimed at communication and avoiding conflict and misunderstanding. The Pluralism Project works with the premise that engagement is required to move from mere knowledge and recognition of diversity to a more cohesive and inclusive pluralistic social context. Hopefully, the burden of presenting and explaining one's religious difference, often adopting terms from the dominant religious paradigms, can shift to one of open-minded curiosity as people become aware of and more responsible for their pre-conceived notions and misinformation.

My religious background is a source of support for my work managing everything from finances, supervision of staff and researchers, information technology, and web and database design, to research, editing, and extensive networking for a complex project with very fluid staffing patterns. As a Wiccan priestess, I am trained in noticing energy flows, and I design processes to support these flows. In practice, this has meant broadening our inclusion, redesigning processes of research submission, and bringing in more outside expertise to support student researchers. Imagery from my tradition suggests my work may be considered like that of a spider, not so much a locus of power, but a central agent in monitoring, diagnosing, and maintaining the strength of the larger web. This web includes over ninety university-based affiliates, many of whom work with their own set of student researchers. We also include museum curators, independent researchers, photographers, high school teachers, and film makers as affiliates, to acknowledge that the work of studying religious diversity reaches beyond the academy. Through the inclusion of these affiliates, we can offer a wide range of pedagogical tools to a broad constituency of educators, thus helping to fulfill educational objectives in many arenas.

Supporting Student Researchers

The Pluralism Project provides student researchers with an array of resources and opportunities. Initially, we encourage students from across the country to apply with a straight-forward application, with advice and consultation available upon request. For many, this is their first grant-writing experience, and we assume it will not be their last. Simplicity and directness in the application itself has many benefits; besides avoiding the creation of obstacles and "hoops to jump through," this simplicity encourages the focusing and honing of vision. I have recently heard from an applicant (whom we were unable to fund) that the process of applying itself was useful to her in that she clarified her vision and goals in a brief proposal. This clarification helped her attract other resources and proceed with her project.

We offer encouragement and give advice about the basic expectations for the budget and for research products, with the main focus on the youth's development of their own ideas for the research. We may work with an applicant and adjust a proposal to meet specific Project needs, but the initiative and inspiration come from the student. We define "student" very broadly, including those who are in college, those who have recently completed college, those who are considering or are in graduate programs—in short, any person with some substantial background in the study of religion and a compelling research interest in line with our mission is encouraged to apply. Most applicants are youth, also defined broadly. Ours is an expansive project.

In addition to very modest funding, student researchers receive a variety of other services from the Project, including a host of online guidelines to assist them, support from the youth staffing our central office, and technical support and encouragement towards the development of a variety of research "deliverables." These deliverables, which build upon and contribute to our existing body of research, may include professional papers, additions to our directory of religious centers or our database of news stories, slide shows with captions and text, articles for newspapers, and other resources. We also encourage them to have a vital relationship with their faculty sponsor, and to anticipate multiple edits of their final work.

Our young researchers produce research that provides innovative windows into the life of diverse religious communities in the United States. For example, Sarina Pasricha prepared a slide show to document the *kumbabishekam*, or temple inauguration, of the Hindu Temple of Delaware (available online at www.pluralism.org/images). Experiencing such inaugurations—even virtually, through the Internet—is one opportunity in the new religious life of America. Eric Barbee began the documentation of the religious diversity of Arkansas, and Clare Giles covered the Jain Temple dedication in Boston.

Profiles of religious centers are one of the building blocks of our research, as are directory listings and news articles, and while not all researchers complete sophisticated analytical papers, each contributes to the growing body of knowledge. We encourage researchers to contact the news writers in their area, because previously written articles may serve to move their research forward. These connections lead to an increased awareness of the Pluralism Project's resources among local news staff, and can possibly result in an invitation for researchers to write or be featured in a news article on their research. As student researchers make the connections required by their research, they represent the Project as well as their respective universities.

We try to develop a community of youth researchers every summer and throughout the year. Summer researchers communicate via e-mail and face-to-face at our annual conferences, both at Harvard University and prior to the American Academy of Religion's annual meetings. These professional presentation opportunities, with an audience of fellow researchers and interested and often very knowledgeable others, give them an opportunity to dialogue about their work. Conversation brings up links across projects, geographical areas, and religious traditions. The value of one focused project is enhanced when seen in a broader context. We offer state-of-the-art presentation facilities; for many of these students this is an important opportunity to present in a professional context, building their experience base and potentially advancing their careers. We provide an entry point for young people into academic circles. We publish much of the research online so as to reach an even larger audience; researchers have earned invitations to present at other conferences based on their research being accessible on our website.

The Internet is a powerful tool by which we share our research, and it is a challenge to pay attention to all the details that keep a website not only up-to-date but vibrant and accessible. This almost immediate public sharing of research is unique to the Project, and it is energizing to have an extremely fast turn-around. New staff members are continually impressed with the opportunity to work so directly with material that is immediately published. We continue to devise interfaces to enhance our editorial control before public viewing on the web. The speed of delivery has been consistently appreciated, particularly by our student researchers, who value seeing their work posted promptly. While other research projects have lengthy time lags before written publication, we harness the energy of the fast turn-around, enabling students to use materials from the web in their professional presentations and to share their work with all their interested audiences, within and outside of the academy. For example, a religious community will have particular interest in the work of a young member, and rightfully so. Serving this interest brings the work of the Project to a wider audience.

We also partner with many affiliates who are engaging in the study of religious diversity without prior work for the Pluralism Project, and support their work. Our network includes many seasoned academics, often the very best in their fields, and it is into this matrix of seasoned scholarship that we bring our younger researchers. Our geographic focus has led us to reach out in areas where we have insufficient coverage, and to cultivate connections with professors in Arkansas, Utah, Kansas, Nebraska, Louisiana, Montana, and Mississippi, among other states.

Director Diana Eck's university students often become informal participants in the Pluralism Project, as do many individuals from within the religious communities we study. While presenting some managerial challenges, our strategy of being widely welcoming has been tremendously successful. Open networking and efficient systems to support this work distinguish our Project in the field. Generous funding from the Ford Foundation and the Rockefeller Foundation has allowed us to conduct and publish our research via our website.

Staff and Management

Our office staff is comprised of youth who contribute to the Project in multiple ways. All conduct direct research as well as performing support functions. There is much work to be done to support the publication of research, and we resist the hierarchical division between "privileged researcher" and "lowly support staff." With our online research submission forms, even our distant researchers can participate in support functions by entering their own research into a database for web publication. This justice-based sharing of different labors is one way the Project has developed such highly functioning equitable teams. We also work with a mutual editing policy, since everyone needs editorial input from others to improve clarity and communication. I routinely ask staff members to review my writing (including this piece) and benefit from this service. Our intention is to respect everyone's work and need for editorial assistance.

The Pluralism Project leverages federal work-study funding to cover a substantial part of the expense for staff associates. With flexible scheduling and an eye towards autonomy in job performance, we understand that our students need to focus on coursework while working for the Project. We utilize many different levels of involvement and skill and honor a wide variety of contributions. Our student staff members give us years of devoted service, working with us to design help documents and operations manuals so that we may more effectively train new staff when current workers graduate. Simple measures like letting staff work out their own work schedules simplifies the management of this young work force, with each member averaging only ten to twelve hours of work per week. I let staff negotiate office coverage using a large whiteboard for the general schedule, and a smaller corkboard for posting the constant small weekly changes. The purpose is to responsibly accomplish the work and let all staff know when to expect people; this isn't an area in which control is necessary. We have a set of in-boxes, and staff know that their projects must be filed there in case the needs or timing change and someone else picks up that task. I insist that staff consider their work in a public context, so that it may be shared with a co-worker on a moment's notice, so everyone documents his or her progress in as clear a way as possible. We use lots of notes for an informal paper trail, so that everyone's brain can rest from the multiple details and projects involved.

We meet the challenge of turnover as students graduate by creating instruction manuals for our databases, and by streamlining and making transparent as many office procedures as possible. Essential forms are stored on a wall in public view, all work stations are kept clean and ready to be shared, and supplies are mostly kept in view on open shelves. Most staff develop an area of responsibility based on a skill set or on a subject area and have responsibility for completing phases of work. Everyone is expected to be flexible and to have "background" projects as well as more time-sensitive projects, so that everyone's work time is used efficiently and staff are not dependent on management to dole out tasks. Management is responsible for giving timely and detailed oversight to all work, and to be readily available for consultation on a myriad of details.

On our team, everyone is familiar with the larger picture of how their work fits into the project as a whole, so even relatively mundane data entry is recognized as important. Updating the data on religious centers ripples through the website, affecting the presentation on the state-by-state map and shifting the maps of religious demography. We share small victories in the office, such as discovering a Buddhist center in Montana that maintains a website with great photographs, or receiving an e-mail from a Buddhist monk who writes that "the Pluralism Project rocks!"

These managerial principles ensure that everyone is involved in the big picture and also maintains his or her individual agency and autonomy. We respect individual needs and schedules, share group successes, and laugh hard while we work hard. These are sound principles in general, and are even more important when working with youth. We have a tremendous flow of information in this research project, with many tasks required in preparing the information for web publication at a profession-al standard. This requires much coordination, oversight, and close work so that bot-tlenecks are minimized.

One highlight of the office in recent years has been the advent of Maxime, the son of our webmaster Alan Wagner. We have welcomed Maxime to the office from the age of a few months to his current toddler status. Despite a few crying days, it has been a joy to have a young child in the office. He has always been curious and entertained; it is well known that children like to play with real things rather than toys. Upheaval has been limited and a small price to pay for the smiles and gurgles of a bright child.

Growth of the Project:
Expanding Networks, Maintaining Old Ties

The Project has expanded according to a network model with many of the affili-ate researchers and projects availing themselves of the talents of a new generation of youthful student researchers. We also stay in close contact with many of our former student researchers and office staff who have continued work in the study of religion or related fields. This growth, along with its multiplier effects, is significantly devel-oping the field of interfaith youth work.

Clare Giles is one example of a student researcher who contributed immensely to the Project and used her own initiative to pursue the opportunities that came to her through work on the Project. We provided her with a like-minded community that was respectful of her talents and of her growing knowledge of Hinduism and with the opportunity to fully participate in the work of the Pluralism Project. Clare was initially a researcher for one of our affiliate projects, and came to visit our office at Harvard in search of a stronger community of interest. When she began her studies at Harvard Divinity School, we hired her to write for our "Religious Diversity News," and with extensive background in our procedures, she interfaced with the entire crew of student researchers one summer. She received funding from the Project in order to research Vedanta centers in the U.S. The web presentation of her work now serves as a model for other researchers; she very effectively presents highlights of her research as well as more in-depth reporting in a highly accessible format. She has recently completed

Fulbright research in Mauritius and we look forward to web presentation of that work. She now co-teaches a summer course at Brandeis on world religions and will begin teaching world religions in a private high school this fall. Obviously her work has flourished, as has her ability to educate others.

Many other staff members go on to teach and become university affiliates of the Project, leading their own local research teams of students. Anne Hansen is conducting research in Milwaukee; Doug Hick's book on religion and the workplace has been released by Oxford University Press, and Duncan Williams is coordinating research on Buddhism in Southern California. Scott Hansen's work on religious diversity in Flushing, New York, is being made into a documentary, and Patrice Brodeur has headed up the Pluralism Project at Connecticut College. Patrice has mentored Dr. Eboo Patel, and their collaboration has brought forth this publication.

Many other young researchers have continued on to publish and create other research projects and opportunities. This is part of how we are expanding the field of research in the area of religious pluralism. Annapurna Astley, for example, is a former staff member who graduated to teach at Kashi Ashram and is now heading an interfaith youth project (see Annapurna's article entitled, "Spirit into Action").

Stephanie Saldana has been writing for "Religious Diversity News" and has been awarded a Fulbright to study Muslim-Christian relations in Syria in the 2004–05 academic year. Although young in years, her writing skills are already recognized with publication and awards. In a recent article published about her in Harvard's *Gazette*, Stephanie says that working with the Pluralism Project has kept her informed about the current issues in religious diversity in the U.S., which she will carry forward in her career.

Challenges and Criticisms

When a project creates as much of an opening as we have, there are bound to be disappointments over our limits. We have been criticized for not sufficiently delving into the multiple diversities and tensions within Islam and within Christianity; with neglecting to give Unitarian Universalism adequate representation as a non-Christian faith; with neglecting the minority status of Christianity, for not including every new religious movement. Our inclusion of Paganism has been derogatorily noted on numerous occasions. In addition to doing our best to address these important points, I have also learned to take most of this criticism as a compliment, because it implies that we are doing so well at what we are doing that surely we should be doing more.

While every profile of a religious center is not written with sophisticated academic nuance, and some are admittedly very basic, each contributes to the documentation we are doing. A young researcher on a summer's project may not write as profoundly as could be desired, particularly when s/he is writing on many traditions. A student reporting on a community of which s/he is a member may offer more description than analysis, and without the "objectivity" that is revered in the academy. However, our methodology of building our research in pieces and with many different products allows varied contributions to all be of value. At times when a student researcher's work has been criticized by the religious community, we are able to receive updates and nuances from the community itself. Offering an invitation to participate allows us to include those who offer constructive suggestions, sometimes improving the work after the preliminary research has been completed. Even when the results are imperfect, they open doors for further development.

We are currently looking forward to expanded research initiatives in the areas of the interfaith movement, the civil square, women's organizations, and the international arena. There is so much work to be done exploring the shifting patterns of religious traditions in the transnational, globalizing world. An open network that supports and enhances the work of local specialists while attending to the larger whole is a model that has a proven record of dynamic success. It is flexible and can expand or contract given the resources available at the time. Meeting the challenge of helping Americans engage with diversity is a huge undertaking, one towards which we have made great strides. Our network continues to grow and serve the needs of those who also serve the network. We tend this vitality, and are pushed forward by it.

9.

Seminarians Interacting: One Model of Multifaith Theological Education

Karen Wood

IN 1985, THE NATIONAL CONFERENCE of Christians and Jews (NCCJ) piloted the Seminarians Interacting (SI) program after having conducted various kinds of interfaith dialogues for almost six decades. These dialogues, for the most part, were carried out amongst the different religious constituencies Will Herberg described in his classic of religious sociology *Catholic, Protestant, Jew*. The SI program reflected the NCCJ's expanded focus on theological education and intergroup dialogue in a multifaith setting. This article provides a snapshot of the Seminarians Interacting Program (SI) during its first ten years, as it expanded, developed, and made an impact on theological education in the U.S.

I began my work with the SI program as a student. I was in the Th.D. program at Harvard Divinity School, pursuing studies in constructive Christian theology, trying to discern how Jewish self-understanding might have an impact on post-Shoah Christian self-expression. My experience of NCCJ's leadership development philosophy went something like this: I was critical of the program, so I was put on the planning committee; after working with the planning committee for some time, I was hired to run the project. Sneaky, eh? It helped me to listen with more grace when students with whom I was working then criticized the program in their turn.

SI grew out of another program, Theology in a Pluralistic Setting. Funded by the Pew Charitable Trusts, and directed by Dr. Ellen Charry, this early program brought together faculty from several theological schools in the Northeast, with representation from Evangelical, Roman Catholic, Greek Orthodox, and Protestant seminaries, and rabbinical schools from the Conservative, Reform and Reconstructionist movements of Judaism. In April of 1986, Dr. Charry expanded this program to include students from several of these schools, gathering the group for an initial conference in Stony Point, New York.

This first conference was organized with three faith groups in mind: Catholic, Protestant and Jew. The issue of identity and self-definition of participants arose immediately at this first conference. Students quickly began to invoke the first rule of dialogue: every participant has the right to her or his own self-definition. African-American Protestants identified their experience, both historical and contemporary, as distinct from that of white Protestants in the U.S. Likewise, Evangelical Protestants wished to self-identify as a different group from more liberal Protestants. Within a year, Orthodox Christian students were participating, as well, bringing the number of self-identified traditions within the program to six: Roman Catholic, Orthodox Christian, Evangelical, Liberal and African-American Protestant, and Jewish.

Seminary Visits

It became clear early on that student participants in the program would benefit greatly from exposure to other religious traditions prior to the large conference held each spring. A series of visits to pairs of geographically proximate schools was added during the autumn and winter months. Groups of twenty to thirty students would spend a day at each of these schools, visiting classes, experiencing worship, meeting with students, and learning about the education offered by the school. A group that included students from several schools up and down the coast might spend twenty-four hours in New York City at Hebrew Union College-Jewish Institute of Religion, and the next twenty-four hours at Union Theological Seminary; others might go to the Boston area to visit Holy Cross Greek Orthodox School of Theology and Gordon-Conwell Theological Seminary. This visit program ensured that every student who arrived for the large conference each spring had some idea of how theological education worked for at least two other traditions, and had met and engaged in some preliminary dialogue with several other participants.

Spring Workshop

With some insight gained from these visits, about 120 students and faculty would gather each spring in Stony Point, New York, for a four-day, intensive workshop, organized around a particular theme chosen by a representative student planning group. Themes for these workshops included "Expressions of Spirituality," "Revitalizing our Traditions in the Post-Modern World," and "Death and Dying in our Traditions." The Spring Workshop had three major components in which each student participated: Tradition Modules, Tradition Groups, and Worship.

Tradition Modules were two-and-a-half-hour segments, each devoted to presentation and study from a particular group. A Tradition Module would begin with a half-hour presentation on the workshop theme by a resource scholar, followed by fifteen minutes of general questions. Then the plenary group would break down into small mixed groups of ten to twelve, diversified by tradition, sex and race, and led by a trained facilitator. A student from the presenting tradition would lead a study of a critical text from scripture or another authoritative source that was relevant to the theme of the conference. Participants would experience the different approaches to texts across the range of traditions. After text-study, the facilitator would lead a reflection/discussion on the presentation of the tradition. This is where the real, intense dialogue took place. Facilitators would guide the discussion, reminding participants of their "Rights, Risks, and Responsibilities of Dialogue," a document of guiding principles for dialogue, which was developed by students, and which evolved as the program grew and changed. In the Spring Workshops in the Northeast, students met in these groups without the faculty, fearing that the presence of faculty might be intimidating, either because of their "expert" status or because of their perceived power over the ordination process of some students. Faculty in SI programs in Texas and the Ohio Valley were welcome participants in small mixed student groups.

Tradition Groups provided opportunities for participants to reflect upon and respond to what they heard from other traditions. Tradition Groups met regularly to prepare responses to two tradition modules at the final plenary: a response usually consisted of positive comments, concerns, and further questions. For instance, the African-American Protestant Tradition Group might choose to respond to the Jewish Tradition Module and the Orthodox Christian Tradition Module, describing in each case points of resonance and disagreement, and, perhaps, asking for further clarification. This final plenary would also provide an opportunity for further brief conversation with members of the module to which they had responded.

Worship was an important component of the Spring Workshop, as well. SI did not aspire to nor did it offer "interfaith" worship. Rather, each tradition would prepare a worship service from within its rites and liturgical practices; each tradition would hold its worship service directly before its Tradition Module. All participants were expected to be present at worship, and it was agreed that presence did not indicate assent. The presenting tradition would describe the extent to which participation of others was possible; it was then up to each participant to decide for her or himself the extent to which they felt comfortable participating.

This rather complex structure of Tradition Module, Tradition Group, and Worship were developed and refined over the course of the first two years of SI in the Northeast; we would joke that it was clearly the product of a committee! When taken as a whole, however, it made sense, in that it included opportunities for experiential and cognitive learning (worship and lecture, discussion and text-study), and opportunities for dialogue on an individual and corporate basis (small mixed groups and tradition groups). A typical workshop schedule would start with a general welcome and overview, and then break down into the components:

1) A meeting of the small mixed groups to do introductions and go over the Rights, Risks, and Responsibilities of Dialogue (i.e., guidelines for dialogue[1])

2) Worship and Tradition Modules for three traditions

3) Tradition Groups meet to formulate response to Tradition Modules

4) Worship and Tradition Modules for three more traditions

5) Tradition Groups meet to formulate response to Tradition Modules

6) Final Plenary—presentation of Tradition Group responses to Tradition Modules

7) Final small mixed group meeting—wrap up.

Geographical Expansion of SI

Starting in 1989, with assistance from another grant from the Pew Charitable Trusts and a generous grant from the Henry Luce Foundation, SI expanded to other seminary-rich areas of the U.S: Texas and the Ohio Valley. Each of these two areas brought a different set of issues and a different texture to the conferences (Seminary visits remained a feature of the Northeast SI, but were not instituted in Texas or the Ohio Valley). In Texas, the lack of a rabbinical school was compensated by the presence of rabbis who were just starting their careers in the Lone Star State. Evangelicals were in the majority in the Texas program; perhaps as a consequence, they tended to take less rigid doctrinal stands in dialogical settings than their counterparts in the Northeast. In the Ohio Valley, various Protestant and Catholic students got on well with the rabbinical students from Hebrew Union College; there was considerable friction, however, between the Catholics and the Protestants on matters of Christian faith.

Meanwhile, in the Northeast, the student participants were expanding the concept of identity to include identity constructed around race, gender and sexual orientation; the result was the formation of caucuses (identity groups) that cut across the lines of religious traditions and added important voices to the conversation. Indeed, alliances formed around these other aspects of identity, with two results: first, the presentations of various traditions on the topic at hand were subject not only to questioning and exploration on a theological basis, but also to a social critique, and second, individuals who might, within their own religious traditions, be quite isolated on the basis on race, gender, or sexual orientation, found a supportive group of students who understood the challenges posed to religious leadership amongst these groups, and could share their own experiences.

Expansion of SI to include Muslims

In 1994, thanks to the efforts of Peter Lawrence, NCCJ began planning to expand SI Northeast to include Muslims. When Patrice Brodeur was hired to replace me as Director of Seminarians Interacting in the following year, the implementation of this expansion included two Muslim institutions (one Baltimore mosque with an advanced education program and an accredited higher education institution based in Virginia, the Graduate School of Islamic and Social Sciences) as well as the Religion Department at Temple University and the Hartford Seminary, because they both had strong Muslim student presence in their respective graduate programs. One more Tradition Module was added to the Spring Workshop program for Muslims. As for the Jewish participants, their small numbers prevented their group from being divided into one or more sub-groups according to a variety of possible variables, as the Christians had done.

The SI Northeast program demonstrated the great need for integrating Muslims into this inter-seminary program. It also raised the challenge of having to find Muslim participants through institutions that are not equivalent to Christian or Jewish seminaries, demonstrating the gap between older and more recently established religious communities. It also made it possible to envision a possible future expansion to include Buddhists since they are beginning to develop American institutions of higher learning to train their own leaders, such as the Naropa Institute in Boulder, Colorado. Apart from the real geographical and therefore financial challenges which such an expansion would have meant, moving beyond the Abrahamic circle of Jews, Christians, and Muslims faced a psychological barrier as much as an intellectual one: monotheistic Abrahamic traditions have a lot more in common with each other than any of them with Buddhism.

Lessons Learned

During SI's first decade, the period in which I was directly involved, we learned a number of lessons, some about the nature of theological education, some about the nature of dialogue, and some about ourselves as future religious leaders.

We learned that seminary curricula are focused, of necessity, inward. In all three incarnations (Northeast, Texas and Ohio Valley), the program remained persistently co-curricular, never reaching a point where students could receive course credit. This meant that those who participated were deeply committed, but it also placed extra demands on students and faculty who were already very busy. In part, this persistence of the program outside the curriculum was a reflection of the increasing need for seminaries to steep their students, many of whom were not practicing in any religious tradition from the cradle, in the traditions, doctrines, history, ethic and esthetics of the community they would be serving as professionals. There was not extra curricular time for examining another tradition.

We learned to tell the truth about the other. SI focused on future religious leaders, because it was seen as essential that truth-telling start from the pulpit, the altar and the bimah. Religious leaders—rabbis, priests and ministers—would have the authority and, now, the experience to correct teachings that came from bias and misunderstanding.

We learned what roles we play in other traditions' stories. On one occasion, when the Greek Orthodox students referred to St. Moses, the rabbinical student next to me winced. When a Protestant student asked what is taught about Jesus at Rabbinical school, the answer, "not much," was very illuminating about how Christians use Judaism to define who they are, but Jews don't need reference to Christianity for their self-definition.

We learned where to set our own boundaries, and how to respect others'. In worship, each participant would have to ask her or himself: "Will I participate?" "How am I welcome to participate?" Jewish students would read ahead and sing along with Christian hymns, and then hit what they called "the Jesus wall": some reference to Jesus as messiah in the verse that they couldn't sing with integrity. Other traditions' boundary setting was sometimes painful; Protestant participants at a Mass at Catholic University repeated all the same prayers that were familiar to them from their own eucharistic worship, then came up against the prohibition, on the part of the Roman Catholic Church, against non-Catholics receiving communion. They were bereft.

We learned what Krister Stendahl calls "holy envy": the appreciation and admiration of another tradition, without conversion to that tradition. This was sometimes tricky; "May I borrow that prayer?" was not an infrequent question after a worship service; often Protestants wanted to use a prayer from a Jewish or another Christian tradition. Discussion would ensue about the integrity of a particular tradition, and the need to plumb the treasures of one's own tradition, to find similar riches there.

We learned that our traditions have developed—a lot!—in the time since we parted, first the church from early forms of Judaism, and then the various difference churches from one another. Almost every time we would gather a new group, a well-meaning Christian student would declare him or herself to be Christian, "but also Jewish, really, because Christianity came out of Judaism." After morning prayers at the Jewish Theological Seminary, we would ask that student if he still considered himself to be Jewish. . . "I had no idea what was going on during those prayers," would be the reply. "Maybe I'm not Jewish, after all."

We learned what was foundational about our faith. The most conservative statements of faith emerged from us in the context of dialogue, surprising many of us. One student from a theologically liberal Christian tradition, in which the role of Jesus is most highly valued as a prophetic teacher, found herself passionately declaring belief in the resurrected Christ to be the core of her faith—something that she said she had never confessed among other skeptical, liberal co-religionists, but that became clear to her when someone from another faith asked about her faith.

We learned what hurts. In the small mixed groups, we learned that some of our most cherished beliefs and stories were a source of great pain to others, either because they had been historically used as a weapon, or because they negated the experience or, sometimes, the very existence of the other.

We learned how messy everybody else's house is, that is, as messy as our own! SI provided a wonderful education about conflict within traditions; one day at Weston School of Theology, a Jesuit seminary, three Roman Catholic students from a conservative diocesan seminary refused to receive the Eucharist because a female faculty member had read a portion of the pastoral prayer. After the service, the Protestant and Jewish students looked on in amazement, as the Roman Catholic students engaged in a massive theological throw-down. For years, in the Northeast, the students from the Conservative, Reform and Reconstructionist rabbinical schools would take turns leading their own prayers, always struggling with the different forms and interpretations. One afternoon, after prayers, the Jewish students came back into the plenary quite excited; they had all felt that they had fulfilled their obligation, praying together, with no struggle, and they shared their delight with the rest of the group.

Did SI achieve any long-lasting results in its first decade? Time will tell. What we do know is that 1,200 participants, in three parts of the U.S.—rabbis, ministers and priests, teachers and educators—know how to tell the truth about one another; they have learned from books, and from experience, and from their relationships with one another. It is not enough, but it is a very good start.

Conclusion

The Seminarians Interacting program, in its three different forms not equally well described in this article, remains one of the jewels of interreligious dialogue worldwide. NCCJ's national headquarters in New York unfortunately decided in 2000 to stop the Northeast program; other regions lost steam as well.

Since September 11, 2001, the call for such programs has only increased, and not only in the United States. There is an urgent need to adapt this model of inter-seminary encounters to various locations around the world. For example, in 2003, discussions around this idea took place among the religious leadership of several countries in the Balkans: mainline Orthodox and Catholic Christians as well as Muslims have realized that key to peacebuilding in this region recently ravaged by war is the formation of all future religious leaders in the skills of interreligious cooperation for peace and justice. The same lesson applies the world over.

NCCJ can play a direct leadership role nationally by strengthening its current Seminarian Interacting program in California, reviving the ones in the Ohio Valley and the Northeast, as well as expanding in other areas of the United States. Internationally, as a key member of the International Council of Christians and Jews, NCCJ can also become a catalyst to help expand the SI model to other regions around the world. Our world is currently in dire need of such institutional leadership.

Notes

1. Various versions of these guidelines exist, with varying names. A later version called Rights, Responsibilities, and Skills of Dialogue (RRSD) was published by Patrice Brodeur in an article entitled "Description of the Guidelines for Interfaith Celebrations" in the *Journal of Ecumenical Studies*, 34:4, Fall 1997, pp. 559–560.

10.

Towards a Multifaith Community at Wellesley College

Victor H. Kazanjian, Jr.

PERHAPS IT WAS THE OPENING WORDS of welcome from Baha'i, Buddhist, Christian, Hindu, Jain, Jewish, Muslim, Sikh, and Unitarian Univeralist students; or the call to worship by Native African drumming offered by the Yanvalou African Drum and Dance Ensemble; or the mystical singing of a Zoltan Kodaly piece by the College Choir; or the scripture read by Buddhist, Catholic, Jewish, Muslim and Protestant chaplains; or the classical Indian song and dance performed by Hindu students; or the inspirational reflections on the theme "Education as a Spiritual Journey" by writer/teacher Parker Palmer; or the echoes of a Hebrew song sung in round; or the prayers for a new president, spoken in seven different languages; perhaps it was one of these things or the inter-wovenness of all of these elements of the service that moved those gathered at the Inaugural Multifaith Celebration to realize that something different was happening at Wellesley College, when Diana Chapman Walsh was inaugurated as Wellesley's twelfth President in the fall of 1993.

This celebration was the most visible manifestation of a revolution in religious and spiritual life taking place at Wellesley College, a revolution that has evolved during the past decade to a comprehensive exploration of the role of religion and spirituality in higher education. In 1993 the Wellesley College community was introduced to an exciting new model of religious and spiritual life. At a time when most colleges and universities, confused by the conflict between a mono-religious institutional history and a multi-religious contemporary college community, were de-emphasizing the religious and spiritual dimensions of their institutions, Wellesley set out on a journey in the opposite direction. Determined to continue to value the role of religion and spirituality in the educational experience which has been so much a part of her past, Wellesley created a new and largely untraveled path for an academic community, (or perhaps any community), the exploration of multifaith community.

How did this happen? First a bit of context.

The Wellesley College that you may think you know or at least that I thought I knew before arriving at Wellesley, is not the Wellesley that I found in February of 1993 when I walked onto campus for the first time. The college whose name conjures up for many images of white New England debutantes, (as evidenced by the recently released Hollywood film, *Mona Lisa Smiles*), is, in fact, one of the most racially and ethnically diverse colleges in the United States. Due to its commitment to need-blind admissions, which enables Wellesley to admit students without regard to financial status, and to an equally strong commitment to multiculturalism as an essential context in which excellent global education takes place, Wellesley College's student body is a microcosm of human diversity. What had not changed as rapidly by 1992, were the institutional structures that were born out of Wellesley's history as a more homogeneous community in which the cultural norms of wealthy, white, Western Protestant Christian society were dominant. One such outdated institutional structure was the college chaplaincy that was a reflection of Wellesley's history and that reflected a much broader history of religion and higher education.

The history of religious and spiritual life in higher education has been complicated at best. It was religiously inspired motivation that led to the founding of many of the earliest colleges and universities in this country and shaped early educational philosophy and pedagogy. The relationship between religion and education persisted, over the growing objections of many scholars who found their academic freedoms restricted by the theological principles rather than educational ones. This continued until the mid-twentieth century, when secular scholarship won out and most colleges and universities severed ties with organized religion or relegated it to the extreme margins of the educational enterprise. In non-religiously affiliated institutions, chaplaincy programs continued to exist either on the margins of academe quietly serving their communities, or in a few remaining places like Duke, Harvard, and Stanford; historically powerful religious programs cling to larger roles within institutions, but in increasingly ceremonial ways.

Wellesley College's religious history was in some ways no different, (and in a few very important ways completely different). Like many similar institutions, by 1993 Wellesley had a College chaplaincy program which was a slightly modified version of its earlier Christian chaplaincy. Religious life at Wellesley was led by a full-time College Chaplain, who was the Protestant Chaplain. The Protestant Chaplain was first and foremost responsible for the Protestant Christian majority on campus and then, only by her own inspiration rather than by design of her role, concerned with the spiritual lives of all students. [In fact, Wellesley's two previous College Chaplains, Paul Santmire and Connie Chandler-Ward, were outstanding examples of spiritual leaders serving all members of the community in spite of their institutional roles.] In addition to the College Chaplain, a part-time Hillel Director/Campus Rabbi and a Roman Catholic priest (both funded for the most part by their own religious communities) served Jewish and Roman Catholic communities on the margins of campus life. In the face of the dissonance between this model and the college's diverse student population, College Chaplain Connie Chandler-Ward, in her final letter to the community in 1991, pleaded with the College to move beyond this outdated model of religious life that failed to respond to the reality of the diversity of the contemporary college community, but rather simply perpetuated the outdated culture of the past.

The religious context of the Wellesley College culture is indeed similar to many New England schools and yet different enough to be fertile ground for experimentation. Founded in 1875 by Henry Durant, a self-proclaimed evangelical Christian and friend of evangelist/educator Dwight Moody who served on Wellesley Board of Trustees in the early years, the language of Wellesley's founding documents is filled with calls for the radical necessity of women's education as a Christian imperative. Listen to the language of Durant's opening address to the college. "The Higher Education of Women is one of the great world battle cries for freedom. . . . I believe that God's hand is in it; that it is one of the great ocean currents of Christian civilization; that He is calling to womanhood to come up higher, to prepare herself for great conflicts, for vast reforms in social life, for noblest usefullness."[1] Although clearly Christian in context, from the beginning the language of Wellesley's mission called for the education of women for full participation in the world. One point to which I will return later in this chapter is that although explicitly Christian, Wellesley was from the beginning also fervently non-denominational and therefore not attached to any organized religion, a fact that has been significant to its multifaith development. Through the years, the Christian context of the College's mission gave way to the values of secular liberal arts education. What did not fall away, however, were the institutional structures that carried the cultural norms of Wellesley's Protestant Christian past. These structures remained largely invisible to those who shared the dominant culture (wealthy, white, western and Protestant Christian) and yet painfully obvious to those who did not fit this cultural profile. Community members were reminded of the dominant culture through the words in the Wellesley logo (*Non ministrare, sed ministrare*, not to be served but to serve from Christian scripture), Christian images in stained glass windows across the campus, and college rituals such as convocation and baccalaureate which followed Christian liturgical forms. Each of these things served as subtle (and not so subtle) reminders not only of the historical culture of Wellesley, but created a sense that Wellesley's contemporary culture is Christian and that all others may be welcome, but are welcomed guests. The college which I discovered in 1993 is best described by Diana Eck in her extraordinary book *Encountering God* in which she presents three forms of interreligious relationship, exclusivist, inclusivist and pluralist. Wellesley was according to this analysis an inclusive community in which "the diversity of peoples and traditions is included in a single worldview that embraces, explains, and supersedes them all."[2] What I found particularly ironic in my first year at Wellesley was to discover that this secular college was unknowingly perpetuating institutional structures that proclaimed Protestant Christian hegemony. My first big challenge was to attempt to bring this factor to light as we tried to move from an inclusivist community to a pluralistic one in which different cultures, traditions and perspectives are equally valued in a grand experiment of educational encounter among different peoples of the world.

In contemplating this process of change, I discovered certain aspects of Wellesley's history that stood apart from these dominant cultural norms and other peer institutions. As it turned out, these historical realities played a crucial role in laying a foundation for the creation of the multifaith religious and spiritual life program. As mentioned above, Wellesley was founded as a women's college in defiance of a male dominated culture. The memory of such a revolutionary spirit of equality through challenging cultural norms remains a part of Wellesley's stated institutional values. This initial value of gender equity has been extended over the years at Wellesley to include those racial, ethnic and religious groups that have historically been excluded from full participation in shaping the culture in institutions of higher education. Wellesley's seventh President, Mildred McAfee Horton illustrated such revolutionary thinking in her farewell address to the College in 1949. When talking about the importance of including all students into the Wellesley community she said, "Because she is a student at Wellesley, that rich girl, that poor girl, that Catholic, Protestant, Jew, Muslim, Hindu, American, Egyptian, Chinese, Iranian (girl) . . . is entitled to all the 'rights, dignities and responsibilities' of this College." At another occasion she added, "The day we learn as a people that differences do not necessarily involve discriminatory evaluations, vast problems of human relations will be solvable."[3] It became clear after a brief introduction to Wellesley's history that the value of equality and the goal of Wellesley as a diverse educational community would play a positive role in the development of a multifaith model.

A second factor that enabled us to build a case for the importance of a multifaith model of religious and spiritual life at Wellesley College was Wellesley's defiantly non-denominational religious beginnings. While the founders of Wellesley were certainly devout Christians, they refused to be attached to any Christian denomination. This meant that from the beginning the religious and spiritual life of the College was entrusted to the president and the faculty rather than an external religious institution. Although this led to the rapid secularization of the College in the mid-1960s, I found that it also enabled me to call upon these early ecumenical roots when suggesting that a multifaith community which included people of all traditions was a better reflection of Wellesley's educational values than a community in which one tradition was privileged over another (the old College Chaplaincy model). The principles underlying Wellesley's ecumenical roots have been translated a century later from inter Christian ecumenism to multifaith ecumenism.

And finally, in the early 1990s while many colleges and universities faced with fiscal challenges were downsizing or curtailing support for their outdated chaplaincy programs, Wellesley chose a different route. Convening a consultation on the religious and spiritual life of the college involving trustees, students, faculty and senior administrators, the college devised a plan to renew its commitment to religious and spiritual life through a multifaith program. The first act of the college in this direction was to create the new position of Dean of Religious and Spiritual Life, the role of which was not to represent any one religious community, but to design and oversee a new structure that would meet the religious and spiritual needs of students, faculty and staff, and consider the role of religion and spirituality in the college's overall educational mission. The second part of this charge proved to be especially important, in that it opened a door to reconsider the relationship between religion/spirituality and education, a process that ultimately moved religious and spiritual life from the margins of the institution to a seat at the table in defining how to implement the college's core educational goals.

In my opening address to the College as Wellesley's first Dean of Religious and Spiritual Life, I offered the following words:

> I believe that it is the awakening of a desire for wholeness, in one's self, in one's relationships, among humanity and in all of creation that is the essential task of all spirituality and religion and the essential work of education. In my first few months at Wellesley, I have been truly inspired by the desire of so many people here to incorporate a spiritual component into their lives in this community, students who seek the support of familiar religious experience, other students who explore the possibilities of spirituality beyond institutionalized religion; faculty who see the educating of the mind as inseparable from the nurturing of the spirit; and staff for whom the place in which they work holds the possibility for the development of

community. In these first months, I have experienced a genuine commitment to include religion and spirituality in the life and learning of this College.

Now for some, the thought of a College embracing any sort of religious or spiritual component in this day and age strikes fear in their hearts and raises critical not to mention constitutional concerns . . . and I might say not without good reason, for in the past the mingling of religion and academia has often meant the establishing of a normative religious perspective centered around a single religious tradition. But we are up to something new at Wellesley, something which springs forth from the rich religious and spiritual traditions of this College and yet something which truly reflects the magnificent montage of religious and spiritual beliefs represented in today's Wellesley College community.

It is my hope that in the years ahead, we will, through the Religious and Spiritual Life Program, nurture a multi-faith environment which truly responds to this rich diversity of religious tradition and experience represented in the Wellesley College community among students, staff and faculty. This means striving to support the spiritual, educational and worship needs of each religious group on campus, while establishing new ways in which people of all religious and spiritual beliefs can learn about and from one another and thereby begin to discover the common threads which bind us together as people of faith. This I might mention is very different from past interfaith efforts where the goal was most often to establish a kind of common, neutral language and practice, which offended no one but which also quickly became unrecognizable to any person of faith. Our hope is to affirm the integrity of each religious tradition while challenging people to see their own experience as simply a part of some greater whole. . . .

But there is more to this challenge than the support of the religious and spiritual lives of people at this College, for I believe that spirituality far transcends the boundaries of institutionalized religion and is a part of the intellectual, moral and personal development of all people. As an academic institution charged with the task of educating women to fully engage in society, the incorporation of a spiritual dimension to this educational process seems essential. What that means . . . how that becomes manifest in this community, is the work of discovery that lies before us. There is much in the recent and past history of this College that will inform us in this process. Some of what has come before, we will incorporate into the future. While some things, we will necessarily need to leave behind. For we are attempting something new and yet something old as well. For the roots of this movement

> towards spiritual wholeness harken back to the beginning, the beginning of creation.
> . . .and that which we create here at Wellesley in our day, will, if we do it well, awak-
> en in us the desire for wholeness and help us rediscover a very essential aspect of
> our common humanity.

And with these words, we began a process of experimentation as to the role of religious and spiritual life in higher education that continues to this day. At the inauguration of Diana Chapman Walsh as Wellesley President in 1993, two ceremonies signi-
fied the beginning of a new era of religious and spiritual life at Wellesley. The first
was the multifaith celebration held the evening before the inauguration. Months in the
planning by a team that included students from the Baha'i, Buddhist, Christian (Evangelical, Orthodox, Protestant and Roman Catholic), Hindu, Jain, Jewish, Muslim,
Native African, Pagan, Sikh, Unitairan Unversalist and Zoroastrian religious communities, this celebration introduced the community to the implications of the inspiration
to multifaith ecumenism that they had followed. For some, it was the realization of a
dream, for others perhaps more of a nightmare, for the door was now opened to decon-
struct one hundred years of Protestant Christian defined college culture and rebuild a
new multifaith community. The next day, at the inauguration ceremonies, President
Walsh was presented with the "keys to the College," an historic Wellesley ritual
unearthed for this occasion. The three keys, to the library, the dormitory and the
chapel, represent the three historic areas of educational development central to a
Wellesley education, the intellectual, the social and the spiritual. The implication of
this ritual embraced by President Walsh was clear. Wellesley was seeking to reclaim
its historic values of a holistic education for women that included the spiritual dimension. At that moment, none of us had any idea how significant this process would
become for Wellesley and for those outside of Wellesley concerned about the role of
religious and spiritual life in higher education.

Space does not permit me to adequately tell the story of the past decade of multi-
faith work at Wellesley. Several years ago I attempted this in a chapter in the book
*Education as Transformation: Religious Pluralism, Spirituality and a New Vision for
Higher Education in America.*[4] For this chapter, rather than retell the tale in narrative
form, I would like to highlight a series of principles that guided our process and in
doing so hopefully provide insights that can be used to develop multifaith programs
in different contexts.

1. Ultimately this is about education, not religion

One of the principles that we discovered only by making many mistakes over
many years, was that ultimately questions about the role of religion and spirituality in

higher education must start and end with the question "How does religion and spirituality enhance the education of our students?" not the question, "How do we support religion on our campuses?" This is a principle that religious folk often find hard to swallow. But if you can't get past this question, stop! because your efforts will most likely lead to the perpetuating of old dysfunctional processes, not the birth of new constructive ones. For too long, religious professionals working in higher education have spent inordinate amounts of time bemoaning the fact that they feel marginalized on campuses, voicing frustration that faculty members have all the power, and nostalgically reflecting back on the good old days when "religion really mattered." Having wasted far too much time participating in these musings myself, I learned my lesson one fall day when a faculty friend clearly tired of listening to my whining about the marginalized state of religion on campus said, "Did you ever consider that maybe it is your job to think about how religion and spirituality fit into education, not ours?" Oops. I sat silent. Fifty years after secular colleges and universities rejected religious control over their educational institutions, I was still carrying the notion that religion and spirituality should be assumed to be an important part of the educational process. This gentle confrontation early in my time at Wellesley changed my entire orientation to the work of religious and spiritual life on campus. What became clear was that a new dialogue was needed as to why religion and spirituality are relevant to education. The first step for us was to initiate a conversation about this question so that we could explore the possibility of a partnership between academics and religious folks working together to enhance our students' learning. We found it useful to start such a conversation by reflecting on questions that students are asking about religion, spirituality and education. For example, in a survey of Wellesley students in 1995 these questions emerged.

"I am a scholar and I am spiritual. Are these two parts of one person? Or I am two people separated from myself by the split in education between mind and spirit?"

"Why must I leave the religious part of myself outside the door of my classes, only to enter and encounter writings of those who were inspired by their religious faith?"

"How can I understand the role that religion plays in the world around me, if I do not have the opportunity to understand the role that religion plays in the life of my classmates?"

"In terms of my religion, I am invisible. My professors, they look at me, see the color of my skin and think they know my story. I am African-American and I am

Jewish. How can they see me, if they do not know me? and how can they teach me, if they do not see me?"

To adequately take up questions such as these, educators and religious professionals must come together with students and talk about the relationship between religious/spiritual identity and intellectual development. Academics have long recognized the philosophies and practices of the world's religious traditions as formative in the establishment of various systems upon which societies are organized, including systems of law, governance, education, and other dimensions of the total complex of human relations. However, in most of our colleges and universities the influence of these same philosophies and practices on the formation of individual students has gone largely unrecognized by educators. The role of religious identity in students' lives has most often been separated from the education of students and relegated to religious communities who have set up outposts, (called chaplaincies) on college and university campuses. Often these programs have little relationship to the educational program of their institutions. They are seen by many faculty as vestiges of a past entanglement between institutional religion and institutions of higher education and therefore are looked at as either irrelevant or antithetical to contemporary secular education. While issues of racial and cultural identity are finally being seen as central to a comprehensive understanding of the intellectual development of students, by and large religious/spiritual identity has not been included in these discussions. This, however, is beginning to change.

Researchers and writers such as Beverly Daniel Tatum and Daryl Smith, who work on the impact of identity on intellectual development, have begun to include religion as a significant category of identity relevant to education. In the Spring 1998 issue of *Diversity Digest*, Daryl Smith includes religion in her analysis of campus diversity. "[D]iversity on campus encompasses complex differences within the campus community and also the individuals who compose that community. It includes such important and intersecting dimensions of human identity as race, ethnicity, national origin, religion, gender, sexual orientation, class, age and ability. These dimensions do not determine or predict any one person's values, orientation, or life choices. But they are by definition closely related patterns of societal experience, socialization and affiliation. They influence ways of understanding and interpreting the world." If this is so; if religious identity impacts the way a student understands and interprets the world, then religious/spiritual identity is an educational issue and needs to be taken up as such. Other resources for the discussion of religion, spirituality and education include the work of the Education as Transformation Project based at Wellesley College (www.educationastransformation.org) and the Higher Education

Research Institute and specifically their Spirituality in Higher Education project (www.spirituality.ucla.edu). The first step, then, to developing multifaith campus programs is to locate this effort in the larger discourse of enhancing education. This means new conversations among faculty, religious professionals and students.

In 1998 we attempted one such conversation at Wellesley. We gathered a group of Wellesley students and asked them to share stories of "moments of meaning" that they had experienced in their classes. At the time I was searching for a way to make the connection between religion/spirituality and education and struggling with the language to use. As I sat with these students and listened to their stories, their words provided a new language for our discussions. The students told of moments of meaning, inspiration, connection, wonder and awe in the classroom and many spoke of these moments as having a religious or spiritual dimension. The classes in which these moments occurred cut across the entire curriculum, from biology to history, from sociology to theater, from ethnic studies to mathematics—story after story of moments when they were awakened to a deeper understanding of themselves, of others around them and of the world which they described as transformational in some way. One student told of a moment in molecular biology during a lab when she suddenly made the connection between the smallest forms of life and the largest living ecosystems of the planet. Another student related an experience of working on a psychology project with her mentor in which the faculty member's encouragement of the student's research resulted in them co-authoring a paper and in the students having a sense of herself as being able to have original thoughts. Still another student shared her experience of her political science studies (and her own understanding of the world) coming alive during a winter session trip to Mexico. Students spoke about transformational moments coming through collaborative work with other students, through service learning opportunities associated with a course, through an encounter with particular texts, through the mentoring of a faculty member.

The next step was to approach faculty members with the stories told by their students. I e-mailed faculty members telling them that a student in their class had described having a transformational experience, a moment of meaning in their class. I then invited these faculty members to a discussion about such moments in the learning and teaching process. Over the course of the next month, fifty-five faculty members met to discuss transformational moments in the classroom and shared similar stories with one another about such moments from their own learning and teaching. Eventually the discussion centered on the reasons for their original choice to become a scholar and a teacher. Some spoke of a passion for seeking truth, others of a desire to kindle a fire within their students, many told stories of having been affirmed as a person whose ideas were of value by a faculty mentor in their own life. Many spoke of the joy of watching students come alive in their classes as connections between self and world began to be made.

A meeting between students and faculty to process the experience led to the formulation of central questions that they felt bring religion and spirituality together with education. These questions included: What is the purpose of our learning? What does it mean to be an educated person? What does my learning/teaching have to do with my living? How is my learning relevant to the lives of others? Embedded in the stories told by students and faculty and in their questions is a vocabulary that seems to bridge the chasm between the language of religion/spirituality and the language of scholarship.

2. You've got to be willing to move beyond tolerance

Perhaps the most profound lesson that we have learned at Wellesley is that tolerance is not the goal that we should seek in forming pluralistic community. In the face of a world punctuated by acts of intolerance, how could tolerance possibly be an unworthy goal for which to strive? After all, throughout history has not tolerance been the goal towards which forward thinking people have worked in seeking to respond to conflict? At a time when tolerance has often been replaced by overt acts of intolerance on our campuses, a little tolerance seems a worthy goal. Our experience (and numerous historical examples) tells us otherwise. Tolerance, as often practiced in our communities, is little more than conflict arrested. While it is a harness applied to the destructive forces of ignorance, fear and prejudice and provides a kind of wall between warring parties, at best this is a glass wall where protected people can see one another going about parallel lives. In this condition, people exist less able to harm each other, but also unable to interact due to the wall of tolerance dividing them from each other. As such, tolerance is not a basis for healthy human relationships nor will it ever lead to pluralistic community, for tolerance does not allow for learning, or growth or transformation, but rather ultimately keeps people in a state of suspended ignorance and conflict. Rather than tolerance as a goal, we choose to speak about tolerance as only a first step to interdependence.

A program with tolerance as its ultimate goal is satisfied with tinkering with existing models so that previously disenfranchised students feel a little less disenfranchised. While this may serve to mollify students for a while, it fails to examine both the structural ways in which religious life programs were created to serve particular groups of students (and not others), and that interreligious dialogue may be one of the most significant skills that students learn at college in preparation for work in today's multi-religious realities.

The multifaith program at Wellesley College is entitled "Beyond Tolerance." For us this means that in moving beyond tolerance we seek ways in which religious diversity can be a resource rather than a barrier to building multifaith community. In developing this program, we started with the assumption that to move from a mono-religious community to a multi-religious community would take people from all traditions building new relationships and providing leadership for the college as a whole. This required building two leadership teams: The Religious Life Team of chaplains and advisors, and the Multifaith Student Council. The Religious Life Team at Wellesley College is now comprised of a Buddhist Advisor, Catholic Chaplain, Hillel Director, Hindu Advisor, Muslim Advisor, Protestant Christian Chaplain and Unitarian Universalist Chaplain. This team meets weekly with the Dean not simply to coordinate our work but also to examine together issues of religious and spiritual life that affect the lives and learning of our students. The religious life team meets regularly with other religious advisors on campus such as the advisors to Intervarsity Christian Fellowship, Real Life, and the Mormon student group so that all religious professionals on campus are in touch and working collaboratively. The group also works regularly in partnership with student life professionals (including residence life staff, counseling services, and cultural advisors) and faculty members interested in supporting the whole lives of students as they go through their college years.

The multifaith student council is a second leadership group in the Beyond Tolerance Program. This group is comprised of students from the various religious traditions on campus. Representation is based on equity of voice, not proportional representation (more like the U.S. Senate than the House of Representatives). There may be two Bahai's on campus and 1,000 Roman Catholic Christians on campus, but both groups have an equal number of representatives on the council. The goals of the council are as follows:

- To engage in an exploration of the possibility of religious pluralism at Wellesley College as women from different religious and spiritual traditions.
  Religious pluralism in this context is nurturing and celebrating all particular religious traditions and spiritual practices represented in the Wellesley College community and actively engaging this diversity in ways that build community by exploring the principles that bind us together in a common life.

- To serve as an advisory council for the Dean of Religious and Spiritual Life.

- The council meets regularly with the Dean of Religious and Spiritual Life and convenes in times of community crisis.

- To serve as a leadership team, along with the Religious Life Team and the Dean of Religious and Spiritual Life, nurturing the religious and spiritual life of the College. To do this the council should:

    meet periodically with Religious Life team;

    participate in the planning of multifaith community worship;

    participate in the development of the Religious and Spiritual Life program;

    plan programs relating to religious, spiritual, ethical issues for the college community;

    seek ways to engage communities outside of Wellesley in this work of religious pluralism.

- To act as a liaison between the sending religious community on campus and this multifaith work. It is essential that each member of multifaith council have an active and engaged relationship with their own community and its leadership.

- To provide advice on issues related to student religious activities by advising on complaints filed under the code for religious organizations and serving as liaison with College Government and Senate.

The religious life team and the multifaith student council are the heart of the religious life program at Wellesley College. The relationships that are built and the conflicts that are engaged among members of these groups provide the insight and inspiration for the work that we do. My job is always to facilitate this process and remind them that just sitting in a room together engaging in creative dialogue is a radical act in and of itself.

3. The Protestants are not going to be happy. In fact, no one may really be happy either (i.e., this isn't about making people happy!)

When dismantling century-old culturally embedded structures and replacing them with new pluralistic ones, it is likely that no one is going to be particularly happy, (at first and probably for a long time). When we began the process of restructuring religious life at Wellesley, it soon became clear that everyone was being asked to reconsider their identity in the system. For Protestant Christians this meant giving up privileged status, much of which was invisible to them until it was taken away. Very much like the process of becoming conscious of issues of race, those with privilege are often unaware of their status until it is challenged. Over the years, I have found myself spending a lot of time helping Protestants grieve the loss of their status of being the normative tradition of the college. A few are outraged at the loss of their

"Christian College," but quite frankly for most it is a subtler change, a sense of loss of the familiar, a slight disorientation from "so much change." Attending to the very real grief process of this community while at the same time not allowing this to slow down the process of transformation is a role that somebody needs to take up, if this issue is to be addressed.

The second part of this principle is in many ways the most unexpected. One would think that a group that has been marginalized for decades if not centuries would heap praises on a process that changes these unjust structures. However, the reality of having a seat at the decision-making table presents new challenges for groups whose identity has been forged as being an outsider for years. Many non-dominant culture groups on our campuses have organized themselves around their marginalized identity, (understandably so). It takes time for this to change.

More than a decade after starting this process at Wellesley, we are just now beginning to see real change in terms of people's sense of identity within the community. in part, this has to do with the transitory nature of student populations, but culture change takes time and we have found it best to remind everyone of that a lot. (Another reason why people can find this work frustrating.)

While I am delivering the "bad news" (or perhaps most challenging aspects) about this work, let me offer another principle.

4. Including everyone at the table means more food

Most of our religious life programs have spaces on our campuses and hold spaces in the budget that reflect old models that serve only particular groups of students. Questions about dividing existing resources or designating new resources can unravel efforts to develop new programs before they get off the ground. Rather than pitting communities against each other over limited resources, we have found it better (although not always successful) to start by considering examples of institutional change within higher education that are somewhat analogous. For example, there was a time when Greek and Latin were the only languages taught in universities. Then a strong case was made to expand opportunities for students to take additional languages because it would enhance their education. German, French, Spanish were added, then Russian, Hebrew and Hindi. At no point in the process was the Latin department asked to teach Hindi, nor the Greek department French. We do not ask sociologists to provide the foundations of chemistry in their classes, nor do we ask academic deans to provide psychological counseling for students. In addition, we create spaces in classroom buildings and dormitories that meet the needs of the students in those settings. Therefore, once we have established that religious and spiritual life is in fact an important part of the educational goals of the institution (see principle number one) then providing resources for the staffing and space needs of religious groups on campus should be no different.

Under the leadership of President Walsh, Wellesley College has found creative ways to support religious and spiritual life on campus. From consistent organizational support from senior administrators to fundraising initiatives including the most recent College Campaign in which religious and spiritual life was a priority, Wellesley has stood behind its vision a decade ago for a renewed religious and spiritual life program through times of conflict as well as celebration.

This leads me to a final comment about our journey towards multifaith community at Wellesley College that has to do with celebration. During the past 12 years, many of the significant moments in people's lives that relate to the religious and spiritual life programs are moments of community ritual and celebration. For some, religious and spiritual celebration is that small gathering of Muslim or Jewish students meeting for weekly prayer or the morning Buddhist meditations, or Christian or Hindu scripture study that they will remember as a meaningful part of their overall educational experience. For others, perhaps most, religious and spiritual celebration will be a time when students, faculty and staff come together to mark a moment of joy or struggle. It is in these gatherings led by the college's spiritual leaders, where people find comfort and community. It is in moments like these, the memorial service for a student or service marking a tragic world event, the multifaith convocation or baccalaureate service that celebrate the beginning and ending of a school year, that questions about the importance of religious and spiritual life vanish and we are reminded of the kind of ways in which the search for meaning through our learning and in our lives is a task that requires all forms of seeking.

Take a look at the mission statements of any college or university in the country. Somewhere therein you will find reference to the highest vision of education that enables each student to find creative expression for their thoughts and actions in ways that positively contribute to one's community and the world. This is a goal around which scholars and religious folks alike can rally. The search for meaning in this moment in history needs to be a search that draws upon the diversity of human experience and wisdom. As such, it needs to be a multifaith search in which the depth of all religious and spiritual understanding is brought together with the breadth of scholarly inquiry. Perhaps then, by forging a new partnership between these two worlds can we adequately engage the internal and external struggles that face our world.

There is a second inscription that is part of Wellesley College's motto. The words are "Incipit Vita Novae," translated as "Here begins new life," a motto worthy of the highest vision for the spiritual and the scholarly. In our journey towards multifaith community, we have begun to sense the creative possibilities that might be born from a new partnership between these two worlds. It has been a good beginning and we are excited about what our second decade of multifaith community will hold.

Notes

1. Jean Glasscock, *Wellesley College: 1875-1975—A Century of Women*, (Wellesley College, Wellesley, MA 1975) p. 1.

2. Diana Eck, *Encountering God*, (Boston, Beacon Press, 1993) p. 179.

3. Mildred McAfee Horton, *Presidential Addresses* provided by the Wellesley College Archives.

4. Victor Kazanjian and Peter Laurence, *Education as Transformation: Religious Diversity, Spirituality and a New Vision of Higher Education for America*, (New York: Peter Lang Press. 1999).

11.

Bringing Interfaith to the University of Illinois

**Savva Amusin, Sarah Bier, Arielle Hertzberg,
Rozina Kanchwala, Nicholas Price, and Alison Siegel**

DURING THE TWENTIETH CENTURY, universities have played a significant role in major political and social movements. During the 1920s, large numbers of students took part in the suffrage movement, and in the 1960s many were involved with the civil rights movement and the Vietnam War protests. Students engaged in dialogue and activism in order to challenge and strengthen the fabric of our society. These movements have repeatedly advocated for change and social justice. Until recently, however, one critical area has been overlooked: the realm of interfaith work. The United States is the most religiously diverse country in the world, but rarely is the issue of religion discussed in a way that promotes understanding and cooperation between faith communities. As wars are waged around the world in the name of religion, the instance of religiously motivated violence in the United States is increasing. Recent tensions in the Middle East have brought intercultural and interreligious conflict onto the global stage, intensifying inter-group relations all over the world, including those in the United States. As microcosms of U.S. society, American college campuses are no less vulnerable to these clashes than are any other communities. The University of Illinois at Urbana-Champaign is one of many college campuses where students are seeking out positive and innovative ways of dealing with these conflicts, including the advancement of interfaith work as a means of creating a better community.

With the rise in violence in the Middle East several years ago, the campus began to feel the impact of the region's clashes. At a school where the Jewish and Muslim communities are of significant and comparable size, the atmosphere on campus was largely characterized by protests, hate speech, inflammatory chalking of campus side-walks and buildings, and a divestment campaign. Hurt and humiliation fueled anger, verbal assault, and a polarization of students sympathizing with either Israeli or Palestinian concerns. Voices calling for peaceful communication and dialogue were drowned out by those of extremist leaders within both communities. Jewish and Muslim parents alike became concerned about their children's safety, fearing that their children would become targets in the campus version of a battle thousands of miles away. By May 2003, the heated debate on campus had calmed, and Middle East related hate speech had all but disappeared on campus.

How was such a dramatic change achieved?

Peace movements had been ongoing at the university for quite some time, each gathering small numbers of dedicated supporters but quickly ending in defeat. Ultimately, these movements would falter and dwindle as their membership grew older and either moved on from the university or became discouraged and focused their energies elsewhere. One of these efforts was the EPIC initiative from 2000 to 2001, which stood for Education in Palestinian/Israeli Coexistence, which included approximately two hundred students. According to Sara Bokhari, a Palestinian Muslim who was involved with the initiative, "It was very focused on the politics and the history of the event." Yet, while it achieved some mild success in creating connections between organizers, unfortunately many of the discussions at EPIC broke down due to the bias and emotion that are unavoidable for many when discussing these sensitive topics.

In response to these issues the Bridges Dialogue Group on Middle East Issues was born in 2002. Bridges was an effort to create a space for political conversations and experience-sharing designed to foster mutual understanding and build friendships across communities. Bridges grew from a small cluster of five interested students up to about fifteen, but ultimately fell back to a small grouping of frustrated and tired members. In response, Bridges' leadership decided to change course. According to Lauren Kidwell, a Bridges organizer, "We decided it might be more effective to start building relationships between people by helping them learn about each others' cultures, history, and traditions which meant avoiding politics until trust had already been built among the group."

In an attempt to achieve this mutual understanding, Common Ground in the Holy Land was founded in May of 2003. In only three weeks, the organizers mobilized fifty university students, representative of multiple religious and ethnic communities present in Israel, to create a cultural symposium on Israel/Palestine. While many people were initially hesitant to work across cultural and religious divisions, support was quickly gathered after the first meeting. Common Ground volunteers created displays on demographics, arts, religions, social issues, languages, and peace initiatives in Israel/Palestine. This cultural initiative succeeded in calming many of the tensions that had been clouding the campus, and relaxed political conflicts for the remainder of the year.

However, seven months after Common Ground in the Holy Land took place the university began to see the resurgence of political tensions. Letters flew back and forth in the campus newspaper, mainly expounding political viewpoints on the Middle East conflict. The introduction of Dr. Daniel Pipes, a right-wing pro-Israel presenter, onto campus served to ignite a new era of political activism that had been relatively quiet over the previous year. As a result of this provocative event, students recognized the need for continued religious-based interactions in order to provide a forum for constructive dialogue.

A vision for how to build this type of ongoing dialogue was developed in the summer of 2003 when three students from the University of Illinois—Savva Amusin, Sarah Bier, and Rozina Kanchwala—took part in a summer internship at the Chicago offices of the Interfaith Youth Core. The Interfaith Youth Core strives to motivate religiously diverse young people to strengthen their religious identities while nurturing inter-religious cooperation towards social justice. While in Chicago, the interns saw how the interfaith movement works on a large scale. At the Chicago offices, led by founder Dr. Eboo Patel, a variety of service activities and dialogue events are put together for religious youth in the Chicago area. The students who interned at the offices were able not only to lead some of these discussions, but also to carry out much of the background work that goes into organizing these events.

This format became the springboard for a major project of the Interfaith Youth Core, which was the National Day of Interfaith Youth Service. The former interns at the University of Illinois brought the project to campus, where it served as a catalyst for interfaith work in Champaign-Urbana. The National Day encouraged students to come together around the shared faith value of serving others, and to collectively act on that value by going out into the Champaign-Urbana community to do service projects. Over 80 student participants from a diversity of faith backgrounds performed service projects in five local agencies, including the Center for Women in Transition, the Champaign County Nursing Home, and the Eastern Illinois Food Bank. Afterwards, these students took time to discuss with their fellow volunteers the importance of volunteer work and its relationship to the faith values of each participant. This was the first time a conference was organized on campus that had the central goal of interfaith dialogue and that focused on volunteering as a key ingredient in that dialogue process. The model of interfaith work used in the National Day proved so successful that many students were eager to continue the dialogue in the future. The planners of the conference received numerous requests to create a permanent organization on campus dedicated to bringing religiously diverse students together in order to interact with each other, explore their religious experiences, and work together to improve the community through regular service projects. In response, student organizers banded together and formed a new student organization named Interfaith in Action.

Interfaith in Action has adopted a method of dialogue based on the exploration of common faith values, an idea learned from the Interfaith Youth Core. This method of dialogue is crucial to facilitating the communication of religious commitments in a way that allows someone to see another person for who he or she is and to hear his or her story. Interfaith in Action has made it a point to steer away from politics. In a college setting, where people are often busy and meeting attendance is regularly sporadic, strong ties can be difficult to establish. At the University of Illinois, the tackling of political issues in this manner caused participants to see arguments before people and ultimately led to the demise of early inter-group efforts.

Interfaith in Action constantly strives to increase the numbers and diversity of its members. The board consists of five religiously diverse students; Muslim, Hindu, Jewish, Catholic, and Jain. As a new organization, Interfaith in Action is working to establish itself and provide a safe space for people of faith to come together on campus. The organizers also hope it will serve as a catalyst for bringing religious communities on campus together to volunteer and work in harmony.

Meanwhile, during the spring of 2003, tension and trepidation mounted in the Jewish community around the upcoming release of Mel Gibson's film *The Passion of the Christ*. The movie was greeted with anticipation by many Christian students who were interested in the story and concern by many Jewish students who had heard mixed reviews of the film's supposed anti-Semitism. Christian students also had heard of Jewish community concerns about the movie and were curious about these different perspectives. However, many Jews had little vocabulary for interpreting and discussing the issues raised by *The Passion*. Despite this barrier of understanding, the film offered the Jewish community a unique opportunity through which to learn about the story of the Gospels as well as to reach out to Christian students in order to learn about their faith experiences and beliefs. The Hillel Foundation for Jewish Campus Life based at the university and the local Presbyterian center took the film's release as an opportunity to develop an interfaith dialogue encounter. Jewish and Christian students hoped to use the occasion to create a new and positive interfaith relationship in the midst of great debate. Working together, staff and students from both institutions met to discuss goals and concerns for a possible dialogue. Together they created a successful month-long encounter that included introductory sessions around aspects of each faith, a joint screening of the film, and cultural exchange prospects.

As diverse as the University of Illinois is, it is absolutely necessary for religious groups to coexist but also to do what most religions require of their followers: serve humanity with love and respect. Interfaith in Action members strive to volunteer and dialogue in ways that allow people to view their own faith within a pluralistic society and to live harmoniously with people of other faiths.

Partnering in this vision are several different campus organizations including Global Crossroads and the Religious Workers Association. Global Crossroads is a Living/Learning community run through the university housing program that seeks to unite students from a variety of national backgrounds for the purpose of dialogue and understanding. The Religious Workers Association is a council of leaders from different faith communities in Urbana-Champaign who meet monthly in order to share ideas with one another regarding religious work on campus. This year Global Crossroads created an interfaith portion of their program to further education in regards to the diverse faith communities represented here on campus. In conjunction with Interfaith in Action and the Religious Workers Association, Global Crossroads plans to provide a multiplicity of educational opportunities for students including trips to different places of worship, an interfaith spring break service trip, and panel discussions on interfaith issues. Hopefully, the growth of these organizations will encourage understanding, respect, and cooperation among the diverse faith groups at the university and build a common vision of service as well as an appreciation for the beliefs and values of various faith communities.

As the interfaith movement continues to grow at the University of Illinois the dream of achieving a peaceful and diverse society is slowly being realized. It requires hard work, and the movement has had its share of pitfalls and obstacles, but it continues to evolve, gaining momentum as new groups unite to build a common vision of interfaith work and service at the U of I campus.

12.

Articulating What Is at Stake in Interreligious Work

Alison L. Boden

Successful interreligious organizing has the potential to produce friendships and understanding as well as a transformed perspective on the power and value of such relationships. The participants are converted, if you will, to seeing interreligious work as a way of transforming not only the relationship between two or several communities but also the dynamic within each community individually. Participants are made more alive and eventually feel even truer to the ethics of their particular religion. This is a wonderful process to witness.

As we know, however, such success does not always happen. Well-intentioned folks come together for a first meeting or put out feelers in their own groups to try to gauge interest in having a formal relationship or project with others. Often the basic interest is there, but there is not enough enthusiasm to sustain an ongoing relationship.

Several years ago, I tried to create a student interreligious committee at the University of Chicago (we already have one for campus ministers), one made up of representatives of each of our many religious organizations. I spent quite a lot of effort communicating with individual students, asking them to articulate what kind of projects or topics or associations they would like to see. It paid off, initially. A large and diverse group convened to try to kick-start an intentional interreligious student organization. (It probably did not hurt that I put out a lot of gooey desserts, including kosher ones.) But the conversation was rather tepid, and by its end it was clear that the students could not articulate what was really important in having a formal organization. Everything that occurred to them seemed to be a good idea—service projects, topic-based discussion groups, a standing committee that would speak with a unified religious voice on campus, etc. They perceived the whole effort as being genuinely good for them (the cod liver oil argument for doing interreligious work) and also as being just a really good idea (the teeth-flossing argument for doing interreligious work). They agreed to meet to talk about it again. I sent out tons of e-mails and on the appointed day put out more desserts, but the crowd was a quarter of the first meeting. They never met again. Student schedules are so busy—too busy—and meetings and events for this proposed group, while acknowledged to be a great idea, just were not a high enough priority for them, given all the schoolwork they had and their many, many other commitments. The group died on the vine because the participants could not articulate what was really at stake in having a formal relationship with each other. They could not name a compelling enough reason to make time for this.

What Is at Stake?

There are many groups on our campus that putter along, that have few members, that can never seem to generate broad enthusiasm for their programs, no matter how many natural constituents they have in the academic community. I think that their malaise, too, comes from an inability to articulate and share what is at stake in their group's very existence. The groups that are robust are the ones that are able to articulate what is at stake in being a member of their organization. There is something crucial that is offered or supported. Our Muslim Student Association is the fastest growing religious group on campus, thanks to patterns of immigration to the Chicago area from parts of the Middle East and South Asia. But it is also one of our most thriving groups. Not every Muslim on campus takes part—far from it. But a good number do, because what is at stake to them is practicing their faith both individually and in community. Success, salvation, and the critical importance of living a Muslim life are clearly at stake. Similarly, our large Christian evangelical organization is thriving. To its members, salvation is of utmost importance; therefore, so is being part of a religious community whose members share this commitment and can support them in their own efforts. Our Jewish life center flourishes because of an equally deep commitment by some of its members to a number of elements—religious observance, the state of Israel, the Hebrew and Yiddish languages, Jewish culture generally, one's Jewish identity. For members of all of these organizations—and these are only examples—there is very much at stake.

Although the interreligious group I tried to start did not take off, several years later, a very specific group got going through a student initiative and became an important part of the participants' experience here at the University. There was indeed very much at stake. At the beginning of the current intifada, in September 2000, competing rallies were held on our main quadrangle, one dominated by members of our Hillel organization and the other by our Arab Union. There was yelling, but there was also a small number of students from both groups who actually listened to what the others were saying, responded passionately but thoughtfully, and who in the end exchanged e-mail addresses. Those students then went on to create a Jewish/Arab dialogue group that lasted for several years (until its members graduated) and which became a transformative experience for each of the participants. I will say more about the transformative characteristics later, but what made the group experience so powerful and durable was that much was at stake for the participants. The hardest conversations, the most troubling comments by members of the other community, the deepest challenges to one's beliefs and perspectives were borne with relative grace and patience and each person returned again the next week because so much was on the line in terms of what they each valued most: family, land, community, identity.

A new interreligious group has gotten going this past year and it, too, is thriving. Again it is because something very important is at stake. It is a Jewish/Muslim dialogue group (the former group had a Palestinian member who came from an interfaith family and another whose identity was as an Arab not as a Muslim, so their proper designation was as a Jewish/Arab group, although religion was always a central focus). The intifada continues, the level of violence has only escalated, the war in Iraq has real implications for both Jews and Muslims, and the new dialogue group is thriving. There is much to compete with the participants' attention, but the members have situated this organization as a clear and compelling priority. The consequent relationships are wonderful to see.

None of this is probably coming as headline news to you. We all participate in things that really compel us, that win our attention over the cacophony of competing items. The challenge for individuals wanting to promote interreligious work is to articulate and claim what is at stake in participating. I have many ideas about what is at stake, and I found myself in an awkward position when the student group I tried to found a few years ago was unable to name such things for themselves. I—we—cannot tell the people we want to involve what will matter to them. We can share our opinions with them, but we cannot make them own those reasons. They really have to appropriate them for themselves or they are just not going to get involved.

Key Points

I am now going to name a few of the things that I believe are at stake; perhaps the reader will find them helpful. The first thing is the creation of a foundation during times of crisis. This is a rather negative thing to organize around: "Hey, let's get together and create a solid organization so that when really bad things happen in our country or to one another we can support one another and show a unified face to others." But it is a great thing to have. Some years ago when a swastika was painted on the door of our Episcopal campus ministry (ostensibly in reaction to that ministry's proactive support of gays and lesbians), the religious organizations banded together to support that ministry and to present a unified face in opposition to intolerance of all kinds—just what a campus ministry network is for. When our local Metropolitan Community Church kept having its sign (with rainbow flag) defaced, many of the congregations in our local interfaith council put rainbow flags on their own signs in solidarity, and jointly signed a letter to the editor of our local paper. In all its tragedy, September 11, 2001, showed how many interreligious ties we already had, even though we had no formal association of student religious groups or leaders. My staff had worked hard to build connections with all the groups, and so those relationships were there to be used. We had three interreligious observances in that first week alone, and I am certain that the University of Chicago community, in seeing the groups come together so quickly and in such a spirit of partnership, learned a lot about the variety of traditions represented here, the thoughtfulness of the groups, and the good relationships we are privileged to enjoy. More than one person told me that while the presence of the groups together in reflection was a source of comfort, it was also a teaching moment and one of inspiration. It is these ties, especially during times of conflict, that are very much at stake in organizing interreligiously. We have so much to offer.

Another thing that is at stake is transformative potential. I mentioned earlier that it had become a centerpiece of the Jewish/Arab dialogue group here. It happened because the group members made themselves vulnerable to one another, listened deeply even when bothered by the others' comments, built a foundation of respect, and learned to trust one another with their own deepest confidences, fears, hurts, and dreams. Deep friendships evolved, and perspectives on the crisis in the Middle East became infinitely more nuanced as participants learned to think and feel like the other. All this could happen because of the quality of the relationships that were formed. A powerful thing is very much at stake—the opportunity to grow, the opportunity to learn, the opportunity to be transformed, to be larger than who you were. That is a lot! But it is not always easy to describe to busy people over dessert, and again, it has to be something they want (or will make themselves vulnerable to) and own by themselves.

What is at stake is becoming part of a global movement of people who seek to maximize religion's potential to heal and to build and to lift up. Most of our religions are getting (and often earning) a black eye these days for their violence, imperialism, greediness, patriarchy, or any number of real ills. We who participate in this kind of work first acknowledge the negative contributions of our co-religionists (after all, we do not have our heads in the sand) but then we retain our determination to model a very different ethic. We know that violence and subordination are antithetical to the teachings of our religions. We know our traditions' crucial support of social justice movements around the planet, we know the mobilizing potential of religion in societies (both for good and for ill), we know the power of religious communities to speak out against injustice, to promote the common good, to effect peace, to counter all systems of domination, and to push the human community closer to fulfilling its goal of living sustainably, respectfully, and equitably. There is much at stake in having members of various traditions sharing these goals and coming together to mobilize on their behalf. There are many people, young and old, who will want to be a part of this, if we can just help them to own the project.

What is also at stake is the formation of a single religious community unified not in belief but in commitment to the mutual uplift that I have described. That is so important, not just globally, but also on campuses like the one I serve. How important for those here who participate in religious community to know themselves not only as members of the Jewish, Muslim, Baha'i, or Buddhist groups on campus, but also to know themselves as members of a total religious community that includes all groups —to know when they see a member of another community that they are looking at someone with whom they share much in common, the most important things in common. Whether or not their religions have many similarities or none, they can know themselves as members of a broader community, a broader family; they can see the other as a brother or sister. This is not just about feeling even better about yourself and others; this is about establishing the kind of unity by which the social and spiritual goals that I have just mentioned can be brought to pass. It means, too, that when those who are not members of a religious community have contact with those who are, they experience religion not as a series of hard and fast boundaries but as a total community, a positive community, a welcoming community, a unified community. They connect with a total community that models positive and respectful dialogue on divisive issues, be they religious, political, social, or economic. I want to say that a unified religious community will certainly have benefits for its own internal members, but it may also be instructive in important ways for those looking in from the outside.

For those of us working on campuses and/or with young people particularly, I think a terribly important thing at stake is the educating of citizens for a multi-religious world. It is not a world to come; it is here; it has always been here. It is here in more profound ways in the United States than ever before. Interreligious work helps shape citizens for this reality. It is not the same as religion courses, where facts are learned about the tenets of various faiths. This is important, but the interreligious work that interests all of us requires its participants to deeply integrate what they experience of the other. It is about teaching them a manner in which to live and work with the other. It is about teaching them the questions to ask and live by, not necessarily the answers. It is about teaching them how to share the world with one another, and to live side by side with religious truth claims that may be very different from their own. This comes through relationship-building, not rote learning. It is vitally important to pass on to the young leaders who are on our campuses and in our organizations. There is very much at stake.

A last thing I will mention that I believe to be at stake is the surrendering of triumphalism by our particular religions. All religions are culpable, and we have to stop it or all of our hard work will be limited. Arguably, no one who retains a triumphalistic outlook can or will become involved in interreligious work in the first place. How can anyone who essentially disrespects other traditions, who thinks them wrong or inferior, who thinks his or her religion trumps all others, or who wishes to educate others in the "true" way take part in the kind of work for which we advocate? I am certainly not saying that each of us needs to jettison the essential—and exclusive—truth claims of our faiths. We can still retain a deep belief in the promises of our traditions, a special relationship to the divine, we can still know our own religion to be correct or the best over all, without being defensively triumphalistic about it. It is a matter of letting others pursue the truth in the way they best know how, without judging them for it. This all may sound obvious and it may be something that you have done naturally for many years, but I do think it is essential to doing interreligious work and that it lurks under the failures of many an effort. The overcoming of triumphalism is very much at stake—at stake for those who will dare to make relationships across religious boundaries (they risk having their triumphalism challenged) and at stake in that it sometimes thwarts the best intentions.

13.

Teaching World Religions: How and Why

Jane S. Rechtman

ALL RELIGIONS USE STORIES. So I'll begin with a story. When I graduated from college, I taught English as a Second Language in Spain. It was enthralling to be in a place full of so much history, so much art, and so much of the literature and language that I love. I remember at one point going to a very small convent known for its art collection. As I stared at one of the paintings, a tiny nun came up to me and told me I was looking at a very famous artist's picture of the disciple Peter denying knowing Jesus. I must have looked blankly at her, because although I knew the artist to whom she was referring, I was not familiar with the story she was telling me. The look of amazement on that little lady's kind face will stay with me all my life. Here I was, twenty-one years old with a relatively decent education and yet not, in Diana Eck's words, "religiously literate"[1] enough to understand the religious knowledge that formed the artistic, historical and cultural background of the country in which I was living. I had also missed out on a wonderful story about human nature!

One need only pick up a daily newspaper to realize that if we don't learn about each other, we will continue to kill each other. Much of the conflict in this country and in this world is due to the fact that we do not know about or understand each other's religious histories and ideals. One has only to visit another country or a museum, see a dance performance, hear or read a riveting story, listen to music, study history or dream a dream to realize that religions affect—and have always affected—our world. And we need to realize that people from a variety of religions different from our own are no longer exotic strangers in a far away land but are our fellow students, neighbors and countrymen here and in the world at large.

Many still need to recognize that an Irish Catholic's Ten Commandments are the same ones in the Jewish tradition. To understand the devastatingly destructive effects colonialism has had in the Americas, Africa and Asia, we need to understand the religious worldviews of both the colonists and the indigenous cultures. We cannot understand the Holocaust or the creation of the State of Israel unless we understand the pogroms, the blood libels, and the anti-Semitism that preceded them. We must learn that Muslim and terrorists are not synonymous and that the primary meaning of *jihad* is not holy war against others, but first and foremost the internal struggle within each individual to control impulses. Further, we need to understand that all religions—whether they have no god, like Buddhism, or many gods, like Hinduism, have an ethical dimension for behavior.

But what about average high school students? Do you think they are offered an opportunity to study the world's major religions in depth? And, if so, do you think they look forward to taking it as a required course? Rarely. But at the Masters School, a co-ed independent day and boarding school, located just north of New York City, with four hundred high school students from twelve states and fourteen countries, and diverse racial, economic and religious backgrounds, they do come to appreciate such a course.

There are units on symbols, myths and rituals, indigenous traditions, Hinduism, Buddhism, Confucianism/Taoism, Shinto, Judaism, Christianity and Islam. Meeting a number of times every week over a period of a year, we spend about three weeks on each unit. Kids want to learn what real people think and experience and they want to know how it applies to them. So we don't rely upon a textbook description of the religions that we cover. The course includes a great deal of discussion, reflection, reading projects and seeing—whether in videos or field trips or visitors.

At the same time, it is an academically rigorous course with the longtime motto "You don't have to agree; you have to [try] to understand." The purpose is to get kids to see that even though they might not agree with ideas that are different from their own, they can still understand them in a nonjudgmental way. It is a process that happens over time as we talk about, read about and hear about different traditions. By the end of the year, students who were earlier dismissive of religious ideas or those different than their own wrote:

"I recognize that with issues this deep, and personal to many, recognizing each other's beliefs is difficult. . . . I suppose I need to take a step back and realize the other's view on the subject."

"This class has given me the opportunity to expand my knowledge of other people's religions. This has helped me to know, understand and respect others while being able to relate my religion to theirs."

"I can comprehend and understand one's side who has other beliefs than me."

The ideas are presented in an impartial, academic manner, i.e., "this is what Muslims/Buddhists/Christians/Jews believe and these are the symbols that represent those ideas." But if they see contradictory ideas, well, welcome to the real world. Anyone who has two parents or siblings knows from an early age that there are often contradictory views of reality!

An Engaging Curriculum

To present both the academic and the experiential, my colleague Terry Ward (currently Head of Brooklyn Friends Academy) and I put together the *Compendium of World Religions*, published by the Council for Spiritual and Ethical Education. This book is designed to present the overall framework in which religious beginnings are couched: experiences of wonder and awe. It introduces students to the value and uses of symbols, myths, and rituals that have been used by traditional cultures and are still alive today even in our more secular culture. Articles in this section range from a description by ethno-botanist Wade Davis of how the creation myth of the Kogi Indians is reenacted in their daily lives to Joseph Campbell's description of the importance of circles to an interview with George Lucas on *Star Wars*. The book includes primary sources such as sacred texts, stories or ideas. It gives examples of personal experiences/feelings/stories within major religious traditions and describes the practices and rituals of the people within each tradition.

One of the readings we use at the beginning of the year is called "Body Rituals Among the Nacerima." Written in "anthropologese," the article describes a tribe that lives between the Yaqui Indians and the Canadian Cree. The students read about the daily ablution rituals of this group in the fonts in front of their charm boxes. They read about the torturous behavior of their medicine men and the holy mouth men. By this time the students are grossed out to the point of making loud comments about these "weird, sick people." It is at that point that I have them read the word "Nacerima" backwards. And then it dawns on them: they are us. The whole article has described their own American life and, because of the language, the assumptions and the attitude of the "outsider" they didn't even recognize themselves! The reading helps to remind us—all year—that when you are looking from the outside, as either an expert or a student, you're not always getting the complete view of what's going on or why, so be careful before you judge.

We encourage students to pause and reflect upon ideas that are different than—though resonant with—their own. We ask them how an author's bias might color his or her writing. When they jump too quickly to judgment, we invite them to consider alternative conclusions. In other words, our goal is to help students develop critical thinking skills.

It is also important for kids to appreciate the ethical values inherent in all religions; to see that kindness, goodness, and community are a valued part of every tradition. When my students read the Hadith, the sayings of the Prophet Muhammed, they see how passionate he was about taking compassionate care of children, women, neighbors, and orphans. When they read Confucius's *Analects*, they are struck by his version of the golden rule and by the harmony that he desired for society. Reading a Talmudic story about two men in a desert with only a flask of water between them leads to a discussion about making choices in a world of limited resources. The healings that Jesus performs, the idea of Karma yoga or metta sutra, and the social action of the Biblical prophets enliven and support the students' own sense of the importance of community action. And they see that obeying the Ten Commandments doesn't just apply to religiously labeled actions but, as Sister Joan Chittister said in an article entitled "The Twenty-first Century Sin," "When you take an innocent person's joy away, you sin—whether or not you can find your action in a catalog of moral definitions."[2] High school kids who tease each other in the classroom and halls each day can easily relate to THAT kind of sin! And they get the idea. As one student wrote: "every religion is telling people to do the right thing and how to become a better person."

In this class, students begin to realize that religions and human nature are often far more complex than they had previously thought. They start to see a pattern in religious traditions of institutionalizing experiences with a tension between people's conflicting needs to hold onto something tangible and to live with ambiguities. One student wrote, "People are always in search of relevance and context. They want things to have meaning. They also want to feel safe and secure." Another student wrote, "How other religious beliefs are related to each other amazed me. Even though I do not believe it, I am also amazed that religion gives answers to people in their lives. Furthermore, it is interesting that people feel stronger and get strength through religion."

As 14- to 16-year-olds ever watchful for the hypocrisies of their parents, they learn something else true about human nature when they ask, "Well, if that's what they believe, why don't they live their ideals rather than behave in an opposite manner?" Before discussing the different forms of yoga available to Hindus depending upon their interest, students do a mini high school version of the Myers-Briggs personality test. They begin to see that religions incorporate different approaches, tendencies and interests as fully as a school or class. They learn that religions are not monolithic, but full of diverse, sometimes conflicting, approaches.

Course Description

We begin the course with a story and a question which sets the stage for everything else to follow. The story was originally told to me by my father about an old rabbi, but it could as easily have been an old Buddhist monk or Christian monk. The story goes like this: the old rabbi was about to die, so all of the rabbis gathered around him to get the last bit of wisdom he could give. His closest disciple reverently asks him, "Rabbi, please tell us, what is the meaning of life?" The old man pauses to think. Finally he says, "Life—life is like a river!" The words wave through the audience, "life is like a river, life is like a river. . ." until they reach the youngest student at the perimeter of the crowd, who demands to know, "'Life is like a river'?! What does this mean, 'life is like a river'?" And the question comes back until the disciple hesitantly asks, "Rabbi, please, what does it mean, 'life is like a river'?" The old man thinks again for a minute, shrugs his shoulders and says, "So, maybe it's not like a river!"

From that story kids learn that it's okay to question—no matter who you or they are—because you may learn something new and perhaps you'll get someone else thinking in new ways. They also learn that wisdom may come from being willing to reconsider what you hold to be true—even at the moment of death. And they learn that the big questions such as what is the meaning of life may not have pat, easy answers, even to the wise.

Each unit encompasses the questions that all religions ask and try to answer. Why are we here in this life? Why do we die? How might our view of death affect how we live our life? We also read a variety of people's firsthand accounts from different religions regarding all areas of life. By beginning with questions and experiences, we encourage kids to ask their own questions. Furthermore, this approach helps them to begin broadening their definitions of religion beyond "a bunch of rules that people believe in." All year long, they are asked to write reflection papers in which they respond to, question and reflect on the ideas covered. Sometimes this class is the first time they have articulated or shared their feelings about life's mysteries.

Students also encounter the beauty that has been created in the name of religion. Whether it is the drum and flute of original music, Gregorian chants, a cantor's song or the call to prayer, they see that music is an inherent part of religion. A Buddhist mandala in the sand, a Russian Orthodox icon, a Taoist-inspired landscape and a Hindu sculpture are each imbued with beauty inspired by the religious traditions of their creators. When they study Confucius, they are asked to illustrate the qualities he held dear, an assignment which often results in the creation of beautiful art projects.

Students are encouraged to understand and appreciate the important role symbols and rituals play in our lives. It becomes evident that even in a secular society like ours in which we tend to believe that we have done away with "that old stuff," we are still heavily reliant on symbols, as exemplified in movies such as *The Matrix*, advertising or our President's communication.

Studying world religions helps kids understand that the questions they ask and the experiences they have are not always particular to our time and place but have instead been shared over the millennia. A seventeenth-century Sufi poet asks the same question they do: "Who am I?" When we begin our unit on Buddhism, I ask kids to write about their experiences with death, illness, old age, or a wise person. These four things are, in fact, the passing sights that sent Buddha on his journey. The responses I get are awe-inspiring. Students at thirteen or fourteen know firsthand what it's like to lose a parent or sibling. They have experienced a mother or friend with a life threatening illness. They have seen their grandparent age into debility. More rarely, have they met a wise person in their culture. But they begin to realize that they are similar to the mother whose son had died and who goes to the Buddha hoping he'll bring her son back to life. "Okay," he says. "But first, find me a house untouched by death and I'll bring him back." After going all around and finding no one who has been untouched by death, she understands that her plight is the human plight and that she is not alone. Nor are my grief-stricken students. One said: "It helps me deal with the definition and concept of death." Said another: "I understand the heart behind it . . . [the] moral sense . . . value of life . . . life itself is the main core and mystery." And another simply wrote: "We are all so different but yet we are all the same."

Projects

We assign a large quantity of reading and spend a good part of our class time discussing these readings. Additionally, we have the students do independent and group projects which they share with the class. When the students study symbols, myths and rituals at the beginning of the year, each must research a symbol or ritual from a tradition other than his or her own. Often times, students make comparisons between symbols in other traditions with aspects of their own. In the class presentation, students more familiar with the symbol being presented find it interesting to hear it described from the outside.

In "the extra-terrestrial project," borrowed from a professor at Florida State University, students use a wonderful book entitled *Barlowe's Guide to Extraterrestrials* which has descriptions and drawings of extraterrestrials based on a variety of science fiction books. After students choose or are assigned their extraterrestrial, they must create a religion for that culture based on the given history, culture and physiology as well as Ninian Smart's dimensions of the sacred (plus a few more). These are:

ASPECTS	EXAMPLES FROM HUMAN RELIGIONS
sacred narratives or myths	Abraham's journey, Jesus/Buddha's birth
doctrines	Triple Gem, Shahadah

ethical and legal teachings	Shariah, Dhammapada, Talmud, Sermon on the Mt.
ritual practices	kiva ceremony, Passover, communion
religious experience & emotion	feelings at Mecca, enlightenment, meditation
social institutions	sangha, synagogue, mosque, church, temple
sense of "Otherness"	God(s), Goddesses, kami, Tao, Brahman, bohisattvas
emblematic figure(s)	Jesus, Moses, Muhammed, Lao Tzu
symbols, art, music	statues, mandalas, chanting, Cathedrals, cross, star of David
after death belief	reincarnation, resurrection, kami, Judgment day

Each group must present a paper and a visual representation, which can be anything from a reenactment of a ritual, a video, to a model or a picture. With wit, imagination and a great deal of insight, students create a system of thought and practice that reviews major concepts and shows a deep understanding of religious thought and practice. They also have a lot of fun and learn the joys and difficulties of working with a group.

We also bring in speakers, show a number of videos and take trips to religious institutions that are here in our own area. As one student wrote after a visit to a Hindu temple, "It's one thing to read about Hinduism; it's another thing to smell the incense!" The trips also reinforce the idea that these traditions are not in some land far away, but are instead very close. The fact that the mosque and the Thai Buddhist Temple were only 10 minutes away from school and literally around the corner from each other had an impact! Moreover, students were struck by how different the ornamentation of the Russian Orthodox church was from the simplicity of the Quaker meeting place.

Religious Diversity

Because we are at a school that has a diverse population, there are often a number of kids who have been previously influenced by a particular tradition we study. This helps enormously with getting kids to remember that the ideas we study are not just hypothetical but inform the very reality and life of people they know. A number of years ago, this was made clear when we were discussing a book entitled *Why Bad Things Happen to Good People*. Written by a rabbi, it deals with how a loving, caring God can allow so much destruction and despair. The Jewish and the Christian kids who read the book generally like it. But a Thai girl with excellent English and analytical skills, said she didn't understand it. She explained that, to her, there was no issue: from her Buddhist understanding, bad things happen to people because of what they had done in a previous lifetime. It was simple cause and effect. Her insight helped us mutually to understand some key cultural differences. In a book report on Karen Armstrong's book entitled *The History of God*, a Muslim boy wrote: "One fact that absolutely astounded me was just how the idea/belief/faith in/of God had affected people and consequently history so much. . . . This book has convinced me that there are lots of ways of reaching God/Nirvana/Absolute Reality, not just one. . . . Moreover, this book has taught me more about my own religion."

Challenges

Do we accomplish what we set out to do? I think so. And student reactions—both in class and many years afterwards—confirm this.

The biggest challenge presented by doing this course is limited time. How do we cover the histories, ideas, diversity, texts, art, music, thought, and feelings of each tradition as well as have the kids reflect thoughtfully on it all in relatively short sessions, meeting only a couple of times a week for one year? And yet we are lucky to be given even that much time! As a result of our limitations, a number of traditions that should be covered, such as Bahai, Jain, Sikh, and Wicca do not get covered. More independent projects might resolve some of those issues.

We are also lucky because, as an independent school, we are not confined by the church-state separation mandated in public schools. When we study Hinduism or Buddhism, for example, we can practice meditation. Furthermore, our classes tend to be small and are able to gather around a 'Harkness table.' This allows for a good deal of discussion. The bulk of our work, however, could and should easily be translated into a public school setting both legally and educationally. Sophomore year is a good time to get students involved in such a course, because at fifteen or sixteen, they are capable of higher-level thinking and can truly begin to understand ideas that are different than their own.

Somehow in the rush of daily events and in the crush of schedules, despite the kids who do not always do their homework, the pettiness of attendance-taking and adolescent breakdowns, much of what we set out to do does get accomplished. Kids come back, sometimes years later, saying how much they got out of the course. They have really learned that in order to better understand and communicate with each other —here in the U.S. and around the world—they need to know about the religions that shape our views and those of our neighbors. We try our best to help kids to become, as Diana Eck of Harvard University's Pluralism Project says, religiously literate, and to be civically responsible. I think we succeed.

Notes

1. Diane Eck's speech at RSISS conference, Toronto, November 2002.
2. Beliefnet.com 4/10/01.

Bibliography

Armstrong, Karen. 1993. *The History of God*. New York: Ballantine Books.

Barlowe, Wayne Douglas. 1987. *Barlowe's Guide to Extraterrestrials*. New York: Workman.

Kushner, Harold. 1981. *When Bad Things Happen to Good People*. New York: Schochen Books.

Rechtman, Jane S. Baron, and Terry Ward. 2002. *Compendium of Readings in World Reli gions*. Atlanta: Council for Spiritual and Ethical Education.

Smart, Ninian. 1996. *Dimension of the Sacred: An Anatomy of the World's Beliefs*. Berkeley: University of California Press.

14.

Secondary School Teacher Training in Religious Studies: Their Key Role in Interreligious Youth Education

David Streight

AN ALL-TOO-TYPICAL SCENARIO in post-9/11 secondary schools is the principal's meeting with the history—or religion, or humanities—teacher: "We really need to start teaching some Islam," she says, "and your class is the most logical place to put it." That teacher's formal educational preparation took place ten to thirty years ago, and non-Western literature, history, or religion were mentioned only superficially—if at all—even for those majoring in the subject. To complicate matters, the number of institutions of higher learning that teach summer or night classes appropriate for a teacher's education about religion in the country is estimated to be in the low single digits. This scenario is by no means news to religion teachers. At present, the focus is on Islam. In the 1990s it was Hinduism, Buddhism, or "Eastern Religions." Our shrinking world guarantees that the need to understand other worldviews will only swell.

In the mid-1990s, religion and history teacher Tom Collins got permission from his headmaster at St. Francis High School in Louisville, Kentucky, to offer summer seminars for teachers. Collins invited nationally recognized scholars of religion to lead discussions on literary pieces that 1) were seminal texts in a religious tradition, and 2) lent themselves to classroom use. Early gatherings were small. Five to ten teachers met over a three-day period with scholars to examine and discuss the *Bhagavad Gita*, or the *Diamond Sutra*, or the mystical poetry of Rumi, and to learn more about the traditions from which the texts came. Woven into the program was exploration of ways the texts could be used in the secondary school classroom.

Previous to his time at St. Francis, Tom had taught in a religion department with me. One of the issues we had struggled with was finding ways to validate student academic writing in the field of religion. Top grades for excellent papers are fine, but we wanted an avenue to increase recognition for students who excelled in a field that, in the world of academia, was too often marginalized. The primary idea that emerged from that struggle was publication of a review to be called *Journal for Religion in Secondary Schools*—a publication that would never see the light, in view of the time, expense, and logistics in seeking articles from across the country, publishing, distributing, and continuing to get the word out. It was pre-Internet America.

Tom and I reconnected via the St. Francis Summer Seminars. The old "problems" were still there, but the Digital Age had added resources between the late 1980s and the late 1990s, when Religious Studies in Secondary Schools (RSiSS) was born.

RSiSS came into being formally in 1999. Its early commitments were threefold. First, to continue to offer quality workshops/seminars for secondary school teachers, focusing on learning more about religions and ethics, and on sharing and developing ideas on how most effectively to present such materials in the classroom. In most cases, these seminars continued to use nationally and internationally known university colleagues as presenters. Seminars always took place in such a way that they allowed for substantial informal interaction outside formal work sessions.

The second commitment was to be a resource for teachers in a variety of ways. Primarily, however, it was to help teachers deal with the issue that quickly devolved from the scenario outlined in the opening paragraph above: "Now that I've been told I'm responsible for a unit on Chinese religion and culture starting in the fall, how am I supposed to learn what I never studied in my own university education?" The World Wide Web had become a tremendous tool in this regard, as it allows for easy access to recommended resources.

Third, given new resources, RSiSS committed to reviving the idea of validating excellent student writing via an online journal for papers on religion or ethics.

A number of beliefs and assumptions underlie the foundation of RSiSS. In regard to teachers, they include at least:

• Teachers always need continuing education. High quality classroom activities depend on it, as does enthusiasm for one's work.

• Teachers need time, and ways, to interact with colleagues on professional issues.

• Professional liaisons between teachers in universities and secondary schools make sense for a host of reasons.

And in regard to students:

• Students can do high quality work, and they can "engage" in primary texts.

• Working with primary texts in the right way makes education about religions more real, more relevant, and more exciting.

• Engaging students in primary texts teaches valuable skills in literary analysis and critical thinking.

Collaboration

On occasion, seminars and the more pedagogically specific workshops have been aimed at more than one discipline. Teachers of world history and world religions have been invited to gatherings that dealt with individual traditions, like the workshop on Islam and the Qur'an in 2003. One of the 2004 workshops dealt with using important primary texts in the religion or literature classroom; works like Persian author Farid ud-din Attar's *Conference of the Birds*, and the Jataka/Jatakamala tales from the Buddhist tradition. Teachers in a number of schools now incorporate the study of primary religious texts into their literature, or world history, or humanities courses; in many cases, these courses are being team-taught.

In addition to collaboration between university scholars and secondary school teachers, collaboration with other associations has also been a focus; it makes no sense for groups with similar or overlapping foci to try either to "go it alone," or to duplicate others' efforts. Associations like the Pluralism Project at Harvard University, the Harvard Program for Religion in Secondary Education (PRSE), and the Council for Spiritual and Ethical Education (CSEE) all do important work. After an early year or two of hosting an annual meeting for the day before the official beginning of the American Academy of Religion's annual convention, RSiSS quickly joined with Harvard's PRSE and the Pluralism Project to make presentations together. The resources of one organization, the contacts and work-sharing capabilities of others have made for a better AAR pre-conference. Participant numbers went from the teens to over sixty in two years of collaborative presentations. Attendance was bolstered by "return customers" who were excited to revisit issues with colleagues and increase their own professional expertise.

One example of a highly effective collaboration involved work with the Forum on Religion and Ecology at Harvard and Bucknell Universities. FORE's work comes out of the seminal thought of Pierre Teilhard de Chardin in the mid-twentieth century, and application of Teihhard's thinking to late-twentieth-century environmental problems as seen through the eyes of theologian and historian of religions Thomas Berry. The ecological state of the earth is indeed a crisis, and the solution to the problem is as multifaceted as its causes. Significant contributions must be made by both science and public policy. But deep down, religious attitudes hold an important key. From a Judeo-Christian perspective, for example, it is possible to interpret God's communication to Adam in the Garden as "I place you on earth as master over all creation, for you to do with as you wish." In such a worldview, there is nothing religiously or morally wrong with any action that does not overtly contravene other mandates from the Creator. This view of "mastery" sees "master" in the sense of his relationship to slave. If "mastery" is seen in a different light, however, such as the role of a beloved domestic animal's "master," or the independent school headmaster—ideally, one with experience who is in his position to ensure that those in his custody are cared for to the extent possible—a much different set of actions and attitudes is called for. This Creator commanded Adam to be a loving steward over all of creation. Problems of attitude toward the earth arise in most religious traditions, and the intersection of religious and spiritual movements with those in environmental movements is seen as an important one: if certain religious texts can be understood as relevant to care for the earth, tremendous impetus is added to efforts aimed at changing attitudes toward consumerism, ecology, and environmental actions as a whole.

The series of workshops co-hosted by RSiSS and FORE have endeavored to help teachers understand more about the basic worldviews of individual religious traditions, to help clarify how certain important texts can be interpreted, or reinterpreted (back to what they were centuries ago, in some cases), with environmental concerns in mind, and to do program planning with colleagues. These workshops also entailed important, and sometimes groundbreaking, interdisciplinary collaboration, as schools began to send teams of teachers from the science and religion departments, or religion and English departments. A number of interdisciplinary courses have emerged from the RSiSS/FORE collaboration. Teachers have begun to offer courses like "religion and ecology" and "nature writing and religion" in San Francisco and Miami; in Portland, Oregon and Westtown, Pennsylvania, among other places. Interdisciplinary collaboration has been an important focus. As this is being written, the first jointly-sponsored student programs are being planned by RSiSS, FORE, and the Council for Spiritual and Ethical Education.

Website

The Internet has been a key tool to a number of associations, and RSiSS accepts that its website is an ongoing project. In early years work concentrated on the student journal and teacher resources. The latter entailed, primarily, reviews of books deemed important sources for secondary school teachers. In many cases, book titles for review are recommended by university scholars who are experts in the field. Given the frequent lack of educational background of secondary school teachers regarding certain religious traditions, and given the need to find good, helpful, readable, reliable information—and often to find it quickly—the goal of the RSiSS "resources" section of the website has been to offer short reviews of books or electronic media considered to be helpful by RSiSS reviewers, all of whom are in the classroom as teachers. (Books or other resources that do not get favorable reviews never make it to the website, out of respect for the teacher/Internet searcher's time).

A second focus of the early years was the student journal called *Steps*. Teachers from a limited number of schools contributed student writing in the first years. The number of schools contributing grew slightly, but two or three problems hindered progress on *Steps* (see "Challenges").

The third substantial focus of the early website was linking to professional organizations and associations, or simply other websites, that might offer valuable resources to secondary school teachers or their students. The website was also of service in its ability to announce upcoming events sponsored by RSiSS or related associations. These three outreaches should be ongoing.

Texts and Classics Project

The largest project still ahead is continuation of what has been called the "texts and classics project." The endeavor is extensive, and intends to involve both university scholars and secondary school practitioners. But in the long run it will be of tremendous value to secondary schools with high-quality academic programs. Based on the assumption that important learning takes place when, under the guidance of a skilled teacher, students engage in the study of the basic, "primary texts" of a religious tradition, the texts and classics project aims at identifying a handful of key, accessible texts for each religious tradition. Once again, significant dialogue with university colleagues has taken place, and continues to unfold, in order to identify which texts experts feel to be key.

Each text is introduced with a few short paragraphs explaining its place in the religious tradition it represents, followed by an explanation of the text itself and ways the text is effectively used in the classroom. In many cases, a particular text is accompanied by examples of short papers students have written after studying the text.

"Texts" include writings that are foundational to a tradition. It would be inconceivable to study Christianity without key passages from the gospels or the writings of Paul. Genesis is indispensable to the study of the Hebrew Bible, and Hinduism without looking at the Vedas and the Upanisads, for example, would in most cases not constitute a valid introduction to the religion.

A "classic," in contrast, might include passages from Thomas Aquinas, Martin Luther, or Teresa of Avila in Christianity; in Islam it might entail selections from Rumi, Rabia, or Ghazali.

Challenges

Progress at RSiSS has not come easily, despite the efforts of a number of educators from throughout the United States. The biggest obstacle certainly is time. All work at RSiSS, from the beginning, has been done by volunteers, from book reviews to conference organization to webmastering to data base building. Teachers are busy.

Some have as many as five or six classes in a day, and coach a sport. When they get home there are papers to correct and classes to plan. The family needs time. The reviews on the website have been penned by a host of reviewers, from schools large and small, urban and rural, public and private, but far greater participation is seen as desirable.

Lack of financial resources is a related problem, and is, as yet, unresolved. RSiSS board members have liked the model that everyone in the association is a colleague who is also a teacher "out there in the field" dealing with the same issues on a daily basis, but some paid staff might ease the volunteer burden.

At present, the names in the RSiSS database are inordinately those of teachers from private independent schools of the type that belong to the National Association of Independent Schools. As of the six months preceding the writing of this chapter, the majority of teachers requesting inclusion on the RSiSS email list have come from public and Catholic schools; with continuation of this trend, there will be a much broader, much more representative, and much more interesting "member" base.

The online journal of student writing has suffered from lack of a long-term editor. Someone needs to remind busy instructors that the journal exists, and that they should be on the lookout for quality papers from their students. Pieces need to be collected, arranged, and posted on the web. A further difficulty in *Steps* was identified early on when student papers were solicited from teachers. Some teachers tend to assign similar assignments from year to year, and having immediate access to stellar examples of the project on the web has been thought to be a possible impediment to creativity or good research.

Successes

The greatest measure of RSiSS success has been anecdotal. Program evaluations, however, have consistently rendered results of 4 or greater on a scale of 1 through 5, when participants were asked about the interest level or usefulness of the event. Numbers of teachers have reported adding new components to existing courses; and others have begun to teach new courses after feeling more comfortable with subject matter and resources gained through RSiSS.

Students, too, are the richer. One teacher who began teaching a course on Islam reported the interaction between two girls—Sunni Aisha and Shi'ite Zeenat. Both were taking the course to gain an academic knowledge of a religion they had been living at home. Each knew that her branch of the faith—Sunni or Shi'ite—was the "right" one, but neither really knew why. The girls ended the course as good friends, and remained in contact with one another through their college years.

Future Directions

Despite difficulties, the energy at RSiSS has been high. The number of work-shops offered per year has increased, and evaluations—both formal and informal—have uniformly been positive. Clearly, teachers who have participated in seminars have appreciated both the fact that there is plenty of "substance" in RSiSS gatherings, and the opportunity to interact with colleagues in the manner RSiSS events have made possible. The way participation has increased, and the quality of comments, have been patent indications that there has been a void in teacher training in the study of religion.

RSiSS is committed to continuing with high-quality workshops, and to increasing the number of its offerings. These will include both the mainstay "religious texts and classics" seminars, and the annual meeting prior to the AAR conventions. At these latter gatherings, as opposed to in-depth study of a text, the format has typically aimed at having university colleagues address topics like "new issues in Judaism" or "recent findings about Mahayana Buddhism," and at reserving time for a handful of talented secondary school teachers to discuss new programs they have been developing or have otherwise been involved in. An increase in shorter (e.g., one-day) events has also taken place.

As the world shrinks, and as North America becomes more religiously diverse, the focus of teaching religions in the United States will tend increasingly to be via "religion in America." Working with associations like the Pluralism Project, RSiSS will be at the forefront of the movement toward understanding and appreciating the religious diversity of a nation in change.

Similarly, collaboration with the Forum on Religion and Ecology will continue. The interdisciplinary work that RSiSS has begun with FORE has been exciting for the teach-ers involved in it. Many see increased relevance in their teaching when at least part of their study of a religious tradition has looked at the critical issue of how we relate to a world where pure water and fertile land are being lost at alarming rates, and where the new field of "intellectual property rights" allows multinational corporate entities to force third world farmers to purchase seeds from them rather than save certain seeds from last year's crop, as their forebears have been doing since time immemorial.

RSiSS is presently also committed to the continuing search for how to work inter-disciplinarily with colleagues from other departments.

We also want increasingly to be a resource to public school teachers to show how the study *about* religion can be incorporated into the study of an important piece of literature or a key event in history. Separation of church and state in no way applies to such teaching, and court decisions have even suggested that a "free and *appropriate* education" is not taking place if the role of religion and information about religion is left out of events like the founding of the United States or the ongoing crisis in Western Asia.

To date, RSiSS has still not adequately addressed ethics as an academic subject, and its vital role in secondary school education. This area has been "neglected," although certainly woven into a number of offerings, primarily because—once again—of the limited time resouces of the association. But it does deserve attention. As the association continues to grow, the possibilities for offerings—including beginning offerings that include students, too—will similarly increase.

RSiSS has recently joined increasingly with the Council for Spiritual and Ethical Education; their collaborative efforts so far suggest the possibility of greater resources and programs available through both organizations.

15.

Training Teachers in American Religious Diversity

Matthew Weiner and Timur Yuskaev

It is impossible to make sense of the Native-, African-, European-, Asian-, or Hispanic-American peoples and their traditions without engaging in profound exploration of their religious dimensions.
—*Martin Marty,* The One and the Many[1]

Growing up in Missouri, we thought of this New York as Sin City. But there is something beautiful going on here. These religious leaders are doing something moral, and I have to show something of it to my kids.
—*A school teacher from the Religious Diversity in America program*

THE REALITY OF EXTREME RELIGIOUS DIVERSITY in America presents a new paradigm for all of its citizens. It has both deep pitfalls and positive potential. One cannot live here without being exposed to it, in a real or at least virtual sense. Yet informal exposure, while important, is far from a constructive orientation and introduction to this reality that makes sense of it, and fosters the possibility of building positive relationships between religious communities. A primary vehicle for this guidance must finally come through our educators, who will prepare the next generation for our emergent diverse reality. Therefore, there is an urgent need for their social and intellectual interfaith orientation. How Americans face and live with the "religious other" will surely play a vital role in how our shared pluralistic and globalized world develops.

Starting in June 2003, the Interfaith Center of New York[2] has been conducting summer courses for schoolteachers on religious diversity in America. These courses encapsulate our unique approach to practical learning about religious diversity and interfaith.[3] While educators have at their disposal any number of programs about religion, and even a few that address religious diversity, this program creates an opportunity for educators to learn directly, intimately, and systematically from religious leaders themselves.

The Interfaith Center's office itself serves as the doorway to the city as classroom. Located on 30th Street in Midtown Manhattan the location is one of the most nondescript neighborhoods in the city. Yet, across the street to the right is a deli owned by Korean Christians; to the left is a shoe repair shop run by a Bukharian Jewish family; a few shops down are rug stores owned by Tibetans, Zoroastrians, and Shi'i Muslims; around the corner is a Baptist church. New York City is the classroom par excellence in which to teach about American religious diversity. There is no need to add or alter anything—only to explore it, understand it, and in our case introduce its elements to one another.

The course is designed on the premise that teaching religious diversity cannot be accomplished through traditional scholastic methods alone. Today every major American city is home to significant communities of many religious traditions. While the majority of the nation remains Christian, immigration has also changed the face of many Christian denominations. The U.S. is now home to eight million Jews, six to eight million Muslims, over one million Hindus, and close to one million Buddhists. Many metropolitan areas are also home to Africa-derived and Native American religions.

This emergent religious diversity presents teachers and educators with a new set of challenges and opportunities both inside and outside the classroom. What do educators teach about religious traditions that are no longer foreign in America? What do they teach about their neighbors' religions? How do they teach a religiously diverse student body? After the tragedy of September 11, 2001, and the backlash against Muslims and those mistaken for Muslims, many educators realized that it is not enough to teach religious tolerance as a mere theoretical concept. There was also an overall awareness amongst teachers, religious leaders, and religious communities that mutual understanding was neither a given nor a luxury agenda. In order to be effective teachers within this new pluralistic environment, educators need to be able to teach about religion in a more intimate way, beyond the abstractions and towards a more human understanding of those with different worldviews and experiences living in their midst. In a sense teachers need to be able to represent what Ali Asani has called the "human face" of religious life in America.[4] In order to do so, educators must have the experience of interacting with religious practitioners.

Such an experiential education of meeting with and learning from people of other faiths seems useful for teaching any subject that involves religion—such as American history, current events, sociology, ethics, etc.—as well as working with an increasingly diverse student body.

This article articulates how the Interfaith Center designed and implemented its program, describes it, explains the basic methodology behind its design, and presents preliminary outcomes.

Background

The course emerged from the Interfaith Center's core educational initiative, *Religions of New York*.[5] Launched in June 2000, *Religions of New York* hosted semi-annual daylong seminars on one specific religion per seminar for religious leaders of other religions; for example, a seminar on Muslims of New York, for Jewish, Christian, Hindu, Buddhist, and other leaders. Each seminar examined a tradition as it exists "on the ground" in New York.

The idea was not to look at particular doctrinal or theological issues, but rather that the audience understand how, for example, this Chinese Buddhist community came to New York, the role that their temple, monk, and lay leaders play in helping the community, what issues they face, and how they confront them as Chinese Buddhists. Religious community leaders and activists from various traditions were thus given the opportunity to better understand a neighboring community and to acquire the knowledge required for working across community lines. A rabbi in Brooklyn was able to learn about the specific Pakistani Muslim community in her neighborhood—something quite different from reading about Islam in the abstract. The program intends to be practical in this way: to help each leader better serve her or his own constituency by understanding more about one's immediate neighbors.

This approach was developed for two reasons. First, there was a practical need for such a program; indeed, while clergy are trained in theology, doctrine, pastoral counseling, and their faith's history, they are not trained to understand and work with other religious communities in their neighborhood.[6] Second, the Interfaith Center of New York, as a relatively new organization founded only in 1997, needed a working knowledge of lived religion, both for this program and others. In order to develop the program, staff members simply went out into the city and met religious leaders—approximately one hundred per tradition—and through a series of conversations with each one, chose those best suited to represent the diversity within each tradition.

While staff members were recent graduates of religious studies programs, and while their academic studies were certainly useful in synthesizing the information they gained, it was through daily interaction with religious leaders in preparation for the program that the staff gained its expertise in religion "on the ground." Further, while staff members had teaching experience, it was through meeting these leaders, as well as leaders who would serve as an audience, that a pedagogical method was developed. In both cases this was primarily because there was no interfaith education model available through which to work. Program development at the Interfaith Center has remained exploratory in this sense, providing a sophisticated but homespun method and theory for its practical projects.[7]

The Center has organized seminars on Muslim, Hindu, Buddhist, Afro-Caribbean, and Middle-Eastern Christian communities of New York. The pool of some one hundred contacts per faith (many of whom eventually became partners of the Interfaith Center) led to the selection of some twelve diverse leaders within each community who spoke at the seminar. This culminated in a presentation of the astounding diversity within each faith community. For example, in the case of our first seminar, *Muslims of New York* (June 2000), we had representatives of the City's African-American, Arab, South Asian, South-East Asian, and European Muslim communities, including Shi'a and Sunni. In addition to ethnic and doctrinal diversity, the speakers in each seminar included a wide range of leadership functions: clergy, school teacher, social action groups, respected elder, and so on. In the case of Buddhism, Burmese, Chinese, Japanese, Korean, Sri Lankan, and Tibetan Buddhists participated, a broad variety that only hinted at the yet much broader Buddhist community. Besides religious and leadership diversity, the Center attempted to select representatives that collectively mapped the geography of that tradition with in the city. In this way the audience of religious leaders were given a sense of where and in what form that faith manifested itself. The purpose was twofold. First, for everyone to have a general sense of the city at large in relation to that faith. Second, to locate and understand that community in your particular neighborhood. If you were a Latina minister working the South Bronx, these were the Muslims or Buddhists who you might meet.

In addition to finding a diverse array of presenters from each faith community, · much of the organizers' efforts went into creating an audience of religious leaders of other traditions. Therefore, in addition to Muslim, Hindu, Buddhist, Afro-Caribbean, and Middle-Eastern Christian communities that were invited to give presentations and to informally educate us, we also established significant contacts within other religious communities in the city, including Christian, Jewish, Native American, Sikh, and Jain. This experience provided us with important information that has helped us navigate the role of religious institutions, leaders, and activists in communities ever since.

Equally important was the acquired knowledge of what religious leaders want to know about other communities, and why such information is important to them. For example, we learned quickly that most religious leaders were not interested in discussing theological issues. We learned that most would not come if political and international issues were a focus. While there were some who wanted a venue for spiritual exploration, the majority of grassroots leaders explicitly did not. Those who did, usually liberal Protestant and reform Jewish leaders, derived their interest from venues that were already available to them. In general we assessed that most grassroots religious leaders have a practical approach to interfaith relations. For example, Arab Muslim leaders wanted to know local Buddhist leaders in their Brooklyn neighborhood. Their interest was not derived from theological curiosity about Buddhism, but rather a practical need to discuss and organize with other communities around quality of life issues. Jewish and Muslim leaders alike were eager to meet their counterparts in a context that was not focused on the Middle East. Both the general and anecdotal perspectives helped shape what the programs looked like. In this way the personal interaction between the organizers and specific leaders played a central shaping role—one that would have made the program perhaps quite different if different people had met.

Through hundreds, if not now thousands of these meetings, the center's staff became informal experts in New York City's religious diversity, and used this expertise for a variety of projects designed to provide practical education about religious diversity to different constituencies in the city. For the general public, the Interfaith Center offered co-sponsored programs with the Queens Public Library. At the Hunter College School of Social Work, we conducted a workshop for students on the role religion plays in the social lives of communities. For undergraduates we collaborated with Cornell University's Urban Semester Program to create field trip experiences for their students. All of these were successful manifestations of the pedagogy and methodology developed through Religions of New York. We also continue to use this methodology in educating religious leaders in collaborative projects with civic, city, and state run organizations, such as the New York State Unified Court System and the New York City Council of Churches.

In the fall of 2002, we presented our experience and methodology to a meeting of heads of New York City's independent schools organized by Sandra J. Theunick, then head of Chapin School. The group found the project interesting for several reasons. First, it demonstrated a way of teaching religion that they had not yet implemented in their classrooms. While many had been teaching religion through a historical, philosophical, or ethical lens, such an intimate and multi-faceted anthropological approach was new to them. Second, while many were interested in how it could augment the pedagogy of their teachers, others were interested in how it could inform the teachers themselves about their students and the city they live in. How many of them had met a Buddhist monk, an African Imam, a Hasidic Rabbi, or a Vodun priestess—each of who has a substantial community in their city? Through this meeting and subsequent discussions, in which we teased out the specific aspects of the program that would be useful in and for the classroom, we decided to create a training program for independent school teachers.

Project Description

We advertise our course as being important to both teachers and administrators of all levels. Clearly, religious diversity is not only a subject of instruction; it is also reflected in the increasingly diverse student population of classrooms across the country. Indeed, both teachers and administrators choose to take the course. Most who do teach do so in middle school and high school, although elementary school teachers have enrolled as well. The teachers have classes that average around fifteen–seventeen students. Each teacher typically has three or four courses. Most high school and middle school teachers specialize in the humanities, while those who teach in elementary schools have broad subjects. Librarians and physical education teachers attended as well. Among administrators, we had principals, curriculum coordinators, and diversity coordinators.

In 2003, twenty-five educators from eight states attended the course. In 2004, that number grew to twenty-six people from thirteen states. Both years, we extended tuition waiver scholarships to teachers from minority communities. In 2003, we had three Hindu public school teachers and two Muslim teachers; in 2004, we had two Muslim teachers, one Hindu teacher, and the head of an African-American Baptist Sunday School.

Each day of the course focuses on a different faith community as it exists in New York City: Judaism, Christianity, Islam, Buddhism, Hinduism, Afro-Caribbean religions, and Native American traditions.[8] Every day contains three parts. First, an academic specialist from a contemporary religious community in America conducts a one-hour lecture and Q&A period. In 2003 and 2004, our lecturers included: Professor Jack Hawley of Barnard College, who provided an overview of the new religious diversity; Ari Goldman of Columbia University and Michael Paley of the UJA-Federation of New York for the section on Judaism; Zain Abdullah of Rutgers University and Peter Awn of Columbia University for the section on Islam; James Fisher of Fordham University for the section on Christianity; Elizabeth McAlister of Wesleyan University for the section on Afro-Caribbean religions; S.N. Sridhar of Stony Brook University and Kusumita Pedersen of St. Francis College for the section on Hinduism; Chün-fang Yü of Rutgers University for the section on Buddhism; and Andrea Smith of University of Michigan and Michelene Pesantubbee of University of Iowa for the section on Native American religions.

In addition, both times, Rev. Alfonso Wyatt, Vice President of the Fund for the City of New York, moderated formal discussions among teachers on how they intend to utilize the knowledge and experience derived from this course. Relying on his own experience of working with New York's public schools, Rev. Wyatt reflected on why such a program is important for teachers in today's world. He illustrated his point through a personal example:

> There is a program here in the City, called Principal for a Day, in which profession-
> als get to return to their public school and serve as a principal. So I did this, and
> when I returned, the school, which had been primarily black, with some white stu-
> dents, all of whom had English as their primary language, now had over one hun-
> dred languages in use, and people from all over the world.

In the case of each day's tradition, the lecturer's task has been to present a basic introduction as well as a brief historical overview of how that faith exists in America. Each overview provided an orientation to the religion which was augmented by a reading list; a period for questions and answers followed. Then, we held a panel of religious leaders and representatives from each tradition. For example, in the presentation on Buddhism, we had Vietnamese, Japanese, Korean, and Bangladeshi Buddhist leaders giving short presentations on their particular religious communities and the role they each play in their respective neighborhoods. The strategy was to have the introductory lecture present a framework in which the internally diverse religious communities—presented through the panel—could be better understood. The panel was then followed by an extensive question and answer period moderated by the scholar in residence.

Following the panel and a lunch break, participants visit a place of worship from the tradition of the day. On Friday, the teachers visit a mosque, where they observe a weekly congregational prayer and talk with members of the community. In June 2004, we visited Imam Al-Khoei Islamic Center in Jamaica, Queens. In addition to a mosque, the Islamic Center has a full-time Muslim school, and our visit included a tour of the school guided by its principal. In the evening of the same day, the teachers attend a Jewish Sabbath service at a synagogue. They also visit a Hindu and Buddhist temple. In both years the visit to the Hindu temple included a guided tour, lecture, and a demonstration of ritual dance. In the case of every site visit, the teachers see a place of worship and either observe prayer or are guided through the place of worship (in some cases both). On the day when we focused on Native American traditions, we organize a visit to the National Museum of the American Indian in New York City. A part of this tour included a conversation about educational materials on Native American traditions with the staff of the museum's Resource Center Reference Library. For Afro-Caribbean religions—perhaps the most misunderstood faith we looked at—we had each participant sing, and one participant dance, demonstrating the vital role of the asthetic experience in these faiths.[9]

The lunch period, while not an official part of the educational program, provides an opportunity for personal and informal interaction. This often adds and complements formal presentations as well as question and answer periods. As we already mentioned, we place an emphasis on enrolling teachers from minority communities. Our Muslim teachers, for example, have built important connections with other private schools during these periods of informal exchange. For example, in 2004, we had a Muslim physical education teacher who began to plan joint activities, such as basketball games for girls, with her colleague from a prominent New York City private school.

Methodology

The methodology developed through Religions of New York dictates that the educational experience not be limited to a purely theoretical presentation. Rather, the lecture prepares educators to encounter and learn from religious people of diverse faiths. The unquantifiable role that personal contact plays is made central. The focus of our methodology is precisely this practical and educational experience of discovering the humanity of the religious other, enhanced by an academic perspective.

There are several reasons why we stress learning from religious leaders themselves. First, it ensures an authentic perspective on the given faith, and recognizes the diversity and particularity of anyone's perspective, thus forcing stereotypes to be re-examined. Second, such a method is both decidedly different from and complementary to what students can receive in other parallel educational contexts. Whatever was learned before, and whatever might be learned afterwards through classroom or text based education, the experience of hearing directly from religious leaders, often *in situ*, always makes the learning deeply transformative. Finally, as we have said above, by teachers meeting "real" people from these diverse religious communities, their experiences are shaped by the people they meet along with abstract intellectual representations.

Equally important to our approach is an accurate presentation of the internal diversity of each faith. While the overview lectures provide basic information on "What is Buddhism, Hinduism, Islam, etc?", the panels show the "human face" of the faith and help complicate the picture by showing at least pat of its internal diversity. Our purpose is to ensure that the teachers would not think a Jew, a Muslim, a Hindu, is just one thing, and that no one perspective on a faith was the right or only perspective. We wanted to demonstrate that, when one teaches about a religion or a religious people, they must take into account its vast diversity of expressions. When one thinks of Islam, for example, one has to think of both the similarities and differences which exist, say, between an African-American Muslim, a South Asian Muslim, and an Arab Muslim.

One must also see religious leadership beyond official clergy—there are Buddhist monks and nuns, but also lay people. Buddhism is often seen as a meditative, even passive faith, so we introduced a Buddhist priest who plays electric bass, another who is a martial artist, and yet another who runs an orphanage in Burma. Also, one must think of both men and women across religious traditions. When people think of Sikhs, if they do at all, it is most likely of a man with a turban and a beard. This is not in itself incorrect, but it excludes fifty percent of the Sikh population, i.e., Sikh women. What do Sikh women look and sound like? Moreover, not all Sikh men or women adhere to the so-called "traditional" or "religious" dress code. What do they look like? What do the large percentage of American male Sikhs who do not wear turbans or beards have to say about their faith?

Therefore in selecting religious leaders, we make a point of inviting not just clergy to speak, such as a monk, priest, or Imam, but lay leaders as well, such as an after-school teacher, a community elder, a domestic violence councilor. This broad selection is derived from our working definition of "religious leadership" which we understand to be those persons who can represent, reflect, educate, and/or mobilize their community.[10]

Another goal of our program is to depict the internal theological or doctrinal diversity within each religious community—not for its own sake, but rather to demonstrate how different perspectives create unique patterns of living for individuals and communities who would all identify themselves as members of one religion. For example, in the panel on Judaism we had Hasidic, Orthodox, Conservative, and Reform rabbis. The Reform rabbi explained that in her tradition she could be a clergy person; the Orthodox rabbi explained his strict dietary conditions and why he cannot enter a church; the Hasidic rabbi explained their specific dress codes and restrictions on involvement with secular society (such as not watching TV), while pointing out that he has a pilot's license and an official liaison relationship with the police department, as well as personal friendships across religious lines—hardly someone "stuck in the middle ages," to use his own language. We were also able to show the political diversity within Judaism, with a rabbi who staunchly supports Prime Minister Sharon, another who is equally staunchly critical of him, and yet another—the Hasidic rabbi—whose specific community does not recognize the state of Israel at all. The reactions demonstrated the need to present such diversity. One principle of a Muslim school said he was astounded by the diversity of what it meant to be Jewish. Another teacher remarked that "the next time I see a wise old rabbi with a beard, I'll remember that he could be a pilot."

Finally, site visits are an important component of the course. As with many projects at the Interfaith Center, the idea of site visits came from the interest of participants, and from speakers inviting people to come pray, meditate, or just see where they live. Such interactions have led us to institute site visits into our program. The site visits are an important aspect of the educational experience both viscerally—as teachers are often amazed and moved by worship services—and cognitively, as the teachers see and experience the places of worship (as well as, in some cases, the worship itself) and interact with community members.

Furthermore, the visits allow an insight into artistic, social, and aesthetic manifestations of faith, in architecture, prayer, ritual, and music. In some cases the experience is exotic or sublime, as with the Hindu temple in which guests witnessed worship and ritual. Other times seeing the practical way communities adapt was equally important—for example, visiting a Buddhist temple which was a former soy factory in Brooklyn, and discussing how traditional religious demands are kept while adapting to a new environment.

While the intention of site visits was by no means to invoke a spiritual response, our surveys reveal that people were moved by these experiences, which added an intangible yet vital element to their experience. When teachers explained what was important about their time in New York, many gave answers about practical information gained. But as many also said, they were moved by the stories of and encounters with the religious people they met. For most participants, and in unique, personal, and intimate ways, this was the defining learning experience.

Two very different examples will suffice. When asked to summarize the experience, one teacher responded: "We met the people, tasted their food, smelled the incense, and heard the music. We watched them dance." Another teacher reflected on his experience of the city as a whole through who he met: "Growing up in Missouri, we thought of this New York as Sin City. But there is something beautiful going on here. These religious leaders are doing something moral, and I have to show something of it to my kids."

Outcomes

Our assessment of the outcomes of the course relies on a three-part evaluation process: a survey of the educators on the last day of the course, another one distributed six months later, as well as informal yet documented conversation. The results of these evaluations help us to gauge both their immediate impression of the course's effectiveness and its influence on their classroom work over time. In addition, as we work on developing further programs, the surveys help us understand a broad scope of educational professionals for whom our course would be important.

So far, all surveys demonstrate an overwhelmingly positive reaction. For example, of the twenty-one teachers surveyed at the end of the 2003 course, seventeen ranked its overall content as excellent, three as very good, and one as good (with none choosing to rate it as fair or poor). We received similarly positive feedback in their rating of our methodology, format of the course, and its usefulness for curriculum development, especially with reference to reading materials and online resources.

According to the follow-up surveys six months after completion of the 2003 program, most of the respondents indicate that they indeed have changed the way they teach about religion. Some add additional subjects, such as Afro-Caribbean religions. Most teachers now include instruction on religious communities in America in their discussion of world religions. Significantly, when they do this, they draw on experiential components of our course—site visits and interactions with diverse religious leaders. Reflecting on the importance of such an experiential approach, a teacher from South Carolina wrote:

> The studying of other faiths can, of course, be done in an armchair. It was the experiencing of worship and meeting people that made the difference and gave me much material to use in my classes. Students are always more engaged when you can put a "face" on things. The difference between, "Most mosques . . ." and "When I was in a mosque in New York City last summer . . ." is quite extraordinary.

Another teacher, from upstate New York, had a similar reflection:

> The course gave me more information [about] history and practices of world faiths. I have used the notes I took this summer as the basis for my class discussion notes. I also had the "voices" of the members of each religion in my head as I teach my religion course this year.

Significantly, many teachers indicate that they are now better prepared to work with minority students. A teacher from Virginia, who has Muslim students in her class, wrote:

> Because of what I learned at the Interfaith Center, I feel that I can better relate to [my Muslim students] as well as anticipate how the [school] culture may run counter to their religious beliefs. They have been surprised and comforted by my knowledge and interest in them.

Another teacher reflected that, as she is organizing site visits to places of worship, she is now "more comfortable approaching parents who were affiliated with religious organizations, sanctuaries to assist us." Her experience echoed that of other teachers, several of whom have also been involved in extra-curricular activities that involve parents in their surrounding communities.

Conclusion

We return to the experience of Rev. Alfonso Wyatt, who went back to his high school after thirty years to find it completely transformed. Everyone had spoken English—now there were over one hundred languages spoken. There had only been Jewish and Christian students—now there were students from every major religion in the world. As Martin Marty and others have asserted, understanding the communities that make up this diversity is impossible without seeing the integrated component of religious traditions as they are lived in particular places. How educators both comprehend this reality and express it to their students will shape how America presents itself to itself, and to the world at large. An example follows.

Musa Drummeh, the Muslim principal who attended the 2003 course, and was astounded by Jewish diversity, was also a speaker on the day that speakers looked at Islam. Drummeh is from west Africa, where there is virtually no Jewish community. Drummeh is glad to live in New York and to engage its religious diversity. "I thank God every day that I live in the Bronx, with everyone who lives there." When we invited him to speak the next year, he sent a teacher from his school, but had a good excuse for being unable to attend himself—he was taking his class of young African Muslims to the Jewish Museum for a field trip. This story will travel far outside of New York.

More than surveys, anecdotal information such as this validates our efforts to develop further educational opportunities for teachers. We continue to offer intensive summer courses for private school teachers and are developing semester-long courses for both private and public school educators. In addition, starting in the spring of 2005, we will offer day-long workshops for educators on Buddhism and Islam in America.

Notes

1. Martin Marty, *The One and the Many* (Harvard University Press, 1998), p. 196.

2. The Interfaith Center of New York was founded in 1997 by the Very Reverend James Parks Morton, Dean Emeritus, The Cathedral of St. John the Divine.

3. While "interfaith dialogue" and "pluralism" are technical terms, "interfaith" is a widely applied vernacular which is used by religious leaders, communities, activists, and spiritual seekers. It is used both as an adjective, for example "interfaith action," and as a noun, describing an approach that encompass posture, intention, and praxis.

4. Ali Asani used this expression when he moderated our program *Muslims of New York*, June 14, 2002. We have used it ever since. See Muslims of New York at interfaithcenter.org.

5. For a mission statement and explanation of the Interfaith Center's methodology, as well as a fuller description and video footage of *Religions of New York*, see www.interfaithcenter.org. *Religions of New York* was conceived by Matthew Weiner. It was designed by both Weiner and Yuskaev—as was the training program. Yuskaev has served as the lead teacher for the program. For a more detailed description of the history and methodology of *Religions of New York*, see "Religions of New York: A Narrative Explanation of an Evolving Educational Model" by Matthew Weiner (unpublished—available upon request). Also see "Religious Communities of New York: An Educational Program for Religious Leaders in New York City," *The Nexus of Queens*, Fall 2000, Yuskaev and Weiner.

6. Such a program is being put into place at Union Theological Seminary.

7. The logic behind the insistence of an exploratory method of program building as well as the reliance on a personal relationship based approach is further developed in "Investigations and Experiments in Interfaith: A Plausible Guide for Social Ethics, Peacemaking, and Sustainable Development" Keynote address by Matthew Weiner at the 2003 Okayama NGO Summit for International Contribution.

8. A section on Sikhism was added to the day on Hinduism. In addition, we hosted an informal conversation with the first full-time Shinto priest in the Eastern U.S., who also performed a tea ceremony for teachers.

9. The Afro-Caribbean traditions, represented by Vodun, Yoruba, Condomble, Espiritismo, and Rasta, are by far the least accepted in interfaith conversations and meetings. While their community in New York is large, they are continually left out, either intentionally or not. For example, they were not invited to be a part of the Yankee Stadium interfaith service (though Buddhists were left out as well) immediately after the September 11, 2001, tragedy and, recently, they were denied access to an interfaith meeting hosted by a major national ecumenical body for fear of frightening Christian delegates. The Interfaith Center of New York began its work with Afro-Caribbean faiths in its Religions of New York series; we also included Yoruba and Voudu prayers in our Interfaith Service for the United Nations, which the Secretary General Kofi Anan regularly attends.

10. Our definition of religious leadership has evolved on a practical need basis over time, and determined by particular educational and socially oriented programs. For a fuller description of this process, "Religions of New York: A Narrative Explanation of an Evolving Educational Model" by Matthew Weiner. We see "religious actors" in much the same sense that R. Scott Appleby does: "Religious actors (includes) people who have been formed by a religious community and who are acting with the intent to uphold, extend, or defend its values and precepts." (9). It should be noted that our definition of religious leadership is considerably wider than his (283), and our notions of theological pluralism do not necessarily agree with his (13, 14). See *The Ambivalence of the Sacred: Religion, Violence, and Reconciliation.*

16.

The Interfaith Youth Core:
Building Chicago as a Model Interfaith
Youth City

Eboo Patel and Mariah Neuroth

THE EARLY TWENTIETH CENTURY BRITISH WRITER G. K. Chesterton once commented that the United States was a nation with the soul of a church. Mr. Chesterton's insight remains true today, but in a greatly expanded form. America is a nation with the soul of not only a church, but also a mosque, synagogue, temple and gurdwara. The most religiously devout nation in the West is also the most religiously diverse country in the world.

The stability of a diverse society is found in the strength of the relationships between its different communities. While a vibrant interfaith movement has emerged in the United States to encourage positive interaction between religious communities, most of these organizations pay far too little attention to youth and young adults. It was the absence of youth participation that particularly struck me, Eboo Patel, when I first started attending interfaith events in the mid-1990s. In my mind, neglecting to involve young people in interfaith work was especially surprising when considered next to two other observations: 1) Many of the movements that are diametrically opposed to interfaith understanding and cooperation seem to be swarming with youth and young adults; and 2) So many of our role models of interfaith understanding and cooperation—King, Gandhi, His Holiness the Dalai Lama, Dietrich Bonhoeffer, His Highness the Aga Khan, and Dorothy Day—to name a few—became influential leaders when they were relatively young.

I knew that there were other young people who, like me, were committed both to their faith identities and to creating respectful and appreciative relations across religious communities. And I knew that my generation, religious and non-religious, felt called to serve. Most of my college friends were involved in some sort of volunteer service, and many of them joined Teach for America, City Year, Public Allies or other full-time volunteer programs after graduating. Moreover, these national service programs intentionally brought people from diverse race, class, gender and geographic communities together, believing that different identity-based perspectives would strengthen the service contribution, and that service was a common table where people from different backgrounds could build understanding. But religion was not a factor that these programs included in their diversity considerations.

In the summer of 1998, at the United Religions Initiative Global Summit at Stanford University, I had a big idea: What if we built an organization that brought young people from different religious communities together to do service projects? It would add a youth dimension and a service component to interfaith work, and a religion aspect to the youth-service-diversity movement.

A number of other young people who were present resonated with the idea. We decided to discuss the shape of an interfaith youth organization more thoroughly at a separate conference sponsored by three major interfaith organizations—the Council for a Parliament of the World's Religions, the Interfaith Center of New York and the United Religions Initiative. In June 1999, at Menlo Park College, sixteen young people from four countries and six religious traditions gathered to build the foundations of an organization called the Interfaith Youth Core. After two days of intense conversation, we decided upon the basic principles of Interfaith Youth Core programs—a dynamic, integrated process of intercultural encounter, social action and interfaith reflection.

Since June 1999, the Interfaith Youth Core has made an impact on three levels: 1) In Chicago, we are building a "model interfaith youth city" (discussed in more detail later in this article); 2) Across the United States, we are catalyzing, resourcing and networking a national interfaith youth movement; and 3) Internationally, we are an advocate for interfaith youth programs through publications, conference presentations, and workshops. Over the past five years, the Interfaith Youth Core has educated, involved and/or trained tens of thousands of people across multiple layers of leadership: teenagers; youth advisors; college and seminary students; congregational leaders; interfaith professionals; and leaders of national and international religious and civic institutions.

The Interfaith Youth Core articulates its vision and mission this way: There are hundreds of millions of religiously diverse young people in our world, and they are interacting with increasing frequency and intensity. This interaction tends in one of two directions—conflict or cooperation. The Interfaith Youth Core is nurturing this interaction in the direction of strengthening religious identity, encouraging understanding between religious communities and facilitating cooperative service for the common good.

Theory

The Interfaith Youth Core operates on nine integrated theories. These were discussed in more detail in an article earlier in this book entitled, "Affirming Identity, Achieving Pluralism."

1. A Theory of Encounter—From Anthony Giddens, we learn that, "In a cosmopolitan world, more people than ever before are regularly in contact with others who think differently from them." We believe that encounters between people from different traditions are "reflexive" moments, meaning that individuals in interaction are incited to reflect upon their own worldviews. The IFYC seeks to create spaces where young people from different religions experience these reflexive encounters in a manner: 1) where each individual is strengthened in his or her own tradition; 2) where they learn about the other tradition in a way that is enriching rather than competitive; and 3) where they discover "common-ground" areas within their traditions where they can cooperate in ways that serve others.

2. A Theory of Interfaith—"Interfaith" work is different from the "study of world religions" because it is focused on relationships between diverse faith communities and individuals rather than knowledge of religious systems. A theory of interfaith work is intimated by the term itself. Let us take the "inter" part to mean our interactions with people who are different from us—a fact of our lives in a diverse society. Let us understand the "faith" part in the Cantwell Smith sense, meaning the way a religious person connects to the cumulative historical tradition of his or her religion. There is plenty of "inter" in our society, and a good bit of "faith," but not enough interfaith. "Interfaith" is when our experience of the diversity of modern life and our connections to our religious traditions cohere such that we develop faith identities which encourage us to interact with others in intentional and appreciative ways. It is the goal of being rooted in our own traditions and in relationship with others.

Interfaith work, particularly with youth, must be respectful of the "private space" of a religious community. Items that belong in this space include prayer and other forms of devotion, ideas about the nature of the divine and matters concerning salvation.

3. A Theory of Identity—Identities can be understood as ways of being, believing and belonging. From Peter Berger, we take the idea that identities are nurtured by institutions. If there are vegetarian restaurants, grocery stores, clubs and cookbooks in an area, chances are there will be a lot of vegetarians in that area. Totalitarian religious identities—ones that believe that only their interpretation of connection to the divine is correct and every other one needs to be either converted or destroyed—are nurtured by institutions. If we want religious identities that seek to build understanding and cooperate with those from other traditions to grow, we have to build institutions which nurture such identities.

4. A Theory of a Pluralist Civil Society—We hold that the ideal of a diverse society is a "community of communities." This means, as Michael Walzer has said, that the diverse society must embrace its differences while maintaining a common life. This suggests a responsibility upon the constituent communities of that diverse society, that they maintain their difference while embracing a common life. There is both danger and opportunity in a diverse society. The danger is when ignorance, prejudice or bias characterizes relations between diverse people—a situation which tends towards conflict. The opportunity is for diverse faith communities to bridge their tremendous social capital, thus multiplying the impact. From Diana Eck we take the notion that diversity must be intentionally and positively engaged if we are to avoid the dangers and achieve the opportunities of a pluralist society. From Varshney, we recognize that it is "networks of engagement"—strong and cooperative relationships between diverse people and communities—that prevent conflict when communal tensions flare. And we are inspired by Martin Luther King's vision of a "beloved community," where diverse religious communities cooperate in a spirit of love to achieve the brotherhood on Earth that God meant for us.

Embedded within the view of a civil society as a "community of communities," is a belief that the community (in this case, the religious community) is an important part of a civil society. Programs seeking to build a pluralist civil society should take care to strengthen communities in the process.

5. An Assets-Based Theory of Youth Development—For too long, approaches to working with young people were dominated by views of youth as a range of problems to be solved, or a set of needs to be met. An assets-based theory of youth development views young people as coming to the table with much to contribute. The Interfaith Youth Core believes that the experiences religious young people have in their faith communities has given them both an interest and an expertise in serving others and taking leadership. The Interfaith Youth Core creates a space where young people can tell personal stories based on their experiences. In this way, Interfaith Youth Core participants recognize the knowledge that they already have about their life as a young person of faith is of great value. These young people become "scholars of their own experience." They use their scholarship to teach and to learn from their peers about the faith inspiration to serve, becoming both student and teacher through the sharing of stories.

6. A Theory of Religion—From Wilfred Cantwell Smith, the IFYC takes the notion that religion is best understood as a "cumulative historical tradition" with many facets, including prayer, theology, heroes, symbols and inspiration for social action. Also from Cantwell Smith, the IFYC emphasizes not the religious system as such, but the religious community and individual, with particular attention to how religious

people connect to and are sustained by their cumulative historical tradition. In our methodology, we are especially focused on how religious people are inspired by their traditions to engage in social action, and how we can bring individuals and communities from different traditions together on the common ground of faith-inspired social action.

7. A Theory of Service—From Millard Fuller, the Founder of Habitat for Humanity, we take the idea of "the theology of the hammer." This means that serving others is a shared value between different traditions and communities, providing common ground for them to meet on. By doing service with people from diverse religious backgrounds, we build uniquely strong bonds with one another. Furthermore, when diverse people gather to do service, the nature of the service is often strengthened because a range of perspectives can help solve problems.

8. A Theory of Constructive Alternative-Building—At this stage in its development, the Interfaith Youth Core concentrates its energies on creating spaces where people from diverse religious backgrounds can interact in ways characterized by understanding and cooperation. Our programs do not directly engage the violence, bigotry, and discrimination that too often occur between religious communities. Even if handled with delicacy and expertise, such discussions often become messy. When it comes to sensitive issues, such as conflicts in the Middle East, South Asia or Northern Ireland, religious communities are understandably inclined to promote their own narratives. We believe that focusing on these issues is, more often than not, a recipe for increased tension rather than increased appreciation. Moreover, the Interfaith Youth Core believes that, too often, religious communities see one another only through the prism of these divisive issues. Our commitment to build constructive alternatives seeks to illustrate that religious communities do not only have to interact over polarizing matters. Possibilities for positive conversations on common ground matters exist as well.

9. A Theory of Religious Discourse—The Interfaith Youth Core believes that one of the most profound problems in our society is what Robert Bellah calls the "privatization" of mainstream religion. This is the sense, especially prevalent amongst young people, that what one learns in a faith community has little relevance to the broader society, and vice versa. This reluctance to express religious ideals on the part of the mainstream faithful has allowed our public discourse to become dominated by those who seek to promote negative interaction between people from different faiths. To rectify this situation, the Interfaith Youth Core seeks to nurture a "positive public language of religion." This language helps religious young people articulate how being a more faithful Jew, Christian or Muslim also makes them a better citizen. This positive public language of religion is a basic tool of interfaith work, and is taught

through the methodology described below.

Methodology

The Interfaith Youth Core combines two approaches—shared-values and service-learning—into one model. We bring religiously diverse 14- to 25-year-olds together, mostly through their congregation—or campus-based youth groups, to discuss how their different traditions "speak to" shared values such as hospitality, service, pluralism and peace, and participate in service projects which put those values in action.

The simple genius of the shared values approach is that it highlights things we share universally while creating the space for each community to articulate its unique riff on the value. In a discussion on the shared value of hospitality, Muslims might cite what they do for *iftar* and a *Hadith* of the Prophet, Jews might talk about their shabbat practice and scripture from Exodus, and Christians might discuss their church's tradition on Christmas and the example of Jesus in Matthew 25.

By speaking from their own traditions, participants deepen their faith. This directly addresses the most pressing fear that parents and religious leaders have regarding interfaith youth work—the "you better not turn my Muslim into a Buddhist" problem. It also avoids the pitfall of immediately getting into competing claims—the "it was Isaac, no it was Ishmael" disagreement. We call this creating the space for the "mutually enriching" conversation about religion, rather than the "mutually exclusive" conversation.

Young people in our programs also find that shared values is a language of faith that is relevant to the diversity of the broader society, and not confined to their own narrow community. Jews, Muslims and Christians can all cite how their scriptures and holidays command them to provide hospitality. Articulating how one's faith tradition calls them to cooperate with and serve others is a positive public language of religion.

A Global Vision, a Local Program

The Interfaith Youth Core thinks big. We are building an organization that puts an idea in the culture—if you are young and religious, part of what you should be about is coming together with people who are like you and different than you to strengthen your own religious identity, to build understanding between religious communities, and to cooperate to serve others. We are building an organization that, amidst very real theological differences and political problems, keeps alive the possibility that the world's diverse religious communities can choose to relate on their shared values rather than their myriad differences.

We are building an organization that encourages every hometown in America with religious diversity to engage that diversity in a way that builds pluralism. And we are starting here in Chicago, one of the most religiously diverse cities in the world and the birthplace of the Parliament of the World's Religions.

Each Tuesday at a Christian church on the north side of Chicago, volunteers gather to feed hundreds of homeless and hungry members of their community. It is a time for that congregation to serve, to come together as people of faith to strengthen their community. While circling the food pantry to pack bags of groceries, introductions are casually made. "What is your name? Do you go to the 9am or 11am service? Tell me about yourself."

Two volunteers are of special interest on this particular Tuesday. "My name is Adina, I don't attend church here, I attend synagogue in Skokie, and I am part of the Interfaith Youth Core." "My name is Zeeshan, I attend jamat khana in Rogers Park, and I am also here with the Interfaith Youth Core." Adina takes her station at the top of the stairs with two volunteers from the church. They hand out bags of groceries and milk to the homeless. Adina turns to one of the adult parishioners and says: "My synagogue has a soup kitchen. I know Zeeshan's jamat khana does service programs like this too. I would love to bring kids from your church to my synagogue and maybe to Zeeshan's mosque. We could see how each faith community does this; we could talk about each of our faith traditions' call to serve."

The idea of service is not new to this socially active faith community. But the idea that other faith communities from different religions are serving in similar ways may be new.

Chicago

All across Chicago, members of churches, mosques, synagogues, temples and gurdwaras make it a regular practice to be of service to people outside their own religious community. In addition to this tradition of faith-based social action, Chicago has a long history of interfaith dialogue, beginning with the first Parliament of the World's Religions in 1893, and continuing until today with the work of the Council for a Parliament for the World's Religions, the National Conference for Community and Justice, the Council of Religious Leaders of Metropolitan Chicago and the Bernadin Center at Catholic Theological Union. Positive social justice work and dialogue in Chicago has been dampened by incidents of bigotry and hatred. In 1999 Benjamin Smith, a white supremacist, went on a shooting rampage that targeted African Americans, Jews and Asian Americans in Chicago. In the immediate aftermath of September 11, several mosques were threatened by violence and discrimination. To build on this positive tradition of faith-based social action and inter-religious cooperation, and to make sure that incidents of bigotry do not happen again, the Interfaith Youth Core is building a model interfaith youth city in Chicago.

A Model Interfaith Youth City

A model interfaith youth city is a place where diverse faith-based youth groups come together to strengthen their religious identity, build understanding across religious traditions and cooperate to serve the common good. This model interfaith youth city is created through programs at six levels:

1) Chicago Outreach—This program invites faith communities into the Chicago network through meetings with and presentations to their leaders at their houses of worship. The Interfaith Youth Core has found that involving congregational leaders (from youth advisors to active parishioners to the head of the house of worship) is crucial to building a sustainable relationship with a community. Meeting with them at their house of worship indicates a desire on our part to get to know them in the context of their religious lives, and to make sure they are comfortable while learning about Interfaith Youth Core programs.

2) Education Workshops—This program introduces the youth group to the Interfaith Youth Core shared values/service-learning model through an interactive education workshop, presented at their house of worship, often during their normal religious education time. The Interfaith Youth Core has developed a curriculum called "Good Neighbors in Service," which highlights shared values such as hospitality and harmony. In these workshops, we ask young people to tell stories about how their personal religious practice, their religious community's programs and their religious tradition's scripture and rituals enact these shared values. Note, this second step also occurs at the house of worship, communicating that the whole youth group should learn about interfaith work. Moreover, our education workshops get young people excited about interfaith work and introduce them to a "positive public language of religion," which is a basic tool of interfaith dialogue.

3) Days of Interfaith Youth Service—The Interfaith Youth Core organizes two large-scale events annually in Chicago that bring hundreds of young people from different religious communities together to do service projects and share how their different traditions inspire them to engage in such work. A typical Day of Interfaith Youth Service begins with a kick-off ceremony in a large auditorium featuring speakers and performers from different faith traditions. The "ground rules" of interfaith work, including such basics as no proselytizing and exhibiting respect for others, are read aloud from the podium. Youth are then organized into religiously diverse groups and bused to service sites across the city. Service projects range from tutoring refugee children to building houses together to engaging in neighborhood clean-ups. Each group is led by an Interfaith Youth Core-trained facilitator, often a college student or young adult. After one to two hours of service, the facilitator leads a small group interfaith discussion that asks participants to articulate how their faith inspires them to

engage in service. We gather back in the auditorium at the end of the day to celebrate our service and cooperation.

4) Faith-based Partnerships—After experiencing an Education Workshop and engaging in a Day of Interfaith Youth Service, many faith-based youth groups decide they want a deeper involvement in interfaith work. The Interfaith Youth Core helps arrange faith-based partnerships, where two or more diverse youth groups come together on a monthly or quarterly basis for interfaith service-learning. One such partnership is based in the suburbs directly north of Chicago and involves the Chicagoland Jewish High School, the Muslim Education Center and Loyola Catholic Academy. In phase one, each school hosts the other two for a hospitality meal, and uses the opportunity to articulate their faith-based approach to hospitality. In phase two. student leaders from each school come together to plan hospitality projects, such as cleaning a local park or spending time at a nursing home, that their larger school communities participate in. The Interfaith Youth Core hopes to catalyze faith-based partnerships in neighborhoods across the Chicagoland area.

5) Interfaith Trainings—The Interfaith Youth Core trains college and seminary students, youth group advisors and other faith-based leaders, in the skills and knowledge-base of leading interfaith programs. Participants acquire a basic knowledge of social action inspirations across religious traditions and learn how to facilitate mutually enriching interfaith youth dialogue. They work with the professional staff of the Interfaith Youth Core in our Education Workshops and our Days of Interfaith Youth Service.

6) The Chicago Youth Council—This is the IFYC's most intensive Chicago program. It involves a religiously diverse group of high school students who gather on a weekly basis to learn leadership skills in interfaith youth work. Not only do these students participate in interfaith service-learning projects, they help the Interfaith Youth Core professional staff design and lead the Days of Interfaith Youth Service that hundreds of their peers from across the city experience. The Chicago Youth Council also participates in special projects, such as creating a "spoken word" CD of how faith traditions inspire youth to engage in social action and making a presentation at Mayor Daley's Annual Interfaith Prayer Breakfast. Like those involved in our training programs, members of the Chicago Youth Council learn interfaith organizing and facilitation skills, as well as an appreciative knowledge of other religious traditions. Moreover, they are the most eloquent spokespeople of the Interfaith Youth Core. The graduates of the Chicago Youth Council have gone on to start interfaith groups on college campuses and weave interfaith work into the life of their religious communities.

Collectively, we call this multi-layered approach to building a model interfaith youth city the Chicago Action Program. As is clear from both the above articulation,

Collectively, we call this multi-layered approach to building a model interfaith youth city the Chicago Action Program. As is clear from both the above articulation, and the map below, we have arranged the activities in a "ladder of social engagement," ranging from introductory contact with the Interfaith Youth Core to weekly participation by faith-based youth.

As we have hinted earlier, the Chicago Action Program is by no means exclusively focused on young people. The Interfaith Youth Core seeks the support and guidance of leaders at multiple levels of religious communities. In some cases, the Interfaith Youth Core creates a formal body for this purpose. For example, the Days of Interfaith Youth Service has a steering committee chaired by the Associate Chaplain at Northwestern University and involving staff and active volunteers of institutions

Chicago Action Program

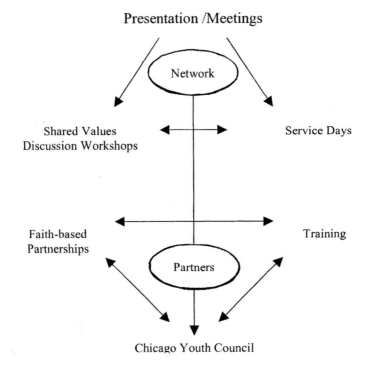

Presentation /Meetings

Network

Shared Values
Discussion Workshops

Service Days

Faith-based
Partnerships

Training

Partners

Chicago Youth Council

Partnership

In the fall of 2004, the Interfaith Youth Core has built a partnership with DePaul University that we hope will provide a national model for collaboration between a community organization and a university in building a model interfaith youth city. DePaul University is the largest Catholic institution in the country and has one of the most diverse student bodies in the nation. The Interfaith Youth Core, working with DePaul faculty and staff, will provide special training opportunities for DePaul students. These will take place at student organizations such as the faith-based social justice community called Amate House, and through curricular efforts such as DePaul's Service Learning and Peace Studies programs. DePaul will host the Days of Interfaith Youth Service and the Chicago Youth Council. IFYC-trained DePaul students will play a leadership and mentoring role in both programs. Moreover, IFYC and DePaul staff will collaborate to help DePaul's Student Religious Organizations engage in interfaith work with each other, including organizing an "Interfaith Awareness Week" at DePaul. A steering committee, made up of IFYC senior staff and DePaul University faculty and administrators, guides the partnership, ensuring the quality of the program and integrating the vision into the life of both DePaul University and the city of Chicago.

Conclusion

The ultimate goal of the Chicago Action Program is to permanently alter the way young people from different religions interact with one another, from the current reality characterized by ignorance and occasional conflict, to our vision of understanding and cooperative service. To achieve this goal, the Chicago Action Program will have to encourage religious communities to include within their institutional patterns an involvement with interfaith service-learning. As the ladder of social engagement model indicates, we hope that religious communities begin their involvement by meeting with an Interfaith Youth Core representative, hosting an education workshop and participating in a Day of Interfaith Youth Service, and then deepen their involvement by engaging in a faith-based partnership, receiving training in interfaith leadership and nominating youth to participate in the Chicago Youth Council.

Chicago is the laboratory for what the Interfaith Youth Core hopes is an international interfaith youth movement. Cities all over the United States are doing the Day of Interfaith Youth Service. As we spread the Day of Interfaith Youth Service program nationally and internationally, we also want to encourage cities to deepen their interfaith youth work, and attempt to become a model interfaith youth city, by starting an outreach education program, a faith-based partnerships program, training opportunities for faith-based leaders and a youth council model. These are first steps towards building an interfaith youth world!

Bibliography

Bellah, Robert N. (with Madsen, Richard; Sullivan, William M.; Swidler, Ann; and Tipton, Steven, M.) 1985/1996. *Habits of the Heart: Individualism and Commitment in American Life.* London: University of California, Ltd.

Berger, Peter. 1967/1969. *The Social Reality of Religion.* London: Faber and Faber.

Eck, Diana L. 2003. *Encountering God: A Spiritual Journey from Bozeman to Banaras.* Boston: Beacon Press.

Giddens, Anthony. 1999. *Runaway World.* London: Profile.

Smith, Wilfred Cantwell. 1963. *The Faith of Other Men.* New York: Harper & Row.

Varshney, Ashutosh. 2003. *Ethnic Conflict and Civic Life.* New Haven: Yale University Press.

Walzer, Michael. 1996. *What It Means to Be an American.* New York: Marsilio.

17.

The Interfaith Youth Leadership Council of the Interfaith Ministries for Greater Houston

Julie Eberly

INTERFAITH MINISTRIES FOR GREATER HOUSTON (IM) is Houston's oldest interfaith-based, social service organization. Founded in 1955 as the Church Welfare League and officially chartered as Houston Metropolitan Ministries (HMM) in 1969, IM has been a leading force in bringing together people of all faiths to serve people in need in the greater Houston area. Renamed Interfaith Ministries for Greater Houston in 1992 to reflect support from increasingly diverse faith traditions, IM works with ten communities of faith: Baha'i, Buddhist, Christian, Hindu, Jain, Jewish, Muslim, Sikh, Unitarian Universalist and Zoroastrian communities of faith. IM provides opportunities and activities that foster relationships and provide interfaith worship and learning experiences. Through its framework for addressing critical human needs, IM brings together people from these ten diverse faiths to express and fulfill shared religious beliefs. IM serves as the connection between communities of faith and the community at large to make Houston a place of hope and dignity for all.

Interfaith Ministries for Greater Houston envisions a society in which people of all faiths come together in service to the community. Cultivating a more tolerant and understanding society must begin with young people. Instilling in youth a sense of understanding and respect for people of various faiths and cultures benefits every aspect of the world they will soon lead. IM's Interfaith Youth Leadership Council, in short, the Youth Council, is a place where diversity is celebrated, community is served and ideas are nurtured. The Youth Council is a dynamic panel of high school leaders, representing a multitude of faiths from across the Greater Houston area who come together to discuss topical issues of faith; travel to various houses of worship and plan exciting and fun interfaith activities. Reaching beyond tolerance to respect is the goal of this group whose members will be the ones who will truly change the world.

The Youth Council began monthly meetings in the fall of 2002. Since then, the members have been educated by guest speakers whose lessons sparked discussions; they have experienced a lock-in retreat to build team camaraderie; they have participated in service projects that allow youth from all faiths to work together for the single purpose of community service, and they have created activities that educate on various faiths and cultures.

With great excitement, the students gathered for their first meeting in the home of a refugee family from Afghanistan. They shared a meal and heard the refugee's compelling story of survival and faith. They then discussed what each one's personal faith community says about *welcoming the stranger*. The following month found them in the home of the Jesuit Volunteer Corps, a group of eight recent college graduates who have chosen to live in community and work in public service areas. As the Corps members shared about the four tenets they live under—simplicity, spirituality, community, and social justice—the students were able to discuss what their individual faith community says about finding meaning and purpose in life.

By the third meeting, the group had completely bonded. One of the girls told how her Islamic school had closed for a few weeks after September 11. A co-council member, a Christian girl, looked at her closely and with tears in her eyes said that had this group been meeting prior to that tragic day her school would not have had to close, because the council members would have been there showing support and standing as friends. Fears and prejudices that perhaps would otherwise remain instilled in someone forever are able to be dispelled as these youth build relationships and friendships. This is the kind of core change taking place in the hearts of the participating Youth Council members.

But it is not without challenges. The idea of the Council is to have several opportunities in which they can invite their peers from their schools, clubs or religious groups to an activity that shares with them the interfaith experience. With excitement the group planned a youth Iftar dinner, a traditional Muslim gathering to break the daily fast during Ramadan. Three of the Jewish students got permission from their private Jewish school to make this a planned school activity. It was at this point that the school headmaster and Interfaith Youth Leadership Council advisor received a hate letter from an angry parent: full of accusations as to the thinking behind such an outlandish event, the parent refused to allow his student to attend.

Left with the option of canceling attendance or forging forward knowing there was much concern, the decision was made to continue. Arrangements were made for a Muslim woman and former teacher to join the students at the Jewish school for a special assembly. She taught briefly about Ramadan and what it means to Muslim people, and explained other pillars of her faith. When finished, the headmaster slowly made his way to the front of the room and full of passion for his own Jewish faith, he reminded the students of the meaning of Tikkun Olam; or literally, their charge from God to be reconcilers of a broken world. He almost quivered as he said that here was a Muslim woman standing in front of a board written in Hebrew, extending her hand in an invitation to join her in her faith celebration. What better way of reconciling a broken world than by taking that hand?

The following day, eighty-five Jewish students entered into a mosque for the first time to observe Muslim prayers, and to join them in a dinner to break their fast. Unfortunately, the girl who most wanted to attend was the daughter of the angry father who forbade it. Still, nothing could squelch the stories brought back to her by her peers. Perhaps in the future, she too will get to experience her missed opportunity.

Analysis

The goals of the council are to harness the energy of diverse youth leaders in order to create a heightened awareness of faith and cultural issues, to encourage productive discussions that lead to improved understanding of various issues of faith and culture and to encourage the dissemination of this information in the individual communities of each youth. The council plays a significant role in building the leaders of tomorrow by teaching them to build relationships and communicate with people of different faiths and cultures. Most important, the council teaches youth the value of such relationships and the value of community service.

Skills developed through the Interfaith Youth Leadership Council:

Leadership and diplomacy skills to work with peers of many religious and cultural backgrounds; communication skills to convey information about oneself and one's faith, and to provide useful and intelligent input in discussions; critical-thinking skills to process information on diverse topics and apply lessons learned to one's own community; facilitation skills to lead diverse groups in discussion, encourage mutual respect and express dissenting opinions productively; a sense of civic-mindedness that recognizes the importance of public service.

In a pre/post survey, the students were asked the following questions. Answers from a Hindu representative are included for perspective.

1. **How has your understanding of others increased?** *"Tremendously! My eyes have opened up and are better suited to understanding the emotions, fears, or hopes I can see in another's eyes. I think my ability to place myself in another's shoes has also improved. The examples come from hearing the hardships endured and overcome by the Afghanistan refugees, the discrimination dealt Muslims after September 11, and the ways Jewish people feel in regard to discrimination felt in the twenty-first*

century. After the realization of all of their struggles, my feelings of sympathy and empathy have truly opened up."

2. **What prejudices have you recognized in yourself this past year?** *"I noticed that at the beginning of last year my perspective of the world and other world religions beside my own, were very rigid and compact. I also discovered that I wasn't well informed about or familiar with followers of any beliefs other than Hinduism, Christianity, Islam or Judaism. I had simply overlooked the others in possibly a negative way."*

3. **List ways the above prejudices have changed.** *"My perspective has become more flexible and has expanded greatly. I have taken the time to better understand the belief systems of familiar faiths and familiarize myself with those that were previously unconsidered."*

Implications

The success thus far of the Interfaith Youth Leadership Council speaks to the necessity of interfaith dialogue and shared activities, as well as the willingness of young people to venture into areas of discussion that their parents have often chosen to avoid. In the very short time that the Council has been in existence, we have seen how dangerous perceptions are eradicated and how this kind of "early intervention" can go far in planting the seeds of peace in our world. The challenges we have experienced speak to the need for such activities and collaborations between people of diverse faiths and cultures.

While there has been incredible support and commitment to the goals of the Council, all do not hold the same opinion. In fact, as mentioned earlier, one parent adamantly opposed his daughter's participation in a religious celebration with a different faith community. His unwillingness to allow this shared experience to take place perpetuates the very stereotypes and fear that need to be eliminated. This reveals the depth of the challenge. Therefore, the Council will make progress by framing the various learning opportunities in terms of education rather than advocacy. It needs to be okay to disagree, while exploring how to do this in ways that respect the value of human life.

Conclusion

A positive sign of the growing acceptance has been an invitation from Houston's City Council to merge an existing program of the City's "Youth Cultural Exchange Program" with the Interfaith Youth Leadership Council. This type of recognition from the leaders of the Houston community demonstrates both an understanding of the importance of this type of work and the effectiveness of Interfaith Ministries for Greater Houston's pilot program. As the students in the initial program have completed their two year commitment, a new class of youth is being recruited to further this important work.

18.

The High School Youth Program of the InterFaith Conference of Metropolitan Washington

Michael Goggin

WHEN MSGR. RALPH KUEHNER ENCOURAGED ME to attend an interfaith youth retreat with some teenagers from the Catholic parish where I worked in 1995, I hardly expected that the experience would greatly affect my future in ministry. Msgr. Kuehner was at the time the Director of Ecumenical and Interreligious Affairs for the Archdiocese of Washington, D.C., a position that placed him on the Board of Directors of the InterFaith Conference of Metropolitan Washington (IFC). I was a first-year Youth Minister at St. Francis of Assisi Catholic Community in Derwood, Maryland—a parish where Msgr. Kuehner (or Fr. Ralph, as everyone in that parish knew him) helped out on the weekends.

Fr. Ralph's invitation awakened in me the realization that my long-standing interest in interfaith understanding and dialogue could be nurtured in the context of Roman Catholic youth ministry. To this day, Catholic parents and pastors alike tend to look askance at ecumenical and interfaith activities that involve young people. Typically, this attitude is based on the fear of losing their children to another Christian confession that might be a little more demonstrative in its worship or an Eastern tradition that might offer a completely different religious worldview. Catholic parents continue to promise to raise their children in the faith of their birth, a mandate that parents and youth pastors both tend to approach earnestly. When a person's salvation is tied up with the choices made by one's children, parents cannot be faulted for treading cautiously in this area.

The key to greater acceptance of interfaith activities among Catholic youth is better adult catechesis on the documents of the Second Vatican Council. The teachings of Vatican II so changed the Catholic Church that many Catholics growing up in the early 1960s were not adequately catechized on the changes confronting the church. Forty years later, these are the parents of today's Catholic teenagers, and many of them have never appropriated a faith identity of their own. Many of their teenagers who long for some sense of Catholic identity have turned to nostalgic, conservative practices that recall the Church militant of their grandparents' generation—marked by liturgy in Latin, rosary beads and all-night adoration of Jesus in the Eucharist.

If either generation was busy studying the documents of Vatican II alongside *The Catechism of the Catholic Church*, they might see the Holy Spirit nudging us out of the church pews and into the world. The Catholic Church radically altered its view of the modern world in the documents of Vatican II. Gone were the *Index of Forbidden Books* and *The Syllabus of Errors*. Replacing them was *Gaudium Et Spes*, the Pastoral Constitution on the Church in the Modern World. The fundamental paradigm shift was that the Catholic Church affirmed that it was no longer the enemy of modernity. By extension, I would argue that Catholicism is also a friend of the post-modern world we now inhabit. As Harvard University scholar Diana Eck has written, religious pluralism is one of the most distinguishable features of the post-modern world. So the Catholic Church has affirmed its connection to the great religions of the world and to the ecumenical movement within the one Christian family. This was true forty years ago in the documents of Vatican II, and it has been affirmed by more recent teachings such as Pope John Paul II's encyclical *Ut Unum Sint*—Encyclical Letter on Commitment to Ecumenism, 1995.

Too often, Catholic involvement in ecumenical and interreligious dialogue has been left to theologians. The vast majority of American Catholics probably have no knowledge of the agreement on justification that was reached between the Catholic Church and numerous Lutheran bodies in the late 1990s. They probably have little knowledge of the ongoing dialogue between Catholic and Buddhist scholars as well. It might be easier to retreat into what makes us unique as Catholics—such as the Real Presence of Jesus Christ in the Eucharist—but the Catholic Church at its most scholarly levels is engaged in dialogue with men and women from the different world religions. It is incongruous to disparage our young people for engaging in similar discussions at their own level.

In Washington, D.C., the dialogue has continued on many levels for more than twenty-five years. IFC was founded in 1978 as the first staffed organization in the world to invite the Muslim community into interfaith dialogue and social justice work with Protestants, Catholics and Jews. Since its founding, IFC has become even more diverse—welcoming the Baha'i, Sikh, Church of Jesus Christ of Latter-day Saints (the Mormons' first such local interfaith involvement anywhere in the world!), Hindu/Jain and Zoroastrian faith traditions into full membership. The InterFaith Conference works on the basis of a two-fold mission statement—to build greater understanding between people who practice each of these great faith traditions and to work collaboratively for social justice. The high school youth program that the InterFaith Conference first created in the mid-1990s aims to serve both purposes.

The weekend retreat that I attended in the spring of 1995 encouraged greater understanding between the faith traditions by utilizing something as simple as a game of show and tell. Each participant on the retreat was asked to bring an object that was important to him or her personally in the context of one's faith tradition. On Sunday morning, we gathered around a fireplace to share our items, our stories and ourselves. I never fully understood the use of a prayer shawl in Judaism before seeing a young man on the retreat treat it with the reverence one reserves for something profoundly holy. Likewise, non-Christians and even Christians of other confessions learned the importance of the crucifix that a Catholic girl wore around her neck. I was greatly impressed by the knowledge that the teenagers had of their own traditions, and I was very proud of the respect each one afforded to the other retreatants as everyone talked about their sacred object. As a Catholic attending an interfaith retreat for the first time, I initially felt odd not attending Mass that Sunday morning. But this time for sharing provided everyone with a really outstanding worship experience!

The same retreat tackled some important social justice issues. The National Coalition Building Institute (NCBI) provided the InterFaith Conference with trained youth facilitators for a workshop on stereotyping. Using a simple exercise in which people stood when they agreed with a statement and sat down when they did not, we were able to see for ourselves the various prejudices and preconceptions we hold about people who are different from us in some way. These stereotypes did not only deal with religious differences between people. The youth facilitators also drew out from us our stereotypes of people who might differ from us in matters of socio-economic class, sexual orientation, and race.

Racial conflict is the main reason why the InterFaith Conference of Metropolitan Washington launched its high school youth program. In a grant proposal to the Robert Wood Johnson Foundation, IFC Executive Director Rev. Clark Lobenstine wrote in 1995, "In recent years, a number of incidents with racial overtones (e.g., the response to the Rodney King verdict and the Oklahoma [Murrah Federal Building] bombing)—have exacerbated strained relationships, locally and nationally, among ethnic groups."[1] In Washington, D.C., there were riots in the predominantly Hispanic Mount Pleasant neighborhood after a Metropolitan Police officer shot an unarmed Latino man.

The first weekend interfaith youth retreat, held in the spring of 1995, reached its goal of bringing together a diverse community of teenagers and adult advisors. African-American Muslims, South Asian Sikhs, Baha'is of Persian extraction and

Protestants of many different backgrounds formed a panoply of believers and seekers who worked together to build unity and overcome racism.

Social justice concerns remained a priority as the program grew. On *Tzedakah* Day, a Jewish celebration of service to the community, an interfaith team of youth and adults gathered to repaint the walls at the Community for Creative Non-Violence, a D.C. shelter founded by activist Mitch Snyder. The presence of the Holocaust Museum in our city gives our youth the opportunity to witness the tragedy of a breakdown in human compassion, and taking part in interfaith prayer services on the occasion of *Yom Ha'Shoah* (Holocaust Memorial Day) gives young people the voice to testify, "Never again!" In the fall of 2003, we raised the frame on an interfaith Habitat for Humanity house to be built in the Northeast Boundary section of the city. It will be the first Habitat home anywhere in the world that will be labored over by members of ten world religions, and our youth and young adults will be active in its construction.

Several other weekend youth retreats were held in the mid-1990s in both the fall and the spring. Different groups of young people essentially experienced the same program that the first group enjoyed. Some of the young people from that first retreat were trained by the National Coalition Building Institute to lead the prejudice reduction work of future weekends. I became a consistent participant in the retreats and a frequent contributor to the monthly planning meetings that were held on weekday afternoons or evenings at the InterFaith Conference's offices in Washington, D.C. By seeking primary input on the program from youth themselves, the InterFaith Conference's High School Youth Program had established itself on the solid ground of developing young leaders.

Occasionally, IFC holds "Why I Love to Be . . ." dialogues with high school students. It is an informal opportunity for teens to get together over pizza for a heart-to-heart conversation about their faith. The conversation intentionally stresses the positive aspects of all of our faith traditions. This is not a forum for debate about the politics of our religions; nor is it an academic exercise more appropriate for a classroom. Rather, it is an opportunity for the young people to tell their own story about what they love about being a Sikh, Muslim, Unitarian Universalist, etc. As each person talks, the others in the group listen intently. Questions are fair game after each person speaks, and often we will include questions that really encourage conversation such as "when was a time when being a Quaker really helped you?" or "when did the moral code of Islam really challenge you?"

As the interfaith youth program of the InterFaith Conference of Metropolitan Washington nears the completion of its first decade of activity, the stories of several youth we have met along the journey stand out. Three stories are illustrative of the amazingly talented and resilient young people we have encountered.

Awakening to the Faith of One's Birth: Bethany's Story

Our Executive Director is fond of relating the experience of Bethany, a youth from the Church of the Brethren who attended one of our "Why I Love to Be" dialogues with some other Protestant friends. When it was her turn to talk in her small group, she was not sure what she would say about why she loved to be a member of the Brethren. She just started talking and the words that came out surprised even her. She finally understood for herself the importance of the figure of Jesus Christ in her life and the value of upholding Christian ideals like love of neighbor. She was never able to achieve such an epiphany when talking among her Christian peers. It was the excitement of sharing her faith and her particular place in the Christian story that enabled Bethany to profess her love of that religion to others who did not share her experience. Many of the young people we have encountered in the first decade of the interfaith youth program can relate similar stories. The experience of interfaith dialogue typically makes a youth a more committed Jain, Zoroastrian or Jew.

The most amazing part of Bethany's story above is that is her confession of faith in Jesus Christ and the Church of the Brethren came at a time when she could have simply passed on her opportunity to speak. Several youth on our planning team come to the dialogue prepared to speak so that the conversation does not deteriorate from the outset, but no one is ever pressured to say anything insincere.

Claiming Stakeholders for Interfaith Youth Work Beyond High School: Manik's Story

A young Hindu named Manik exercised the leadership skills he learned in the interfaith youth program by taking the best aspects of the program to his college campus. Not long after I began working full-time at the InterFaith Conference in January 2001, this first-year student at the University of Maryland-College Park wrote to me about his desire to host an interfaith conference of his own on campus. I worked with Manik and a small core group of Maryland students to create a "Why I Love to Be" dialogue for college students. An evening event in April of 2001 drew about thirty students, mostly Manik's personal friends and fellow freshmen. It was a small but encouraging turnout at a large, secular state school.

By the time the spring of 2002 rolled around, Manik had recruited many more stakeholders in his vision of student-led interfaith dialogue. He became active in the Hindu Student Council and many of his friends from that group helped to plan the dialogue and coordinate logistics on the night of the event. The Nichiren Buddhists of Soka Gakkai International (SGI-USA) cancelled a previously scheduled meeting so that their chorus could provide music for the evening. A Unificationist student group called World Carp showed up in full force and respected the ground rules of the dialogue by refraining from proselytization. Representation by students from minority religious groups outstripped that of the more mainstream Christian and Jewish groups on campus, but the overall crowd more than doubled to include eighty students. Manik's thought to offer a buffet of international foods representing the mother countries of many of the world's religions was a brilliant addition to the evening.

The most recent dialogue, during the spring of 2003, was somewhat less inspiring. The exotic foods returned but the musicians did not. Several chaplains lamented the fact that the date of the dialogue conflicted with previously scheduled events of the Muslim Students Association and several Protestant groups.

At the time of this writing, Manik is in his senior year at College Park. Among other challenges and decisions facing him as graduation looms will be reconnecting with the student leaders and campus ministers from the many chaplaincies represented on the campus of this huge state school. They are the necessary stakeholders that can once again make this annual event a great example of student leadership and the thirst for greater understanding of the world's religions among the student population. Manik will also confront the need to share his vision with younger students so that his event can continue to grow and thrive among new generations of college students, just as IFC's youth program needs to do better outreach to younger high school students.

Forging a Faith Identity for Oneself: Leah's Story

Leah went from being a marginal Jew to an enthusiastic member of the Baha'i Faith during her high school years. That statement might rankle some who read it, and conversions are certainly not something we encourage at IFC! Our statement on proselytization recognizes the right of our member faith traditions to share their version of religious truth with others, but it takes a hard stance against movements that force conversions on people and put down other faith traditions. Leah's conversion was solidified by her experience with the Interfaith Youth Program but not caused by it. I first met Leah when she accompanied some Baha'i friends from her Maryland public school to one of our Presidents' Day workshops. She had already started attending Baha'i firesides (weekly gatherings in a Baha'i home for fellowship and teaching) on a regular basis, yet she remained nominally Jewish. Her parents were divorced and she lived with her mother at the time. Religion was not a big factor in her home life.

We first divided the students up into small groups of people from the same faith tradition. Leah made the free choice to leave her Baha'i friends and meet with her fellow Jews. After the dialogue, she realized that she could not call herself Jewish anymore. She had been just going through the motions in her faith. She realized that the little she knew about the religion of her birth had come through conversations with peers who were Baha'i. The Baha'i faith recognizes the sacred nature of all religious texts, and young Baha'is tend to be quite knowledgeable about the Hebrew and Christian Scriptures. The interfaith youth workshop gave Leah the opportunity to meet peers who were passionate about their faith, and it gave her the freedom to pursue a new spiritual path about which she could also feel deep conviction.

At the same workshop the following year, Leah sat in on the Baha'i discussion of core values. Her conversion had made such a positive difference in her life that even her mother adopted the Baha'i faith. Leah's conversion gave her the strength to weather several challenges before she graduated from high school. At one point, she and her mother were forced to consider moving to a homeless shelter. After spending time living with family friends apart from both her mother and father, Leah moved north to Baltimore to live with her dad, which also meant spending her senior year as a newcomer at a Baltimore public high school. She is now attending the prestigious Vanderbilt University, a testament to her strength of character and trust in God's will for her life.

Leah is a consistently cheerful and upbeat person who is extremely grateful for her involvement in the InterFaith Conference's youth program. In late 2001, she delivered a remarkable speech to some of our donors who had gathered at the Kiplinger Washington Editors building in downtown Washington, D.C.

"I was talking to my friend about IFC activities and she was so grateful for the fact that these activities are ongoing. It's like a continuation and revival of hope that youth can move the world towards a new paradigm of fellowship and unity. That is just how IFC has affected my life. It is the empowerment it gives youth to make this transformation in society that convinces me that I too can contribute in my own humble way and know that my contribution will not go in vain. IFC events have fostered love and unity in every event that I have attended, a unity and spirituality that many youth in school are deprived of and thirsty for. Before my involvement in IFC activities my religious education of the world's religions was extremely limited. From presentation to discussion, I learned a great amount and have been able to recognize the underlying unity of the different expressions of God's eternal faith."[2]

Leah's conversion experience is a unique phenomenon in my experience of interfaith youth work. More commonly, becoming involved in interfaith deepens the personal commitment to one's own faith tradition. Interfaith dialogue certainly requires a young person to become more knowledgeable about his or her chosen faith tradition because no one wants to share false information about his or her religion with friends and peers. On a deeper level, interfaith dialogue can awaken in young people a real love and respect for the tradition that they chose for themselves or the one in which they were raised.

One might wonder if Leah's story would have been any different if her exposure to the InterFaith Conference's youth program had been through a "Why I Love to Be . . ." dialogue. By forcing her to reflect on what she loved about Judaism, would Leah have become a more committed Jewish youth? No one attends any IFC program by conscription, at least not on the part of the staff of the InterFaith Conference. It is hard to imagine that Leah's mother would have forced her to attend such a dialogue, and Leah was by no means connected to any synagogue that actively supported our program. The most likely scenario is that Leah simply would not have been present for the dialogue. Even if she were there, she would have been under no pressure to speak.

Mentoring: A Key Ingredient

Besides being blessed with the amazing youth leaders named above, the InterFaith Conference youth program also benefited from the early guidance of two gifted adult youth leaders, both of whom were quite a bit older than the youth with whom they were working. Pete Schenck initially coordinated the program for three years as a part-time staff member of the InterFaith Conference. Pete was an ideal father figure for the program. He was a Quaker who was quite sincere about his personal search for discernment and one's inner light. He was a great listener and was well respected by the young people and adult volunteers whom he introduced to the Interfaith Conference. He was also indefatigable in visiting different houses of worship in the suburbs as well as the city, despite not owning a car! He always made hospitality his top priority and was generous with his time and talents. When Pete decided to leave the staff of the InterFaith Conference, all of us wondered what would become of the program he had shepherded from its inception.

When we met Dr. Diane Sherwood, we knew all would be well. Diane was hired as Assistant Director of the InterFaith Conference in 1998 and worked on the youth program directly with initial assistance provided by intern Katie Campbell. In addition to earning a doctorate in English Literature and serving as a professor for a time, Diane brought experience in coordinating global events like the multi-media show at the 1992 Earth Summit in Rio de Janeiro, Brazil, to her new role at the InterFaith Conference. Her expansive vision of building interfaith understanding and her natural ability to bring people together through networking allowed the Interfaith Youth Program to dream bigger dreams. Under her leadership, a one-day youth workshop on the Presidents' Day holiday evolved from its initial focus on prejudice reduction and conflict resolution to a new concentration on shared core values. This transformation of the program coincided with the arrival of what Diane believed would become known as the "interfaith millennium."

Facing New Challenges

The InterFaith Conference's youth program hit its stride early in 1999. Nearly 100 high school students from Washington, D.C., and Pittsburgh met on Presidents' Day at the Chevy Chase Chapel of Latter-day Saints. The participants were treated to an all-new program inspired by Diane with considerable input from our high school youth. As you read above, intergenerational leadership has always been a hallmark of the program! We started the day with a game called People Bingo. We had about fifteen minutes to introduce ourselves to others and collect autographs under the heading of categories that each applied to only a few of us in attendance. Some of these categories were expressly religious while others focused on particular talents and skills that a wide variety of young people could possess regardless of their faith tradition. People Bingo proved to be such a popular way of mixing people together that it continues to be used at most of our high school workshops today.

Workshop attendees then were introduced to shared core values. The shared core values model attempts to show that although our religious beliefs might be different from one tradition to the next, the values that form the foundation of those beliefs are things we hold in common as young people of faith. The shared core values workshop begins with small group brainstorming sessions of young people from the same faith tradition. They are asked to write down on newsprint the values that they consider most essential as Christians, Hindus, Buddhists, etc. When everyone at the table agrees on each item on the list, they present their list of values to the entire group and post their list of core values somewhere around the meeting room. This model works best with a religiously diverse crowd of at least fifty youth, so that no youth has to stand alone as the sole spokesperson for his or her tradition.

The youth are then divided into mixed-faith small groups with people from each of the faith traditions represented in the room. Each group considers the core values of all of our faith traditions. The task is to identify the values that everyone in the small group can agree upon. Each small group shares their list with the larger group and the result is a list of shared core values that takes into account the beliefs of every faith tradition present. With Y2K on everyone's mind at the time of this first shared core values workshop, the youth participants committed themselves to be agents of positive change, reciting this pledge. "We pledge to act from our core values, to promote harmony among all religious traditions, and to be Champions of the Millennium—working to create a better world."[3] With unabashed hyperbole, Diane and her youth planning committee titled this workshop, "Coming Together to Lead the World." Diane believed that young people were capable of assuming this burden and this blessing and the young people who came to know her during her five years at the InterFaith Conference felt inspired to the task by her determination and love. Leadership begins locally, so the first task of these young leaders of the new millennium was to introduce the shared core values model and administer the millennial pledge to more than 100 adults who convened at Adas Israel Congregation for the InterFaith Conference's Spring Public Dialogue in 1999. Youth of each faith led a prayer, song or chant from their tradition at this event. The small group dialogue topics dealt with issues of social justice such as debt forgiveness for Third World countries, racism and care for the environment.

Diane's vision brought our group as far as the General Assembly of the United Nations in the summer of 2000! About twenty-five members of the D.C. interfaith youth program journeyed to New York City for the opening session of the Millennium Summit of Religious and Spiritual Leaders. For two days prior to the United Nations visit, Diane orchestrated a gathering of high school students from Washington, D.C., Pittsburgh, Long Island, New York and Boston at St. Bartholomew's Episcopal Church in Manhattan. Our D.C. contingent shared what we had been doing with shared core values and the youth from the other cities also had ample time to demonstrate the best practices of their programs. We had the chance to meet a number of the leaders who would play such a pivotal role at the United Nations meeting, including men and women from Alaska, Greenland and Africa.

We traveled to New York on a bus that bore the insignia "New World," which reminded us all of the task at hand while giving our group plenty of time to get to know each other well. The trip was another outstanding bonding experience. Winds of change were beginning to blow through the program, however. Most of the young people on the trip were just about to start college. Many others were entering their senior year of high school. Not enough was being done intentionally to replace those lost to graduation with younger students. Being able to engage in a dialogue on shared core values requires a level of maturity and knowledge of one's own faith that often only older high school youth possess. While we are always eager to welcome more 9th grade students into our program, it is difficult to assume that all high school freshmen could contribute in a meaningful way to our dialogues. We also face the challenge of living in an extremely transitory area. Families come and go annually, coinciding with new assignments in the military, federal government, diplomatic corps and major corporations. One solution to this problem is to always cast a wide net in interfaith youth work. It is important for the program director to always be meeting new people, staying in touch with them by phone and e-mail and constantly inviting them to interfaith activities while also being available to meet youth on their own turf, such as at their own house of worship.

By early 2001, I had been hired to direct the high school youth program for the InterFaith Conference along with a college campus ministry network of university chaplains and student leaders from campuses in and around D.C. This was to be my full-time job, the first time that IFC had been able to afford to hire a full-time youth and young adult worker. Of course, Dr. Diane Sherwood remained the source of most of our really good ideas!

Diane's next big dream for the Washington, D.C., Interfaith Youth Program was a weeklong summer camp in 2001 that would attract youth from all around the country. The InterFaith Conference reserved space at a large Episcopal retreat center in the Shenandoah Mountains of Virginia. We hoped to bring high school students together for a program called, "To Lead Is to Serve," five days of activities on the concept of servant leadership, including community service opportunities in the small town that would be our host. We thought that we surely had enough local interest in Washington, D.C., to give flight to the program. We were wrong.

Despite Diane's strength of determination and my full-time status, the InterFaith Conference failed in its efforts to launch a weeklong summer camp. Many of the students upon whom we were relying for local leadership came down with a bad case of "senioritis" soon after the 2001 Presidents' Day Workshop. Earlier in the school year, the success of this new summer camp was extremely important to a number of these students. Come spring, they had moved on to thoughts of college acceptance and rejection letters, senior prom, and graduation. We were also suddenly unable to mobilize the same network of supporters that had rallied around our visit to the United Nations the previous summer. Nationwide, we noted with disappointment the fact that not a lot of interfaith organizations were intentionally working with young people. It was time to scale back our ambitious goals.

We did manage to launch a new annual workshop in 2001. Once again, it was Diane who had the foresight to see the need for a fall workshop to compliment the Presidents' Day workshop in the winter. So the Columbus Day workshop was born, just one month after the tragedy of September 11. We had already begun making plans for the workshop when four hijacked planes hit the World Trade Center in New York City, the Pentagon in suburban Washington, D.C. and a field in western Pennsylvania, killing one of my college classmates[4] and three thousand other precious souls. In the days that followed, we heard stories about Muslim-Americans, Americans of Arab descent and even Sikh-Americans being targeted as victims of hate crimes by jingoists who were both angry and ignorant. High school students were not exempt from taunts and slander in their schools, so the interfaith youth program returned to its roots by once again focusing on stereotyping and prejudice reduction at the new October workshop.

The Columbus Day Workshop remains in its nascent stages. It had to be cancelled in 2002 as the entire Washington, D.C., area lived in fear of two indiscriminate snipers for three weeks that October. An ongoing challenge to this workshop is the fact that more and more school districts are holding classes on this federal holiday in exchange for days off in September on the Jewish high holy days and the inevitable snow days. It is unclear just what the future will hold for this new youth initiative, although a successful workshop for about thirty youth was held at a northern Virginia synagogue in 2003.

Dr. Diane Sherwood stepped back from regular involvement in the Interfaith Youth Program in early 2002. In late spring of that same year, Diane was diagnosed with cervical cancer. Her health was extremely unpredictable for the next thirteen months, with periods of aggressive growth of her cancer followed by strong rallies when it seemed that Diane would win the battle against her disease. Diane died peacefully on July 3, 2003, at age sixty-six, but only after a true interfaith community had gathered by her bedside. In the last moments of her life, two Christian colleagues (including this writer) had the privilege of reading a psalm from the Hebrew Scriptures to Diane while her Indian dentist and interfaith colleague played the harmonium, a keyboard instrument, and chanted a Sikh scripture passage. Diane's sister, Donna, and the other friends who were at her side when she gently took her last breath then anointed and washed Diane's hands, feet and head. It was a small gesture of love and reverence extended to a woman who radiated those same qualities to all whom she met.

A current college student who was part of our youth program under Diane's guidance sums up her contributions this way. "In my mind, I still see her smiling, as she always did when we (the kids) would talk about our views on absolutely anything. She is one of the best listeners that I have ever known. Another thing I greatly admired her for was her quality to value everyone's opinion in a way that moved them, and then inspiring him/her to achieve something greater with that idea. She is really a positive force that still inspires me a lot. Since my involvement in the InterFaith Conference, I have evolved as a person and it is all because of Diane's effort that she put in the program."[5] To say that we will miss Diane's presence and inspiration cannot begin to adequately describe the sense of loss we feel.

Conclusion

In its eight years of existence, the high school youth program of the InterFaith Conference of Metropolitan Washington has evolved from a program grounded in prejudice reduction to one that celebrates the values that young people of all faith traditions share in common. Along the way, our high school students have contributed great leadership to our program during their journey to college and adulthood. There also has been transition among our adult leaders, and we continue to mourn the recent loss of our greatest visionary. The one constant in the program has been the respect shown by the leadership of the InterFaith Conference for the young people whom we acknowledge to be essential partners in bringing about an interfaith millennium of respect and understanding. When I said yes to Msgr. Kuehner's invitation to take part in the first interfaith youth retreat in 1995, little did I know that interfaith dialogue among young people would become my unique ministry. After the joy of getting to know great young people like Leah, Bethany, and Manik and phenomenal adult colleagues like Pete and Diane, it is hard to imagine ministering anywhere else.

Notes

1. *Youth Program Grant Proposal to the George Preston Marshall Foundation*, InterFaith Conference of Metropolitan Washington, 1995.

2. Leah Lewis, speaking at the Kiplinger Washington Editors building in D.C., on December 11, 2001.

3. As quoted on the website of the North American Interfaith Network (NAIN).

4. Sara Manley Harvey was working on the 92nd floor of World Trade Center Tower II on the morning of September 11, putting her directly in the flight path of American Airlines flight 11 from Boston. She had just returned to work the previous week from her honeymoon. RIP. Her widower, Bill Harvey, was also a Georgetown classmate of mine.

5. Personal e-mail correspondence from Ashley Owen, July 24, 2003.

19.

The Sacred Stories Project of the Ghetto Film School

Joe Hall and Andrew Unger

FADE UP FROM BLACK and we are on the East River promenade, the dark water to our left, headlights shooting along the highway to the right. This is the city, so no stars can be seen, but street lights form constellations in the night sky. There she is: the warrior in red running towards us furiously fast, and just as we are about to collide, cut to title: Chase.

"What we did was try to re-teach an ancient parable to our generation. But, at the same time, it became personal the moment we chose it. That's when people started putting their own thoughts and ideas into the stories. In my case that meant choosing to make it about a girl who leaves home."

The Ghetto Film School

The Ghetto Film School (GFS) was founded June 2000 as part of a growing national movement that develops young people by honoring their skills, interests, talents and evolving contributions to community. Located in the heart of the South Bronx, GFS students produce high-quality film, video and multi-media projects through a rigorous training grounded in an appreciative study of cinematic masterworks. All students are celebrated along with their projects in regular GFS Public Screenings held throughout the United States and abroad; the organization, its students and programs have been featured in *VIBE* and independent film and video magazines, as well as CNN World News.

The School's founder, Joe Hall, studied at the prestigious graduate film production program at the University of Southern California (USC) in Los Angeles. Encouraged by the wonderful faculty and overall student experience at USC, Joe returned to his Hunts Point neighborhood to start GFS, the idea being that youth could have the opportunity to learn and develop as filmmakers and become competitive for university-based film programs or jobs in the industry. Using assets-based and appreciative inquiry approaches (first for the development of the organization, and now as the basis of our training pedagogy), we learned that talented students having new opportunities for success was but one side of a coin that also included the contribution of new voices and perspectives to an often "ghetto-ized" world of cinema. The GFS Board of Directors and Advisory Board include industry professionals and filmmakers dedicated to realizing our mission. GFS students are typically Hispanic- and African-Americans aged fourteen to nineteen, of mostly Catholic and Pentecostal traditions.

GFS students come from word-of-mouth, presentations at local schools, churches, and community-based youth organizations. All new students complete a creative application, interview and family orientation for the required first course, the nine-week introductory Summer Production Workshop.

At its core, the Ghetto Film School (GFS) has always been about giving young people the opportunity to tell stories they feel compelled to tell. But when we first informed a group of our students that they were going to adapt sacred parables into a contemporary context, they responded with some skepticism. People were not immediately convinced that age-old stories from around the globe related to their lives in twenty-first century New York City. The project was implemented for two reasons: 1) GFS was in the final segment of a three-year curriculum design phase and we wanted to evaluate a course on story development through cinematic adaptation; and 2) GFS board members strongly believe that, as well as promoting intellectual, emotional and spiritual growth, producing (and appreciating) art is a method for making sense of, and engaging with, ideas and emotions which might be otherwise inaccessible. Thus, sacred parables were chosen.

We are close to the ground now, a worms-eye view in a rare patch of urban grass. The warrior trips, and as she falls into the frame we see desperation and dirt streaked across her face. She pauses in a moment of defeat, and we hear a mother's scolding voice ringing in her ears. "You make me sick!" Maybe it is fear fueling her, maybe anger, but as she pushes herself up from the ground we see great strength in her arms. We rise with her, first face to face, then slowly revolving until we are looking over her shoulder, seeing what she sees: the glittering Manhattan skyline gazing down at its reflection in the water below.

"I wasn't so excited about the project at first because I'd grown so used to creating from scratch. I wasn't sure how it would be to pick something and adapt it. But when we started working on it and learning about more and more parables, I got pretty excited. I loved going around to the temples and learning about the different religions, because in high school there's a point where you learn a little about each, but not enough to know where anyone else is really coming from. You just assume other religions are either like your own or completely different, foreign and strange."

A Unique Methodology: the Sacred Stories Project

After our first few field trips to various houses of worship, we quickly realized that we could not have asked for a better place to study the religions of the world than in New York City. At the same time, it became apparent that everyone in our group, instructors and students alike, had not fully explored the city's diverse cultural riches until our summer together. As we turned the corner of Holly Avenue and Browne Street, not one of us was prepared for what we saw. Rising from between a row of the modest houses that line the streets of Flushing, Queens, intricately carved images of Hindu deities rose high from the roof of Ganapathi Temple. We were no less amazed by the Tibet Center in midtown Manhattan. The day of our visit there was a power outage in the entire building, and after walking up five dark flights of stairs flooded by the sprinklers, we followed a warm glow into a room illuminated by a gold plated Kalacharkra Statue that stood majestically under a glass skylight. Our host then began to tell us about the silk Thankas scrolls hanging from the walls which depicted a number of Buddhist Goddesses.

The frame is filled with a man's mouth aggressively devouring a piece of meat. We pull out and see that the fierce jaws belong to a large muscular cyclops, who begins to stagger off into the distance. The running warrior fades onto the screen, and for a brief moment, as their paths cross, the hunter and the hunted become one. The warrior continues on, running frantically through the streets, and then darting into an alley for safety. Waiting there is the cyclops, who quickly pushes her up against a concrete wall and begins to forcefully kiss her ear. Watching her fight back, we soon realize that the warrior is tremendously strong and exceptionally skilled at defending herself. She pushes the cyclops to the ground and runs back onto the streets, running until she is able to stop and catch her breath in the quiet of a nearby park. Before she can fully exhale, the sound of numinous voices suddenly echoes through the air. When the warrior looks towards the sound she sees a green glow emanating from a tiny figure, which upon approaching she sees is a frightened little girl shrouded in a shimmering green cloth.

"I learned that in Buddhist cultures red represents good things. In our culture, red is bad; red means blood and stop and danger. I wanted to switch that around. Also before that we had watched *American Beauty* in class and in that film red seems to represent similar things in my film, how the beauty of life is so hard to appreciate until you are about to lose it. In my film, red also means protection; the main character's sweatshirt is red; it is a symbol of protection. At first we had a red helmet, but that didn't look too good. In the original script, the mother was painting her nails red, which represented her growing and becoming a better person."

The purpose of our visits to the various houses of worship was the telling of a sacred story by a member of each faith tradition. The oldest form of entertainment— sitting in a circle listening to a master storyteller—would guide our students' digital-age creative process. At a synagogue on the Upper West Side of Manhattan a young female rabbi told us a number of Jewish folk tales as well as exploring some narrative passages from the Old Testament. We ate Northern African food at a mosque in the Bronx while a Senegalese man told us the tale of Muhammad receiving his first revelation on the mountain of Hiraut.

Instructors facilitated a reflection session following each visit, a common practice at GFS throughout all activities; we retain and use knowledge more easily after we have taken the time to think about and name our experiences. Students first took part in a journal writing session, considering such questions as, "What was the most striking story you heard? Why did this particular story appeal to you? How might you translate this story into a contemporary context?" Using an appreciative inquiry (AI) methodology we always found the path marked by positive, provocative questions as the quickest route towards understanding, integrating and using new materials or information, whether that meant a new cinematographic technique or a religious concept. We chose the AI approach to religious inquiry and study because our student filmmakers were concerned with communication through art, with creating new constructive connections, rather than reconciling predetermined problems. In this respect, the Sacred Stories Project is markedly different than undertakings that seek to "heal," "understand," "build tolerance" or "promote cooperation," all of which are based on deficit models and perspectives.

Most students chose parables during our structured reflection sessions, but (in line with the spirit of independence that is always promoted at GFS) not everyone found their sacred story though the channels we arranged. Occurrences of such inspiration underscore, and are encouraged by, our basic educational philosophy. We present and organize our staff and equipment as resources for young artists. We do not delineate which materials, sentiments or concepts are acceptable, but rather provide the education our students need to best articulate and communicate their individual creative visions. This is, of course, a shift from the memorization-based, standardized-test-focused curriculum found in the public schools attended by our students. GFS workshop participants take home a $2,500 camera simply because they want to practice while filming a family BBQ that weekend. Equipment is never "signed out," which would hold students legally responsible for technical damage; such a system would promote a fear of (and thus distance from) the filmmaker's tools of creation. We subscribe to a GFS twenty-four-hour notice policy, instructing staff to be available after hours and on weekends for access to, and supervision at, a sunrise shoot or late-night editing session. This policy builds trust, reinforces each student's role as respected artist, and allows every participant the freedom to incorporate the contemporary world he or she encounters into his or her creative work.

"I found my parable one night while watching *King of the Hill* and later found it again in a Buddhist Sutra.—I'm a huge fan of that show, and I know that the creator Mike Judge is big into Buddhism. In the episode, Khan, who is a Laotin character in the show and is also Buddhist, tells his neighbor Hank a Buddhist parable. Bobby, who is Hank's son, wanted to get on the school football team and he wasn't able to make it, and so Kahn was telling Hank the parable to console him. The story went: a long time ago in China there's a man running away from a tiger and as he's running away he falls off a cliff. As he's falling down the cliff, he grabs on to a branch and holds onto it. As he looks down there is another tiger below him and when he looks up there is the other tiger snarling at him. So there's impending doom no matter where he goes. On the same branch that he's hanging on there's a strawberry. He eats the strawberry and it's the sweetest strawberry he's ever tasted. To me that means, what I took away from it at least, was, well, a few things. First, that we only enjoy things when we are about to lose them. The reason why the strawberry was the sweetest he ever tasted was because he knew he was going to die soon and I loved the story because he accepted the fact that he was going to die while in western culture we've been programmed to fear death and look at it as this horrible thing. For me, being young I guess you feel immortal. I just think that people should keep in their minds that death is inevitable. It's not a bad thing, it's not a good thing, it's just something that is, and if we realize that we can live fuller richer lives."

The warrior moves closer towards the little green girl, and with a comforting hand strokes her tear-streaked face. The little girl smiles, but what first seems an innocent and appreciative expression soon distorts into a menacing grin. The warrior cannot look away from the little girl's eyes, which once so seemingly childlike, are now filled with ominous knowledge. The warrior is physically shaken, struck by something from inside. Images of lush green trees, as would be seen shooting past a car window, fade over her pained face as she slips into memory.

It is a rainy day now, many years ago. We are standing behind a young girl wearing a red sweatshirt soaked with rainwater. A man, slightly out of focus, walks away from her, towards a car in the driveway. The young girl's mother is standing in the doorway of a house, looking past her daughter as the man drives off. The little girl turns toward her mother for comfort, but is only met with a look of frustrated anger.

We are back in the park now. The warrior has been hurt by this little girl, and she runs before more pain can be inflicted.

Results

As a creative production, seeking to end up somewhere beyond tolerance and acceptance, the Sacred Stories Project students, staff and audiences found new religious understanding and communication. The difference is akin to that between a lecture and a dialogue. Our students learned about the teachings of unfamiliar religions, but were also prompted to translate the meaning of these teachings into stories which held personal significance. They consequently learned from, as well as about, other faiths. It is one thing to accept or tolerate a foreign perspective and quite another to connect with, use and thus truly appreciate, that perspective.

Imagine, for instance, that you are speaking to a stranger about the recent loss of a loved one. If that individual simply listens and nods, what type of connection has taken place? If, instead, that person tells you her story of loss (the specifics: the ache in her chest, the constant worry that she'll forget the sound of his voice) then you have reason to believe her when she says, "I understand." The assumption, on which the Sacred Stories Project is built, is that the ancient parables we study are as universally meaningful as the common loss of a loved one, that at their core these stories are as relevant to us now, as they were to those who heard them first.

Of course, complete religious concurrence is not necessary for a harmonious society. There is room for the agreement to disagree, and tolerance is often the best compromise that can be reached—though it is no doubt a compromise. Before accepting "acceptance," we can make an honest effort to connect emotionally with each other's beliefs. An organized effort towards such connection fosters greater collective and personal knowledge, stronger interdependent community, and a deeper, more meaningful, understanding of one another.

"You have to look at the components of the story. In *King of the Hill* Hank adapts the parable to tell to his son Bobby. I don't know too much about football, but he was using football references. I chose to make my main character a young woman. I didn't realize this until I put everything together, but I think it was because I adapted the parable and made it really personal. My story is about a girl leaving home, and having to deal with that emotionally. I'm at the age where I'm going to be doing the same thing very soon. And one of the worse things that scares young women leaving home, well you know there are relationship troubles, and living alone you can more easily be robbed or hurt or whatever so then I invented a cyclops who symbolized all of the physical dangers. And the antithesis of that is the pixie who is the spiritual pain. She was sort of a mischievous angel, and I realized when we were learning about Buddhism that she had a lot of the same personality traits of the Buddhist goddess Green Tara. In the Buddhist mythology this goddess appears as a young girl who is wrathful and mischievous, so in a lot of ways that character became Green Tara. Now, I had my two bad guys, but the thing that got me was the end, the strawberry. What is that one thing about life that makes it worth living? In the original parable it was a simple strawberry, but if she's running down the streets of New York City there isn't going to be a strawberry just hanging out there. In the end I had two questions unanswered, first, why does the warrior run away from home, and second, what is the thing in the end she is able to appreciate? I came up with the idea that she has a horrible argument with her mother and in the end I wanted her to come full circle."

The warrior runs back onto the streets. Suddenly the pixie appears on the sidewalk, a green glow emanating from her grinning mouth, and again takes hold of the warrior's consciousness. We are in a teenager's room now, and the same mother is hovering over the warrior. She screams. "Clean up this mess. Dishes on the floor, and dirty clothes everywhere! This makes me sick! You make me sick!" The warrior clutches a red pillow, her face flickering with fear and grief, taking the abuse until she can no longer. She storms out of the room, but this time we do not run with her. Instead, we stay with the mother who is paralyzed in time, her face frozen in an expression of confused suffering.

In the case of the GFS Sacred Stories Project, the dialogue and understanding engendered were not simply that of one individual towards another. From the beginning of the program, each student knew that he or she would be creating a work which would be viewed by hundreds of people at various Public Screenings. This is, in fact, a key component of our pedagogy. On September 10, 2002, student projects were screened in the Assembly Hall of Riverside Church for some 375 guests comprised of everyone from religious youth groups to professional filmmakers. In addition to the usual first-time-filmmaker premier jitters, students also felt pressure about the ethical issues involved in communicating the sacred teachings of a faith tradition that is not one's own. What if I get the meaning of the parable wrong? What it I offend someone of that faith? What if I simply fail to communicate? From the start of the program, GFS students knew that their work as young artists was going to be taken seriously; they'd heard the stories about trips and Public Screenings from veteran GFS participants. They understood that their peers, their instructors and hundreds of audience members were going to consider with sincerity the images put forth on the screen. Such an understanding is as empowering as it is frightening, emotions which were both heightened with the Sacred Stories Project. An Assets-Based developmental approach to working with young people helps redefine the situations which may generate fear into occasions for new possibilities, triumphs and accomplishments. We can rename fear as adrenaline; make it a tool rather than an obstacle, if we truly believe in the students' ability to ultimately succeed.

Conclusion

The courage to accept one's own, and other, personal interpretations of sacred stories is a crucial component in working towards religious harmony. Such courage is derived from, and developed through, opportunities marked by importance and immediacy (like having to make a movie in nine weeks!). Unlike fundamentalist or literalist readings of religious texts, an interpretative eye looking to create something new from the experience can accept the possibility of various meanings. Ultimately, it is the timeless moral relevance of parables which makes such interpretations possible at all. It is that which is sacred about these stories that gives them eternal and universal meaning and which allows for these tales to be translated not only across languages, but across cultures and generations as well.

The challenge in these modern times is that our young people know we fear them; in response to school metal detectors, no arts programs and constant designation as a problem-to-be-fixed, they have constructed a numbing armor of violence, drugs (street-level and prescription) and profound social isolation. Working through this requires activity grounded in young people's compassionate contribution to others (e.g., a community service or arts project), which will begin to melt the cynicism. Giving a South Bronx teenager virtually unlimited access to and control over expensive equipment, script development, production choices, and casting of actors shows them we're not afraid anymore—of them, or of the magnificent mistakes they'll make along the way.

"I think that adapting parables to the medium of digital film worked so well because we could pour personal lives into them and then show it to kids our age, or really any age, because when you modernize something as meaningful as a parable everybody can relate, which is good because in the end we were trying to relate teachings that most people in the west wouldn't regularly be exposed to. Here in America, all the major holidays you get off are Christian or Jewish and you don't learn much about other religions. I thought this was such an effective way to expose younger kids, like the youth groups who saw our film at Riverside Church, to the religions of other cultures. Kids want to be entertained but at the same time they also want to learn something they wouldn't have otherwise. I think they related to our films because we were of the same generation and we put into the parables what we get out of life, what is in our lives, and were able to communicate that through film."

The rain is pouring now as the warrior runs down the city streets, chased by the cyclops, the little girl, and her own memories. She can run no longer, and, gasping for breath stops next to a pay phone. She looks to right and sees the cyclops charging towards her. She looks to left and sees the little pixie glaring threateningly. She picks up the phone, dials a number, and speaks very softly into the receiver "Mom?" We are now with the mother again. She is aglow in a red light, tears falling from her eyes, an expression of overwhelming joy on her face.

The warrior looks up from the phone, takes a deep breath, and stares into the pixie's eyes with composed courage. The cyclops enters the frame. Cut to black.

20.

Spirit into Action:
An Interfaith Weekend Model

Annapurna Astley

SPIRIT INTO ACTION (SiA) HAS ROOTS in the nourishing soil of many organizations that have brought me up to be an interfaith leader over the last ten years—the Unitarian Universalist Church, Harvard's Pluralism Project, Kashi Ashram, CPWR's Next Generation, and the Interfaith Youth Core. At the 1999 Cape Town Parliament, Next Generation youth representatives had presented our commitments to the leaders and elders of the world's religions, and mine was to share this experience of interfaith with more young people. In 2000, I decided that I would continue to express my excitement for the interfaith youth movement by uniting friends I had made in Cape Town with young people in my own community of Kashi Ashram and Indian River County, Florida. Kashi Ashram is a one-hundred-plus resident and international interfaith community founded by Ma Jaya in Sebastian, Florida, in 1976. Situated on eighty acres of sub-tropical jungle, the ashram holds interfaith landscape housing gardens, temples and sacred spaces celebrating the diversity of the world's faiths. It also hosts retreats, conferences, and community service and social involvement programs, and has been active in the struggle with HIV/AIDS since the early 1980s.

Excited by the possibility of a youthful interfaith gathering at Kashi, I started talking about it with everyone—for a while it was all I would talk about. Several people committed to helping facilitate and participate. We had no concrete plan of what we were doing, no business plan, no cash, just an idea. The gestation period for the first one was only about six weeks—and BOOM—SiA was born.

Mission

As stated in the Spirit into Action mission statement, our goal is to create a sacred interfaith space which celebrates our generation's diversity and puts into action our intentions to improve our world. The form this has taken has been a weekend-long event where activities reflect the three principles of the Interfaith Youth Core: Intercultural Encounter, Interfaith Reflection, and Social Action. Each weekend has an event theme such as freedom, peace, compassion, and gratitude. The themes are chosen for their universality among world religions as well as appeal and relevance to young people. We schedule a wide variety of activities that allow space for participants to express, define and explore the theme's meanings, and see it put into action by a peer group. The themes' meanings from different religious, cultural, and linguistic as well as individual perspectives are included.

The weekend-long format has been highly successful. It gives participants enough time to be involved in a variety of activities over a period of two and a half days, time to establish bonds with other participants, and yet leave (as indicated on the feedback forms) feeling like "it should be one more day!" It is always better to have people walk away feeling ready for more, than feel like the event has been overdone. Some other strengths are that we create a flexible and safe space for open discussions, find a place of common ground both for individuals and religious traditions, take action on a common theme, relate world issues to the individual, cultivate an awareness of diversity, teach young people how to dialogue, listen, put their ideals into social action and selfless service, and also create the space for intergenerational dialogue.

Our structure for the weekend is something like this:

Friday p.m.:	Registration, Orientation and Ice-breaking, Introduction of the theme, Logistics
Saturday a.m.:	Team Building Activities/Creative Expressions, Continuing to discuss/express theme (Internet dialogue with other groups)
Saturday afternoon:	Community Social Action Projects—Clean-ups, Church Paintings, Shelter meal-servings, Habitat for Humanity building, etc.
Saturday evening:	Social time (unstructured)
Sunday a.m.:	Sacred Interfaith Happening (ritual, commentary, sacred space)
Sunday p.m.:	Closing discussions, Reflections on the theme and how it has been expressed, Creative project, Feedback forms, Commitments

I will briefly tell the stories of our first four SiA events, the ones I was involved in leading. The stories of individual participants shed a new light on interfaith organizing and have special lessons to teach us. I hope that what I have learned is useful to others venturing onto the path of interfaith organizing.

SiA I: Freedom (Kashi Ashram, Sebastian, Florida)

Eboo Patel, founding director of the Interfaith Youth Core and an Ismaili Muslim, came from Oxford, and Kevin Ross, a young minister from the New-Thought Christian Tradition, came from Miami. The three of us had spent the week together in Cape Town on the Next Generation's Assembly Team. Our hearts, along with those of the 25 other international members of the team, had committed to continuing what had begun there. To me, SiA was how I could put that commitment into action, and we felt the three of us made a diverse yet united core to hold the weekend. I was so grateful that my new friends had come to support this next step. The younger generation at Kashi also began to get excited and meet regularly. We invited everyone we could think of to come and share, contribute, add to the array. I met several times with Radhe Chan, Kashi's thirty-two-year-old Associate Director, throwing around ideas, and she helped tremendously with administration and logistics of the weekend. We made a flyer and sent it to all the databases we could. We made follow-up phone calls. We passed it around. We shared with friends—personal friends, friends of the ashram, friends of the interfaith world. Thirty-five people came, ages eleven to forty. They were Christian, Jewish, Sikh, Muslim, Hindu, and many who did not identify with one or another tradition exclusively.

Our first event, in April of 2001, was very organic and had a magical newness and vibrancy. We wanted to do everything, and packed the schedule to the point of near exhaustion! Our activity list included ice-breaking games and orientation, four off-site service projects (one environmental, one social for each person), board breaking with Tae Kwon Do, drumming, mural painting, group prayer, a dance party, private sessions with Ma Jaya, the founder of Kashi, a Palm Sunday service with "Rev. Kev," celebration of Hanuman Jayanti, a Hindu holy day, with the Kashi community, yoga sessions every morning, and a closing circle with reflections and commitments. All of these activities were tied together with the Passover and the interfaith theme of "Freedom." At the end of the weekend we were more juiced up about interfaith, and vowed to continue, perhaps with fewer activities and more resting time!

Bridget

Each SiA weekend event had many participants, many stories, many experiences. But at our first SiA, our youngest participant added a very special essence, and taught me early on that age is only a number. When first dreaming up this event, we felt a need to define the age range of participants and came up with fifteen to thirty as our target population. Slowly we broadened the range as inquiries and registrations came in—to fourteen, then thirteen, and thirty-two, thirty-five, and thirty-nine. We began to say "teenage to thirty something." On the Friday afternoon, while running last-minute errands, I got a call on my cell phone from one of the teachers at the River School, the PreK-12 school situated at Kashi Ashram. He said that one of his sixth grade students, Bridget, had heard about the event, and was dying to participate, but she was only eleven. She had approached him and asked him to call me and ask if she could come. I was dumbfounded. I was so impressed by her initiative and resourcefulness to find her way to Spirit into Action. In fact, she was Spirit into Action! Who was I to exclude anyone who wanted so badly to be a part? Bridget and her fourteen-year-old sister, Kara, came to the event. This young girl brought not only her enthusiasm and purity to the event, but a wisdom and gratitude far beyond her years. From the first ice-breaker on Friday night, when she thanked us for including her, to offering to give tours of the ashram's interfaith Ganga pond temples, Bridget was present 110 percent of the weekend. We later found out it was her first sleepover experience.

SiA II: Peace (Kashi Ashram, Sebastian, Florida)

The second SiA event was in November of 2001, just following the 9/11 terrorist attacks. We decided the theme of this weekend would be "Peace." Again the Interfaith Youth Core sent a facilitator, the then-executive director Jeff Pinzino. We had other leadership in Crystal Henderson, a university student from Indianapolis who had led hiking programs with challenged youth. Another addition to the SiA family was the IFYC Action Group in Amman, Jordan. Anas Adabi, a facilitator of this group, was active on the IFYC Internet line, and wanted to get involved with Spirit into Action from the Middle East. We chose a time on the weekend to do a speaker-phone call and then a computer chat-room, all with the discussion theme of Peace, and what it means to us as individuals and from our traditions. We shifted to only one session of community social action projects, and allowed more time for relaxation. Forty-five people came to our second event.

Tray

After the first Spirit into Action event, I had made a personal goal of visiting and participating in local religious services to which I had not previously been. In September I attended a Sunday service at the Church of God by Faith, a Pentecostal African-American church in the nearby town of Gifford. I had been invited by Lisa, a staff member at a summer camp with whom I had worked for two years. She had mentioned that her husband was a preacher, and when I began asking about her church, she invited me. As it happened, the Sunday that I had arranged to attend turned out to be the very first Sunday after 9/11, a time when I was feeling sad, scared, and upset. At the Church of God by Faith, I found not only a joyful and welcoming community, but, for the first time since the attacks, I felt a certain peace and comfort. I also met Lisa's wonderful teenage sons, who were leaders of the music in the church. Antravious ("Tray") was sixteen and had a clear and powerful singing voice, while his brother Leon played a drum set, keeping the beat for the clapping congregation. With such positive energy, I knew these boys would have a lot to add to Spirit into Action, so I invited them. I went back to the church for another service in October, where Lisa and her husband invited me to play my bagpipes during the service, and sang along to "Amazing Grace." I repeated my invitation for the boys to come to the November SiA event. I was thrilled when Tray called me asking for a ride. I picked him up at his house on Sunday morning—he was missing Church to come, no small feat for the son of a family so involved with the leadership of a congregation. I invited him to sing that morning at Spirit into Action.

Tray jumped right into the morning's activities with the other participants—reflecting on Peace, drumming on African-style drums, breaking a board with their fears written on them, making bracelets, painting a mural, and listening to a guest speaker from Uganda. (As it happened, there was an international conference happening at Kashi the same weekend, AIDSETI (AIDS Education Training International), complete with 100 doctors, activists, and organizers from Africa and the Islands.) Tray had become shy about singing in a crowd outside of his own church, so I gently encouraged him again after he got to know everyone a little through the activities. Finally, a friend from Kashi made a request that he sing a particular song she remembered when she had come to his church with me. I think that was the key that opened Tray up. The room filled with his proud and confident gospel voice, and soon everyone was clapping and joining in on the chorus. "I love You, I lift You up, and I magnify Your name; That's why my heart is filled with praise." It was almost noon, and we were heading over to the dining room to join the AIDSETI conference for lunch. I had been asked to introduce Spirit into Action to the other group, and I invited Tray to come up with me and sing "Amazing Grace" with me. He did beautifully—I don't think he woke up that morning knowing he would be singing for an international conference!

The following month, Lisa called me and asked me to play my bagpipes at a Christmas service she was organizing. Our relationship has continued to be warm and accepting, a reciprocal sharing of our respective cultures and traditions. Tray and Lisa both worked at the camp the following two summers. I think the most valuable concept of building interfaith relationships that I learned with Lisa and Tray was the importance of the invitation. Would I have gone to Lisa's church if I had not been invited? Would Tray have come to Spirit into Action if he had not been invited? Would he have sung or would I have played if we had not been invited? In building communities of trust, we must invite our neighbors and do our best to make them feel as welcome guests, and, on the other hand, honor them by visiting their own sacred places. I have been told that it is rare to see Pentecostal participants at interfaith events, which adds to the value of such direct and intimate involvement and reciprocal hospitality.

Ananda Devi and Wilhelmina

An account of SiA II would be incomplete without including the story of one of the community social action projects. The young people who were there are still talking about it, such was its impact upon them nearly two years ago. Ananda Devi, who runs an outreach program at Kashi Ashram called Feed Everyone, offered to help us organize a service project. She contacted a friend of hers, Wilhelmina, who had many local connections, and told her of our group of interfaith young people looking for hands-on social action projects. Wilhelmina, a young and energetic woman in her 60s who has raised 16 of her own children and grandchildren, offered to help us, and indeed set us up to clean the apartment of a disabled woman. When we pulled up to this apartment, located in a housing project, our volunteers, some as young as 12, had never seen a place so filthy. They took turns scrubbing, vacuuming, and dodging vermin while others played with the neighborhood kids and distributed canned food to neighbors who expressed a need. I wasn't sure what their reactions would be—how can you predict? They loved it. At one point I walked into the living room to find an eighth-grader with a toddler on her hip vacuuming the carpet, while others scrubbed the walls, cleaned the dishes and took out the trash. One sixteen-year-old said later that she had done many service projects before, but had never before understood the point. Perhaps she was saying she never felt that she could make a difference, but in this case it was impossible not to see the impact that we were making in this woman's environment. This was an important lesson for us in setting up other projects—the personal interaction as well as seeing the impact were the key strengths of this project that we felt crucial to the success the young people felt.

After SiA II, Wilhelmina expressed a need for her own church to be painted, and we joined her youth group in cleaning and painting the Kingdom Church of Jesus in Gifford as one of our projects in SiA III.

SiA III: Compassion (Kashi Ashram, Sebastian, Florida)

For our third SiA event, we chose the theme of Compassion. The theme was suggested on-line by Anas Adabi from the Jordan IFYC group. I felt it was another wonderful theme that not only young people could relate to but that all religious traditions could trace to their beliefs as well. The leadership for this event, in addition to the Kashi facilitators (myself and Radhe), came from Anastasia White from the Chicago IFYC house, and again Rev. Kevin Ross from Miami. We based our activities around the interfaith theme of compassion and sought to define compassion as individuals, as members of a group learning together, and as members of religious traditions. We made our schedule from what we had learned from the previous two events, trying to achieve a balance between overbooking and getting everything done that we wanted to accomplish. We learned we could not please everyone with the diversity of backgrounds and ages present, but we tried to be as accommodating as possible to the input we had received from the feedback questionnaires.

Anas

Our Internet dialogue with Jordan for this event changed forms in that we decided, instead of one large, chaotic chat-room (as fun and energetic as it was) to set up several small instant message dialogues. We set up small groups on our end, since we outnumbered the Jordanians. We gave a list of suggested dialogue questions and a time frame. We then came back together as a large group and shared our experiences with our on-line conversations, and what we had learned about young people in the Middle East, in Jordan, from the Muslim tradition, and their thoughts about compassion. This Internet dialogue (and the one from the previous SiA event) for me were very exciting, and really gave the event an international impact. I spent weeks setting up the dialogues with Anas and his friend Nada, and in doing so got to know them better than anyone. At one point Anas even tried out a Web-Cam in Aqaba at an Internet Cafe and made funny faces at me from there. To me, this was a glimpse of the lighter side of the interfaith youth movement and yet it made a profound statement about our generation and its ability to use technology for interfaith exchange. Anas and I continue to correspond over the Internet and I think he would agree that the exchanges we have coordinated at Spirit into Action have been as inspiring and meaningful to him as they have been for me. Of course, in Internet dialogue there are several factors that are missing from face-to-face interactions: all the unspoken parts of conversation are missing, and the sensory experiences are removed as well. The subtleties of seeing a reaction in someone's face, or even hearing their voice in a conversation, are lost. Hand gestures and facial expressions are no longer helpful communication tools. However, instant messaging does allow for more focus on the content of the dialogue and the words themselves. And it certainly is better than no interaction at all!

SiA IV: Gratitude (Miami, Florida)

One of my goals for Spirit into Action had been to develop a program that not only would be successful at Kashi Ashram, but could travel to any location. In November of 2002, for our fourth Spirit into Action event, it was time to see if SiA was ready to fly out of the nest. Kashi Ashram had been a wonderful place for an interfaith youth program to be born. The community of one hundred-plus residents was supportive in many ways, from office support, food preparation and service, facilities, sleeping quarters, flexibility, and the interfaith Ganga grounds at which you can experience gardens and temples honoring many sacred traditions, in a peaceful, natural setting. Organizing an event in Miami was almost like starting from scratch in many ways.

Rev. Kevin Ross and his congregation, the Lighthouse for Empowered Living, who had participated in two of the three first events, were based in Miami, and seemed a natural place to turn for building a Miami SiA. In the summer of 2002, young people came to Kashi for some initial planning meetings and we were on our way. One of the highlights for me was the process of deciding the theme for the Miami SiA event. Three of us—Kathia, Lisa, and I—sat around a dining room table and had the intention of brainstorming possible themes. For about twenty minutes, we just threw out words that came to mind, like a free association, which had the underlying intention of the event theme. We came up with some great ones, and after we felt we had come to a stopping point in that process, we went over our list, which I had been writing down. We narrowed it down. We talked about our favorites. And then it just hit us. Gratitude. It grabbed us all, and suddenly all the other themes paled in comparison. It seemed even more perfect when we realized later that the event was in proximity to the American holiday of Thanksgiving. To me, consensus building is so important in team leadership. It does not always come as easily as it did to us that day, but it felt to me like a powerful way to start building an interfaith event. To agree on one word in a magical moment unified the event and gave it form.

As the fall progressed, it became clear that while the Lighthouse would participate and help promote the Miami SiA, leadership for the event itself would come from Radhe and myself. It was a new challenge, especially considering the distance (Miami is a three-hour drive from Kashi). It was a stretch in many ways, but it was a great and worthwhile experience.

For many people, the concept of interfaith is an unknown quantity (and therefore somewhat scary) and many adults are especially protective of their teenaged children. Therefore, one of the challenges we have found in this work is in reaching out to new participants, particularly ones with whom we do not have an established, trusting relationship, or for whom interfaith itself is a new concept.

For the Miami event, for example, we sent out hundreds of flyers and letters about our exciting interfaith youth event. We got only one phone call in response to the mailing. It was from a Wiccan coven, the leadership of which ended up coming to our Sacred Interfaith Happening at the Miami SiA after I met with them and discussed the possibilities. The other flyers from our initial mailing were followed up with phone calls, and some with subsequent meetings or communications, but none yielded participants. This just shows me that more time needs to be spent developing relationships, visiting and getting to know youth leaders in other communities. Also, I think that many organizations are so focused on building their own youth programs, and that their priorities are internal rather than external interfaith networking.

Another challenge has been to create a time and space which is accessible to people of the full range of faith traditions. Over the course of a weekend, different organizations have religious services, so our weekend-long model is long enough, and flexible enough that participants can attend the sections that fit their schedules. I think the more we are aware of each other's boundaries and concerns, the more likely it will be that we reach a solution to issues such as these.

Conclusion

Organizing Spirit into Action events has taught me several very important lessons about the journey of interfaith togetherness: Showing up (the most important step); seeing the interfaith journey as a creative process; continually inviting others; and using many forms of activities. What I mean by "showing up" is not just to be present physically, but showing up with your heart and mind open to the creative process of interfaith. How is interfaith like a creative process? It is a dance that hasn't been choreographed, a blank canvas ready to take form, an improvisational jam session. To many people, the unknown is scary. But we are all artists in one form or another. And the more we hone the skills of expressing our truest selves, the more comfortable we will be to do so with "strangers." Finally, the lesson of the invitation asks: Would I have played the bagpipes in an African-American Pentacostal Church if I had not been invited? Would Tray have sung "Amazing Grace" at the AIDSETI conference if he had not been invited? Sometimes it takes a genuine encouraging welcome, or indeed a patient and insistent one, to help us stretch out of a comfort zone into the unknown. Sometimes it takes an outstretched hand to help us show up. Finally, I have experienced the most success with activities that engage young people on many levels. It is important to keep a balance of varied activities within the weekend program. The more diverse ways we can find to share the time together (in dialogue, social-action projects, creative expression, recreational time, quiet reflection, spiritual and sacred ritual), the better we get to know one another and ourselves. Young adults are always on the quest for more understanding of themselves and their place in the world. Having a meaningful experience at an interfaith event at a young age can open up a young person's world forever.

21.

E Pluribus Unum: A Model High School Seniors' Two-Week Interreligious Program[1]

Sidney Schwarz

THE E PLURIBUS UNUM (EPU) PROJECT EMERGED from three distinct but interrelated observations. As a rabbi, I came to realize how easily religion loses its way. By tending to focus on the customs, ceremonies, and forms that give institutional religions continuity rather than the ethical *raison d'être* of their respective faith tradition, many people of conscience turn away from organized religion. I found that many people doing the most important God-work in the world will never set foot in a church, mosque, or a synagogue. Many of us are looking for God in the wrong places.

As one committed to social change, I became discouraged when others engaged in political and social change work were dismissive of religion and spirituality. Given how challenging and difficult such work can be, I observed that those who stayed with it were sustained by a deep faith that comes from another dimension of reality, from a transcendent source. To be able to access that source requires an openness of the spirit to alternate ways of seeing a hard world.

As an educator of young people, I experienced how successfully Jewish texts and values could be used to inspire greater commitment to issues of social justice and political activism. I was eager to explore whether the same approach could be used successfully by other faith traditions. Given how much energy the religious communities of America commit to community service and social change, it seemed only natural to explore ways that a diverse group of young people could be motivated to pursue the

This essay is adapted from an article that originally appeared in *The Reconstructionist*.

common good in a setting where the primary learning rubric was the religious social teachings of the respective faiths.

Level 1

When the EPU project was launched in the summer of 1997, the expressed objectives were as follows: 1) To raise students' awareness of their respective religious traditions as a source of ethics and values that have direct bearing on a variety of major issues confronting our society today; 2) to allow students to explore both the similarities and differences between their respective faith traditions and discover those areas of common interest which might form the basis for a stronger civic fabric in America; 3) to give students an understanding that a democracy rewards those who are most informed and active on issues and to specifically teach the students how they can become more effective advocates for responsible social and political change, informed by the teachings of religion.

The EPU program consisted of four programmatic tracks: 1) the academic track; 2) spiritual arts and worship; 3) volunteer service; and 4) advocacy and a community life experience. Each one of these four discrete EPU strands was designed to maximize the chance that participants came to see the connection between their respective faith traditions and the need for any practice of that faith tradition to be in the service of some greater social good.

In the original design of the three-week EPU program for entering college freshmen, each morning the sixty rising freshmen were divided by faith group into three faith-alike classes with a faculty member expert in the tradition. Three topical areas served as the themes for each of the respective weeks—human rights, poverty, and the environment. Policy experts were invited to address the entire community in a plenary session, grounding the students in the specifics of the given issue. Each faculty member had a good deal of autonomy to determine how best to introduce the students to the particular teachings of that faith tradition as it pertained to the particular policy theme of the week. Every few days, students gathered together to participate in education exercises which challenged them to learn, compare, and contrast the teachings of their own faith tradition with those of the other two traditions.

Despite the fact that the recruitment process brought to the program young people who were far more connected to their religion than the average young adult, it was surprising how little most students knew about the social application of their respective faith traditions. It suggested to the project organizers that none of the three faith communities was particularly effective at conveying the social message of their respective traditions.

In the questionnaire administered prior to the start of the program, fewer than two-thirds of participants could name even three teachings from their own faith tradition that spoke to any social issue. Over 95 percent could answer that question by the end of the program. It was less surprising that less than a third of participants could cite three religious social teachings of faiths other than their own on the intake interviews. That number rose to over 80 percent by the end of the program. There was considerable evidence that the EPU educational environment helped students "find their voice" in relating religious teachings to pressing social issues of the day.

Initial Findings

A somewhat counter-intuitive finding of our three-year EPU experiment involved the relationship between commitment to faith and the ability of participants to fully engage with others who did not share their religious heritage. From EPU's inception, one of the commitments of the program was that we would not sacrifice the passionate embrace of one's own faith tradition in the process of creating an environment that encouraged pluralistic expressions of faith, ethnicity, and ideology. We were committed to avoid this common pitfall of so many well-intentioned interfaith programs. The organizers were not unaware of the peculiar brand of intolerance born out of religious passion and fervor. Yet we believed that, before participants engaged in any interfaith approach to pursue the common good, they would need to be grounded in the social teachings of their own respective faith traditions. Not only did our program design abide by this principle, but in a six-month follow-up study of alumni, we found that those most grounded in their own tradition were able to create the strongest relationships with people of other faith traditions in the pursuit of some social-justice cause. Essentially, they were more inclined to look to religious cohorts for allies because their experience of faith through EPU bore witness to the relationship between religion and social justice.

It is not that the EPU experience did not challenge every participant's understanding of their own and of other religious traditions. It was programmed to do so. In some cases, the expression of a viewpoint from one faith tradition helped a fellow EPU participant understand or articulate a belief or position from his/her own tradition for the first time. This phenomenon tended to strengthen commitment to one's own faith. At other times, however, the array of ideas about faith and religion from so many different perspectives challenged deeply held views and beliefs. One participant wrote: "I am flooded with new ideas and not sure where I stand with my own (faith) anymore."

While participants may have, at times, found themselves confused, the faculty was confident that it was the kind of confusion that would help them grow, both in faith and in maturity. The challenge articulated to the community was to be able to stand in one's own truth while simultaneously being able to acknowledge another's truth. Clearly, it was the focus on the theme of social justice that got participants to look past the particular elements of their respective faith traditions and encourage them to engage in some "boundary crossing" to find common ethical elements among all traditions.

Level 2

Perhaps the richest evidence and testimony to the effect of the EPU project was the group of nine 1997 alumni who were brought back during the summer of 1998 to participate in a specially designed Level II program. After several days of getting reoriented to one another and to the themes of EPU, this extraordinary group of young people created their own interactive program integrating drama, music, and discussion to convey the lessons of EPU. They then had the opportunity to present the program to over three hundred teens in a variety of Catholic, Protestant, and Jewish settings during the summer of 1998.

An added dividend to the Level 2 program was having a group of alumni in residence one year after their initial EPU experience, and subsequent to their freshman year of college. Our conference evaluator, Dr. James Keen, was able to spend considerable time with the group, mining from them critical insights and determining the longer-term impact of the EPU experience.[2]

Level II students came to us as rising college sophomores. They reported that in the year following their initial EPU experience they found that a major shift in their religious self-perception had taken place. They found that they now framed their statements of belief and commitment from a much deeper place within themselves, coming to feel that they more fully "owned" their convictions of faith. They had moved decisively beyond the stage during which such statements parroted that which they got from their parents and teachers. This self-conscious internalizing of deeply felt life commitments, they largely attributed to EPU. The group, as a whole, and the individuals that were part of it, were more solidly reflective of James Fowler's post-conventional, "individuative/reflective" faith stage characterized by the ability to live with religious doubts (*Stages of Faith: The Psychology of Human Development and the Quest for Meaning*, 1981). EPU's dance faculty member invoked a West African proverb to describe the kind of spiritual learning that was engendered at EPU—"The opposite of truth is not falsehood, but another profound truth."

"Justice, Justice. . ."

These alumni had also more fully embraced the "servant leader" ethic that the EPU model promoted. One student said, "We all discovered that the idea of working for the community and (for) the common good and going out and making a difference is something that is common in all our religions. . . . Before last summer I'd have been against working collaboratively. I would have only worked to support [my religion's] organizations." A second student said, "Something I got out of EPU last year is looking at the religious texts from our various backgrounds and what our faith in general has to say about the quest for social justice. When you realize that they are so similar . . .you realize how much bigger a group of people you have to work for the common good from different faith backgrounds. It is a very empowering thing."

In several EPU reunions held during the winter of 2000 with alumni from all three years, this theme recurred with significant regularity. Even as these alumni bemoaned the fact that they could not devote as much time to community service and social justice causes as they would have liked (owing to their commitment to their undergraduate regimen), virtually all reported on the impact of the EPU experience on their thinking. Some had changed their majors; some had developed new ideas about career goals. All had been challenged to reassess the way they thought about religion, social justice, and the common good.

Results

As we consider the impact of the EPU project on the thinking and behavior of 160 young people, all of whom are now moving through their college careers with varying relationships with churches, synagogues, and the communities in which they find themselves, we are given pause to consider the ways in which EPU's unique configuration of themes and disciplines might benefit other fields. To the extent that higher education is concerned about "character education," can colleges and universities afford not to integrate the social teachings of the world's historic religions? To the extent that social change organizations seek to provide impetus to and support for people who are committed to the work of peace and justice, how might they marshal the support of religious social teachings?

Last, but perhaps most important, given the galvanizing impact of exploring the social teachings of one's own and other faith traditions, how might churches, synagogues, seminaries, and parochial schools reassess the way that they teach religion? Might it be that the most compelling aspects of each of our faith traditions lie precisely at the intersection between faith and the common good? Is not the purpose of religion to help people tread the very narrow ridge between attention to one's own needs and self-interest and devoting energies to the needs of those less fortunate than ourselves? Must religion not serve both as a balm for the afflicted soul as well as a spur to the complacent conscience?

These are the kinds of questions that EPU poses. It is in our response to these and other questions that we might find some important answers for creating a more just and peaceful world.

Notes

1. Sections of this article originally appeared in *The Reconstructionist*, Fall 2000, reprinted with permission and sections of this article first appeared as "Religious Social Teachings" in "The E Pluribus Unum Project: Exploring Religion, Social Justice and the Common Good in an Interfaith Context."

2. See the results of these conversations in Jim Keen's article.

22.

The Chicago Interfaith Service House

Lori Eisenberg

IN 1997, WHEN I WAS EIGHTEEN, I participated in the inaugural E Pluribus Unum (EPU) conference in Washington, D.C. This project brought sixty Jewish, Catholic, and Protestant recent high school graduates to explore the nexus between faith and social justice. The following summer, I was one of nine alumni who were invited to explore the mission of the program at a deeper level than the summer before. Part of the three-week program was to visit various sites that practiced the relationship between faith and social justice. I remember hearing the story of a Lutheran volunteer at N Street Village, a transitional women's shelter. She explained how she had recently finished college and had started a year of service driven by her Lutheran faith convictions.

A few days later, I was riding in a van with my fellow EPU alumni after giving a presentation to other young people about the importance of interfaith relationships while doing service work. I was learning more about myself and how I wanted to shape my life around this mission. Because we were learning about ourselves by being part of this group and because we were having fun doing service work together, I could not imagine the experience being limited to those few weeks. I proposed the idea to the group that we spend a year together after college doing faith-based service, much like the Lutheran volunteer had explained, only in an interfaith framework.

Around that time, I heard the words of Gandhi: "You must be the change you wish to see in the world." Those words have not left my mind since I first heard them. Young adults are faced with challenges as they attend college and choose a career path. The big question remains: How am I going to make a difference in the world? Living in an intentional community composed of young people from different religious, cultural, and national backgrounds challenges one to see the world from different points of view. When these different perspectives converge, one finds the common good and each individual begins to define his or her role in being the change he or she wishes to see.

Two years later, as a college student, I pursued this idea of starting an intentional community with the mission of promoting interfaith-based service.

The E Pluribus Unum staff supported my efforts. After much research and development by EPU alumni, staff, and other partners, the Interfaith Service House (ISH) was launched in Chicago, Illinois, in the fall of 2001. With the help and eventual sponsorship of the Council for a Parliament of the World's Religions (CPWR), I joined six other Fellows in forming a community with members from seven different faith traditions and three different countries.

Goals

Three goals guided the mission of the Interfaith Service House:

1) To provide a supportive environment for young people committed to working for social justice and social service organizations in the non-profit sector;

2) To provide a religiously and culturally diverse living environment which encourages young people to learn about other religions and to more deeply examine their own; and

3) To provide opportunities for young people to process their service work through the lens of their faith in order to grow spiritually, intellectually, emotionally, and professionally.

Selection Process

Each person interested in participating in the program was asked to submit an application, which included biographical information, short essay questions, a resume, and letters of recommendation. Staff at the CPWR reviewed the applications. The essay questions were perhaps the most revealing, suggesting who might thrive best in the program. Questions were asked to get a sense of the applicants' ideas regarding their faith tradition, interfaith experiences, community living, and social justice work. CPWR staff members were not looking for "right" answers. They were looking to see if the applicant was thinking critically about these ideas and if he or she could articulate them. The applicants should bring that critical thinking to the Interfaith Service House and share it with others, even if the ideas were not congruent to those of the other Fellows.

The following year, instead of relying upon the CPWR staff, the first-year Fellows in ISH residence selected the next year's Fellows. We created a review system based on both the ISH goals and our experiences living them out. We reviewed and discussed each application, taking into account the overall religious and cultural diversity of the newly selected Fellows. As the future program coordinator, I conducted a phone interview to assess the international applicants' conversational English skills. In addition, job placements were arranged during the selection process: it was important to consider the skills and interests required for each placement and then look for applicants with the right skills and interests to match the placement.

Beginnings

Once we all moved in, the first year Fellows had the challenge of setting up a community. We all agreed that autonomy was going to be a core value of our collective. Because the first challenge of the house was to create community from the mix of our differences, we had to begin with establishing our own guidelines. We first discussed and listed each person's expectations for everyone's behavior. It proved to be a very successful strategy: based on these expectations, we developed a set of guidelines, for which we held each other accountable, as well as goals for our year together.

We had to establish a structure to carry out these goals and expectations. When does the group meet and what purpose does each meeting have? Will the group eat meals together, and when? How does the group pay bills? Does the group share food expenses? How will the group divide housework? Should each person be assigned a role in order to ensure that the internal structure of the program runs smoothly (i.e., treasurer, historian, meeting facilitator, public relations representative, etc.)?

During the first year, we, the seven Fellows, discussed how to pay for the monthly rent and the expenses of running the house. All of us had already agreed to work for a modest salary of $15,000 for the eleven months of the program. There was no room for any extravagance! The majority of the group decided that we should break down the expenses based on what we used. Each bill was divided seven ways and we were each to reimburse the person who paid the bills. Receipts were collected and an extensive process was carried out to divide the costs evenly. At this point though, only four of us had jobs and those who were employed made slightly different salaries. Many arguments arose based on who was responsible for what expense and who owed money to whom.

Shortly after the decision to divide our expenses evenly was made, a discussion took place that significantly changed our financial plan. Eddie Kornegay was our guest for dinner one night and soon became a mentor to us all. He discussed our collective and the idea of looking after our brothers and sisters in the house. He explained that although we were making different amounts of money, we could use this opportunity to live justly by sharing the money we did have so that every person could live equally and have the same economic choices.

From that point on, we pooled our money into one account with one person managing our finances. From one month's salary, each person would keep $500 and deposit the rest of their paycheck into the common account. From that money, rent, utilities, food for common meals, and supplemental programs were covered. We were able to pay for a group facilitator during a workshop mid-year as well as a weekend retreat for ourselves. When a Fellow lost her job just prior to the end of the program, she still received a stipend of $500 per month and had her living expenses covered, all of which was funded by the common account. There was even some money left at the end of the year to hand to the next group of Fellows to assist them with some start-up costs. This key decision about finances brought us together and helped us realize that we were, in many ways, responsible for each other as members of the same community. In this case, we were being the change we wanted to see by taking care of one another despite our different incomes.

From the first year, the Fellows met twice a week, one time for business and once for spiritual reflection, both preceded by a meal and fellowship. The business meetings always had an agenda and were facilitated by a house member. They were a time to check in about the workings of the house as well as to plan and prepare any future activity.

Spiritual nights varied over the two years. The first year, Jamie Harris, a student at a local seminary, did her field study through the Council for a Parliament of the World's Religions as the facilitator for our weekly spiritual reflections. In addition, she met with one of us each week, so that we would see her on a one-to-one basis approximately once every two months. The second year, the Fellows decided to meet every other week in the house with Jamie and on alternate weeks, attend a religious service, celebration, or other spiritually enriching event. This schedule was designed to explore each other's faith traditions in depth and to engage in outside community services and festivals of traditions including those not represented in the house.

In-house spiritual reflection evenings varied in form. For the most part, Jamie facilitated these meetings. At the beginning of the year, they were structured. Later on, Jamie asked each person to host an evening where they explained their spiritual practice to others and invited them to participate in some activity. For example, Mark led a bible study. Carrie invited her house members to walk around the neighborhood and name those places where they saw God. A favorite activity was to put questions in a bowl and draw from it to spark discussion. Topics included economic justice and the afterlife, among others. Typical meetings with Jamie started with a reading followed by personal reflection. Each person was allowed a period of time to write about the topic. The group would convene and talk about their personal reflections or Jamie would have an activity that involved writing or the visual arts.

Challenges

A less successful goal of the program was to match each Fellow with a mentor from his or her faith tradition. The idea was to meet about once a month to check in about spiritual and professional development. Ideally, the mentor is someone working in a field of social justice who could provide advice and support the Fellow throughout the program year. The challenge was finding those who could serve as mentors and also be suitable matches for the Fellows. Some did take advantage of their suggested mentors, meeting with them quite frequently while others did not meet with anyone. Some found mentors independently, sometimes outside their own faith tradition.

Two issues continuously recurred in the Interfaith Service House: compromising one's faith as well as the question of spiritual practices and marginalization. These issues emerged because we were living in close quarters, sharing one's life with people who had, at times, very different religious practices, brings these issues to the forefront. Towards the beginning of the first year, the seven of us wanted to have a party to introduce our house to the larger community. All of us had different definitions of what a party should look like. For example, Ayse's ideas included sitting with friends and eating. Thobeka wanted to dance all night. Colleen was accustomed to having alcohol at her parties. When these ideas came together, there were conflicts. As an observant Muslim, Ayse did not drink or want to be around alcohol, nor did she dance in front of men. Thobeka, a member of the Baha'i faith, did not drink or like to be around alcohol either. There was talk of compromise in order to accommodate everyone's religious tradition and culture, but it seemed to be a black and white issue; someone in the group had to sacrifice their traditions and had to risk authentically representing themselves. It ended up with food and music, a bit of dancing and no alcohol. The compromise was too difficult for some Fellows resulting in half of them leaving during the course of the evening.

Later, we talked about the issue of compromise. It was agreed that we did not want to ask anyone to compromise his or her customs in order to live together but we could never agree on a solution if a similar situation were to arise. At the end of the year, we hosted a presentation for many of our friends and supporters over the year. As a gesture of gratitude, we wanted to share with them our experiences living in the Interfaith Service House and celebrate a successful first year together. This time, it was much easier to organize because we had spent months coming to know each other.

This example of planning social gatherings illustrates a very important issue in interfaith work, especially in this kind of intense shared living: how far can one compromise? Members of the community had to make sacrifices based on the ideas and expectations they arrived with. As the community grew together, they learned about each other's traditions and priorities at a deeper level. As those identities emerged more clearly to everyone, it was easier to come together and create something as a community that reflected the collective. The principal challenge that year was not only for each person to bring who they were to the table and find common ground, but to find a new way of existing as one community that worked for everyone.

Theoretical Reflections

In the effort to understand the maturation of a small community such as the Interfaith Service House, I find it helpful to look at Peck's theory of community development (Peck, 1987 cited in Eisenberg, 2001). He says that a community develops in four stages: *pseudocommunity, chaos, emptiness*, and *community*. While each community moves through these stages at different speeds, this order in the genesis of community formation usually remains the same. Both the individual members as well as the community as a whole encounter these stages. The group is, indeed, more than the sum of its parts. A whole community must move through this process; it cannot assume that any individual has the responsibility of moving it alone.

Pseudocommunity is the point at which the community first comes together. The members want an instant community and make every attempt to make everyone happy, thus avoiding conflict. Generally, the community ignores differences, minimizes problems, and makes assumptions about one another. In the Interfaith Service House, pseudocommunity was somewhat short-lived because of the intensity of intentionally defining the collective as soon as the Fellows moved into their new space together.

In *chaos*, the members of the community start letting their guard down. Thus, when problems arise, other members attempt to resolve them. This fosters arguments and the problems are not solved calmly. Often the community looks to a leader for direction and then, in turn, questions the skills of the leader. The community lacks organization at this point. The party at the beginning of the first year is an illustration of the transition from pseudocommunity to chaos. There was no clear leader in this case, but we all started to question openly how we respected each others' beliefs and traditions.

According to Peck, *emptiness* is the vehicle out of chaos. In a time of arguments and misunderstandings, the community must learn to communicate openly. Each member must empty themselves of expectations and assumptions and open themselves up to accepting who the other members are and what they have to offer. In the case of the ISH, there was constant movement between chaos and emptiness. In the struggle to respect each other's differences, there was also a struggle to communicate openly and honestly. As soon as the group felt that open and honest communication was achieved, true community emerged.

When *true community* is achieved, a sudden peace ensues in the group. People are vulnerable, but as they participate, they learn to reveal more of themselves and to accept others. At this point, the purpose of coming together as a community becomes

very apparent. There are many struggles as well as joys. The way the group addresses them reflects a true community.

In a community with a dominant culture or stance on an issue, it is easy to marginalize the minority. In many communities, majority rules and the minority must
concede. The challenge in the Interfaith Service House is to avoid marginalization but
sometimes it is hard to see when it exists. In a house with many identities, it is easy
to marginalize the minority when it comes to these factors. In the first year, the ISH
was comprised of five Americans, one Turk, and one South African. The American
culture dominated and a native understanding of English was important to keep up in
heated discussions and decisions that were eventually made. It was hard for the Americans in majority to be patient while our foreign sisters were still trying to understand
the culture. It was also challenging to understand that the cultural frame of reference
did not always have to come from the dominant culture. There were ways that we
could accommodate nonnative English speakers.

A first step was to become more conscious of the speed at which our conversation progressed and check in with every group member to ensure that there was a good
level of understanding. Another step was to provide a written agenda ahead of time so
that every person can follow along in multiple ways (i.e., oral, aural, and written). In
addition, as ideas were discussed, one member of the group wrote key ideas on flip
chart paper for everyone to see. A further step was to share language learning: native
English speakers made an effort to learn the mother tongue of one of the Fellows in
order to ease the conflict of misunderstandings.

Conclusion

The issue of marginalization is not unique to the local challenges of developing
an Interfaith Service House; they are intrinsically related to the social systems that
exist in our society and our world. Interfaith work is not just learning about religious
worldviews different than one's own; it is also about learning how those worldviews
co-exist in the context of these broader social systems. To talk about poverty during a
text study means also to talk about the economic system that exists in our society and
the world. In talking about what our faith traditions teach about poverty and then relating those teachings to our current systems, we can better understand how to come
together on an issue because of newly found similarities across religious worldviews.
One's faith identity is not simply defined by the texts but also by the social systems
that he or she is a part of; identities are not mutually exclusive. For example, a Muslim in Turkey is different from a Muslim in Iran and a Muslim in the Philippines.

In brief, the Interfaith Service House provides a good example of what Daloz,
Keen, Keen and Parks (1996) call a "New Commons." Skills are gained by living in

a community that feeds the responsibility of one living in a new commons, a place where community and identity lines are being redefined, where we must recognize that a "global commons challenges us to broaden and strengthen our understanding of citizenship" (Daloz, et al., p. 4).

It is unfortunate, however, that the Interfaith Service House is no longer in existence. The program lasted from September 2001 to July 2003 with two different groups of Fellows. As a project of the Council for a Parliament of the World's Religions, it could no longer continue due to lack of resources: staff, general funding, as well as job placements, among others. A project such as ISH needs strong leadership from staff and Fellows who are dedicated to the mission and goals of the program. A great deal of funding is necessary to bring a program like this together. Because of its international scale, support must be there to enable young people with limited income to travel long distances to be together for the year. Finances must also be in place for the local programmatic expenses. A core staff must be hired and supplemental programs such as retreats, speakers, and meetings must be funded. There must also be strong roots in the community where job placements open to foreign workers are available and encouraged. The ISH started just as September 11 took its toll on the economy. Beginning in the fall of 2001, fewer jobs were available and U.S. work visas were more difficult to obtain. These changes severely affected the positive factors that contributed to the initial success of this idea. It was difficult to see ISH continue without those factors in place. At this point, the CPWR does not have the capacity to sponsor the program with its focus on and preparation of the World Parliament of Religions in 2004.

Despite the current road blocks, there are hopes that this idea of the Interfaith Service House will spread to other cities in the world. The mission would be the same—to bring young people of different faiths and cultures together to work for social change. The manifestation of the mission may be completely different though. Wherever the house is based, the community will deal with different local issues and integrate in a very different way than what emerged in the Chicago experiment. Eventually, if Interfaith Service Houses emerge in other communities, it will become possible to compare different models of interfaith relationships dedicated to the promotion of social change on the basis of interfaith solidarity among young people.

References

Daloz, L.A.P., Keen, C.H., Keen, J.P., & Parks, S.D. (1996). *Common Fire*. Boston: Beacon Press.

Peck, M.S. (1987). *A Different Drum*. New York: Simon and Schuster, cited in Eisenberg, L. (2001). *Interfaith Service Corps: A Pilot Study*. Sarasota, Florida: New College of the University of South Florida.

23.

Face to Face/Faith to Faith: An International Interreligious Youth Program

Katharine Henderson and Melodye Feldman

Katharine's Story

A QUESTION THAT HAS COMPELLED ME since about age nine is this: *Why, in the face of human suffering and injustice, do some people simply walk away, while others stop, take notice, and act?* This primary question has driven much of my life personally and professionally. It lies at the heart of how the most recent part of my vocation has found me in Face to Face/Faith to Faith, the international multifaith youth leadership program of Auburn Theological Seminary in partnership with a Denver-based peace organization, Seeking Common Ground, and its founder, Melodye Feldman.

The seeds of this interest began early on. Some of my earliest memories are of marching in civil rights marches from the waist-high view of a child's sightline. I realized that my family and I were among the few white-skinned people among a sea of black and brown faces and skin tones. My parents had been exposed to the raw racism of the rural South; my mother's family was harassed by the Ku Klux Klan for my Quaker grandfather's leadership in building a high school for black students; my father had witnessed lynchings firsthand. They marched because their interpretation of the gospel message demanded no less.

From his humble upbringing, my father became a seminary professor teaching Old Testament and Hebrew. In the mid-1950s, he wrote about his concerns about racial injustice and the brewing crisis between Jews and Palestinians. My mother also pushed boundaries by becoming the first woman elder to be ordained in our local Presbyterian Church—a matter that caused a major fight in our church. I learned from both of them that to make peace sometimes means disturbing the peace, that being a person of faith means more than sitting in a pew on Sunday morning. It means acting in concert with one's deepest convictions to bridge the gap between the world as it is and the world as it could be.

At age nine, I traveled to Germany on sabbatical with my parents. We lived in the apartment owned by Dietrich Bonhoeffer's twin sister, Sabina Leibholz. I learned about Bonhoeffer, a Lutheran pastor, whose participation in a plot to assassinate Hitler led to his arrest and death in a concentration camp. I was exposed to the potential for human evil while visiting concentration camp memorials, but was equally over-whelmed with the idea that individual actions matter—that we are called to live beyond ourselves.

I am intrigued with people, particularly women leaders, whose progressive public leadership has been religiously grounded. What their entrepreneurial leadership looks like, how they talk about their work and the factors that went into their forma-tion has been the focus of my research and writing.

Melodye's Story

In grade school, my friend Debbie and I would walk home from school. Daily she would ask me this question, "If a Jew and a Catholic were drowning, whom would you save?" and I would ask her questions like, "Am I a good swimmer? Who was closer to me? Did I have a life saver? Did I have a boat to help me? Could I only save one?" She would quickly get tired of the questions and repeat, through clenched teeth, "Just tell me which one you would save!" Sometimes she would touch the top of my head and rub. Only later when I shared this with my mother would she explain that Debbie was looking for my horns. Debbie had been taught that Jews had horns. I wasn't allowed into her house nor invited to her birthday parties. Our friendship consisted of our walks to and from school.

In junior high, I was one of three Jewish students at a local public middle school. Once again, I was an outsider. A group of girls warned me not to even look at the boys in our class. I was invited to parties only to be reminded that I was a Jew—an unwel-come outsider. One day, I was followed home by a group of students who pushed me and shoved me down into a puddle where they began kicking me and calling me names like "kike," "dirty Jew," "Christ killer," and so on. Scared and confused, I ran home.

The next day, we were all called into the principal's office. The principal wanted to know what I expected from the students by way of apology. I told her that I thought that the students acted out of ignorance, that if they knew me and knew about my reli-gion, they might find out that I wasn't so different from them. I then suggested that we have a class about our religious backgrounds and cultures. The principal readily agreed, and offered a class to interested students. My fellow Jews and I spent a year teaching each other about our traditions, rituals, and beliefs. We shared our holidays and foods. We made friends. I was correct in thinking that if we shared who we were and what we believed, at the very least a new respect and understanding of the other was possible. Of course, since it was junior high school, all I recognized was that I now had friends and going to school was no longer so scary! What I didn't know was that these events would shape my life's work.

I grew up in a liberal Jewish home and belonged to a conservative branch of Judaism. In high school I began to study in an Orthodox Jewish day school for women, and became observant of the Orthodox laws of Judaism such as keeping Kosher and observing the Sabbath and all Jewish holidays.

In December 1987, looking over a hill in Jerusalem, I was witness to the beginning of the first Intifada (Palestinian uprising). I stood there with an orthodox Rabbi who was explaining to me the current political situation facing Israelis and Palestinians. As a Jew, I was terrified of the Arabs and what I interpreted as their call to "destroy the Jewish state and push all the Jews into the sea." In my mind, they were terrorists. This Rabbi turned to me and challenged me to learn about the Palestinian narrative. He was an early activist in the emerging Peace movement. It would take me three more years to pursue this challenge and when I did it would change my life and my vocation.

In 1993, as the Oslo Accords were being signed, I was busy planning a program to bring Palestinian and Israeli high school students to the United States to meet for the first time. This program, Building Bridges for Peace, was a subsidiary of Seeking Common Ground, a grassroots non-profit I founded in order to empower young people to build peaceful communities through meeting with one another and sharing their political, religious, and ethnic backgrounds. We began by bringing together Palestinian, Israeli, and American high school women for a summer program in which they would learn communication skills while building interpersonal relationships and planning year-long follow-up programs to continue addressing the issues that divided them. The more the students taught each other through their personal narratives, the more tolerant they became of each other. Real friendships began to emerge. Enemies became friends committed to working together non-violently to address the conflict between their two countries. They were able to see themselves in the "other." In 2000, when Seeking Common Ground was seven years old and I had just completed our summer Building Bridges for Peace program, Katharine Henderson called my office.

The Beginnings

About three years ago, when I was teaching summer school at Iliff School of Theology in Denver, I wanted my class to have the joy of interviewing a religiously motivated progressive woman leader. My search led me to Melodye. After the class, I asked her if she and her organization would consider partnering with me and Auburn Seminary. Some years prior, Auburn's Board had identified multifaith youth education as a potential growth area for us, expanding on the multifaith education with adults that had become a main focus for Auburn over the past decade.

Melodye expressed interest and came to New York the following fall. We sat in my office at Auburn, where I am Executive Vice President, and Face to Face/Faith to Faith was born. The title comes from Genesis 33 when estranged brothers, Jacob and Esau, meet for the first time after many years, in friendship rather than full of murderous rage against each other. One says to the other: *To see your face is like seeing the face of God.* The spirit of their meeting suggested the kind of hope that is possible even between people who consider themselves mortal enemies. Furthermore, the name suggested that all people are bound to each other as the children of God and therefore bear evidence of the Creator's imprint on the world.

At our initial meeting in October of 2000, we determined that we could begin programming immediately by adapting Seeking Common Ground to the mission, goals, and objectives of Face to Face/Faith to Faith. Face to Face was able to take root and grow only because of the initial financial support from Auburn Board member Mark Hostetter and his partner Alex Habib. The encouragement of the Auburn Board and President for this program has also been critically important, as has the Face to Face Advisory Board and its fundraising committee.

Aims, Expectations, and Selection Process

The purpose of Face to Face/Faith to Faith is to equip the next generation of young leaders with an advanced understanding of how their own religious traditions and those of others can be used to build a more peaceful and just world. The program requires at least a year-long commitment from teenaged, co-ed participants of Jewish, Christian, and Muslim faiths. Participants come from South African, Northern Ireland, the Middle East, and the United States (New York, Denver, and Chicago to date). Many have experienced religiously or politically motivated violence as a matter of course.

The selection of students is facilitated in their home countries by partner organizations there and involves a written application, recommendation, and an interview. Students are chosen based on their leadership potential, intellectual and social maturity, openness to and interest in engaging people of other traditions and cultures, and identification with a religious tradition and community where they have already been identified as leaders.

They come, fifty at a time, to a summer intensive program for two weeks to a camp and conference center north of New York City. Prior to coming, each home group has met together with a "home group leader"—an individual designated and hired by Face to Face/Faith to Faith. Orientation meetings allow home group members to get to know each other, learn about the program from the home group leader and previous participants, and prepare for their summer experience.

The curriculum for the summer intensive involves a multifaceted approach to learning, building community, working, living, playing, and praying together. Students become members of several different groupings—the home groups that they came with, dialogue groups that are religiously mixed, interfaith groups that are made up of all those participants sharing one religious tradition (which may represent enormous diversity: evangelical Christians, Protestants and Catholics from Northern Ireland; Orthodox Jews from Israel and from South Africa and other denominations; and Muslims, who are equally diverse) and cabin groups.

The educational goals for the program are:

    1) To foster meaningful encounters with persons from diverse
       religious, ethnic, and socio-economic groups;

    2) To build relationships that will lead to effective conflict management;

    3) To promote the belief that individuals have the power to
       effect positive social change;

    4) To nurture leadership and self-esteem;

    5) To create a network of progressive, faith-based activists and
       peacemakers around the world.

The first part of the summer program involves skill building, learning to communicate across the lines of religious and other kinds of divisions, understanding the difference between debate and dialogue, and micro labs that focus on understanding the factors of family, ethnicity, culture, and religion that form one's identity as a human being and then being able to tell one's story to others. Workshops are reinforced through art projects. One especially powerful project is the making of masks. Each participant decorates the outside of a mask according to how the world sees them and the inside according to how they see themselves.

After the opening communication sessions, the days are organized according to themes such as sacred tradition, religion and faith, political and religious conflict, waging war, gender and race in religion, power in perspective, making peace in the world, creating sacred space, and looking toward the future. Under these rubrics, students have the opportunity to make presentations to the whole group about life in their own countries. This means, for example, that Israeli Jews and Palestinians work together to create a presentation based on their experiences. While a Jew will tell the story of losing friends in a bombing and facing army service, a Palestinian will be talking about being harassed by an Israeli soldier on his way to school, of being hit with the butt of his rifle and having his school books thrown into a puddle.

A scavenger hunt of Sacred Spaces offers participants the opportunity to see a memorial to peace in Central Park, an African-American burial ground on Wall Street and the Battery Park memorial to victims of 9/11 and all victims of violence throughout the world.

A panel of religious activists shares their own life journeys. Recently, an Episcopal priest from Uganda told of a brother who "disappeared" under the regime of dictator Idi Amin; a progressive Muslim scholar shared his story of growing up in poverty in a township in South Africa, attending a fundamentalist Madrassah in Pakistan, and gradually evolving into a leader of a more progressive Islam. Religious leaders lead worship and prayer services to which all students were invited, telling their stories of being called into professional religious life. They engage students in frank conversations, addressing sensitive topics. A Catholic priest, for example, was questioned about the sexual scandals in the Catholic Church and the mystery of celibacy.

Throughout the program, students are introduced to the religious texts of other traditions and to stories of religious role models and thinkers that help them to search for commonly shared values and practices around peace and justice.

Home group meetings allow students the opportunity to process all that they are learning and to test the applicability to their home situations. Students are also given time to begin to plan for the future and how they will continue the learning, leadership, and activism after returning home.

Equally important are the informal times in which participants may journal, digest in cabin groups at night all that has transpired during the day, and enjoy evening programs—a Sacred Slam night (including performance poetry by artists from different religious and cultural traditions), a concert by a gospel choir that includes Freedom Songs, and a talent show where students work together or perform solo.

Sustaining the Experience

Before returning to their home communities, each home group is asked to develop and commit to an ongoing plan of learning and action for the following year. Most groups plan to meet at least monthly with the supervision and direction of the home group leader, who is supervised by Face to Face staff in partnership with local organizations in the home countries. Our partner organization in Israel, for example, is the Interreligious Coordinating Council of Israel (ICCI), a ten-year-old organization that focuses on peaceful coexistence in Israel and the surrounding region. In Ireland, our primary partner has been an integrated school near Belfast, although we are now branching out to form relationships with other organizations that are involved in cross-community endeavors. In South Africa, the home group leader is a candidate for ordination with the archdiocese of Cape Town. In the United States, Face to Face stays connected to students in Chicago through the Interfaith Youth Core, and to other students through a network of relationships with churches and synagogues in New York City and Denver. These partner organizations, along with the home group leaders, provide a network of ongoing support.

Students are involved in a range of activities when they return home—continuing the dialogue work begun in the summer intensive, hosting and running interfaith workshops for other high school students. One in South Africa focused on multifaith responses to the crisis of HIV/AIDS, which is devastating the country there. In Israel, participants visited religious sites and in each other's homes to learn about and celebrate holidays, such as the end of Ramadan. In many cases, the parents of the students have begun to gather informally to do their own work of dialogue and learning.

In addition to the face to face component of the program, students pursue formal and informal communication through the internet. Students created an informal internet group and, more formally, Face to Face has developed an internet curriculum to keep participants connected to the larger network of Faith to Faith participants, to continue the discourse begun during the summer program, to provide on-going educational experiences and to facilitate discussion between and among the participants. This curriculum supports the on-going work that participants are doing in their home countries. Every month, students receive an assignment asking them to respond via email, bulletin board, or real time messaging with the entire group. Assignments vary from month to month and facilitate on-going communication between the participants, to reflect and respond, or to motivate action.

Philosophy and Methodology

"O humankind, God has created you from male and female into diverse nations and tribes so that you may come to know each other." —The Qur'an

Four principles guide Face to Face. The first is the meeting of Jacob and Esau, described in Genesis. This story offers hope that there can be meeting and connection beyond estrangement and expresses the joy of knowing and being known that comes from genuine engagement.

Second, the Qu'ranic quote cited above describes another core value: that difference is one of God's greatest gifts to humankind, not a curse to be tolerated. The program focuses on the opportunities that a genuine pluralism offers, even as we address its very real challenges.

Our third guiding principle is that all major religions call believers and provide resources—through the interpretation of sacred texts and role models, living and dead—on how to relate to the other and to build a more peaceful and just world. Face to Face/Faith to Faith helps students to uncover shared values and beliefs, while maintaining the differences in tradition and practice.

Finally, and perhaps most important, we hold that there is room in the public arena for a vigorous conversation between different religious voices about how we are to arrange and live out our collective futures as communities, nations, and the wider world. Theologian Paul Knitter, in his book *One Earth, Many Religions*, offers the underlying rationale for this level of multifaith work when he says that the pressing question for all people of faith is: "How shall we build a new and more human world for all the peoples of the earth?" (57) The purpose of dialogue is to heal and repair the world, a world "that calls for global, coordinated action based on commonly recognized values and truths" (55).

Paul Knitter calls this *correlational dialogue*:

> Far from requiring that everyone be the same, a correlational dialogue presumes that the religions are truly diverse; without genuine diversity, dialogue becomes talking to oneself in the mirror. Participants will witness to what makes them distinct, trying to show and convince others of what they have learned in their own tradition. But at the same time they will be truly, courageously, open to the witness to truth that the other makes. This is a mutual back and forth, of speaking and listening, teaching and learning, witnessing and being witnessed to. (16)

It is our experience in this and other programs that this level of engagement with the other often creates a renewed curiosity about one's own religious tradition. For teenagers, it may send them back to their own traditions with a deeper level of questioning and appreciation.

Moreover, for many of the students, the diversity that they encounter in Face to Face/Faith to Faith is beyond anything they have known or imagined. To interact with a black person or a Muslim for the first time is mind-blowing. A Muslim from South Africa may be told before coming not to speak to "those Jews there." She then discovers that the prejudice of her friends and family is misguided and forms bonds that she had not previously imagined.

Beyond individual friendship, there is a new understanding about the interconnectedness of the global reality. Conflicts that students have heard about across the globe begin to take on flesh and blood form through the stories of other students. When home groups make their respective presentations of the situation back home and hear about that of others, they suddenly realize that theirs is not the only conflict. When students from the Middle East learn about post-Apartheid South Africa they begin to see that hope and reconciliation may be possible on a national level out of dire circumstances.

Research has shown that exposure to "otherness"—to a person who is different because of race, ethnicity, or other identity factors—is a key to moral development and to building compassion. Almost equally important is the experience of being "other," that is, being the one who is different from the rest. Face to Face/Faith to Faith offers both opportunities in abundance.

Safe Space: A Case Study

These underlying values shape the methodology of the program, which focuses on effective models of communications. During the intensive two-week summer component and through the yearly ongoing local meetings as well as through the Internet, we try to build a "holding environment," a space that provides enough security and nurture so that students can feel safe and be themselves. For some who come from conflict ridden areas, this is one of the first times they have experienced safety. At the same time, we make room for enough challenge and tension that the participants keep stretching beyond their comfort zones to take risks with each other. We do this in both overt and subtle ways—by verbally encouraging students to step outside of their comfort zones and by having the staff model this kind of courageous behavior with one another. The composition of the staff mirrors the diversity of religions, political ideologies, and ethnicities among the participants. They are required to attend a rigorous staff training prior to working with the participants that parallels the quality and depth of learning that the students will experience.

Students work in dyads and in various intentional groupings to share their own identities and to hear others engage various forms of communication styles which are taught within the first few days of the summer program. Based on Imago Therapy, micro-labs and compassionate or intentional listening theories (otherwise known as basic active listening skills) students begin to learn to "listen" to the other. We encourage students to enter into dialogue. We provide a safe space in which students may slow down the conversation and take the opportunity to tell their story without interruption and/or interpretation from the person designated to listen. The designated listener may only respond to clarify what they have heard and to imagine what the designated speaker must be feeling. Connecting on this level reveals empathy and creates a sense of safety to go deeper into dialogue. Students are not asked to agree with what they are hearing nor are they encouraged to reach resolution to disagreement.

One Transformative Example

Jad and Shmuel grew up within twenty minutes of each other and a world apart. Shmuel grew up in an Orthodox Jewish community in Jerusalem. Jad, a Muslim, comes from the West Bank town of Ramallah and East Jerusalem. Both have ties to the land that one calls Israel and the other Palestine. In the summer of 2002, both young men participated in Face to Face. Jad was extremely quiet and shy. Shmuel appeared to be happy go lucky, shying away from the political and religious tensions between him and the Arab and Muslim students. After learning the techniques of communication and a direct challenge from one of the other participants to take the program more seriously, Shmuel and Jad initiated a dialogue facilitated by a staff member. The two young men sat face to face, knees barely touching and each took turns telling their story. Jad began by telling how prior to the summer his family had to leave Ramallah and return to Jerusalem in order to retain their land and home within the boundaries of East Jerusalem. If they did not return, their home and land could be confiscated by the Israelis. This meant that Jad had to say good-bye to his friends, and, more important, to his extended family including his grandparents, aunts, uncles, and cousins. If he tried to venture back to Ramallah, he would face the humiliation of passing checkpoints and be subject to searches. He was made to feel less than human. He came to Face to Face as Israeli tanks sat in the center of Ramallah. He came scared and terrified that he might never see his family and friends again. He thought about joining the young men his age that rioted daily against the Israeli Occupation throwing stones at the soldiers who occupied his land.

Shmuel listened and reflected back the words that Jad spoke. He asked for clarification when he did not understand. When Jad finished his story and had nothing more to say, Shmuel summarized what he had heard without interpreting or asking questions. He had to empathize by trying to understand the feelings that Jad harbored. Shmuel imagined that Jad was feeling angry, sad, frightened, confused, vengeful, less than human.

Shmuel then told his story. In the spring of 2002, a bomb exploded inside a pizza parlor in central Jerusalem. It was a popular hangout for families and teenagers. Shmuel was not present—but three of his friends were. None survived. He refused to talk or share his feelings about this event with family and friends. He did not share this story with anyone until this moment sitting face to face with the "enemy." He told Jad that he could not wait to enter the army after high school and kill as many Palestinians as he could to avenge the death of his friends. When Shmuel finished his story Jad summarized what he had heard. He too had to imagine how Shmuel might be feeling. He guessed that Shmuel was feeling angry, hurt, sad, and vengeful.

The two young men sat face to face—knee to knee, barely touching and looked into each other's eyes. When the facilitator asked "what comes up for them" they replied that it was as if they saw themselves in the other.

Shmuel and Jad did not become fast friends. Following their conversation, they began to question everything they had been taught about the enemy—the other. They left the summer program confused and both confided that they knew their lives were about to change.

We received emails at the end of the summer from Shmuel's father and Jad's mother both thanking us for changing the course of their children's lives. Neither parent knew the other nor that the other had also sent an email.

During the year-long program, Jad and Shmuel began to spend time together. Their conversation deepened. They were leaders in the group. Both were selected to return to Face to Face in the summer of 2003 as Leaders in Training (LITs) representing the Israeli/Palestinian home group. Their confidence was evident from the moment they arrived. Both had grown and matured over the course of the year. Jad, while still quiet, encouraged shy participants to speak and share their feelings and thoughts. He engaged more with staff and volunteered regularly. Shmuel was more introspective and somber as he talked about entering the Israeli army in a matter of months. He mentored the new participants and spent time meeting participants from within his home group and from other countries. Jad and Shmuel engaged in conversation, laughter, and quiet understanding. They had become true friends. Towards the last days of the summer program, Shmuel and Jad approached us requesting a time to talk. As equal partners, they shared what they had learned over the course of the two years in the program. They were able to honestly assess their growth. Both agreed that they were ready and willing to take the next step in becoming religious and social activists within their communities. They stated that they now were the new generation to take their peers from lives of terror and fear into understanding and peaceful coexistence. They outlined the work they were committed to doing together as role models and asked for our guidance and blessing.

Looking Ahead

There are both programmatic and practical challenges associated with Face to Face/Faith to Faith. Because we had start-up funding that allowed us to move ahead quickly for a trial first year, we have grown rapidly. Creating a base of funding sources is an ongoing process. Part of this involves growing the structure of governance to sustain this growth. The program reports ultimately to the Auburn Seminary Board, but receives ongoing oversight from an advisory board and an active fundraising committee of volunteers, representative of the religious traditions in the program. We are experimenting with ways to have the funders "touch" the program so that they are learning and engaged in appropriate ways as the partners who provide the support to make the program a reality. This program is also labor- and resource-intensive and focuses on fifty students at a time, although previous participants often remain involved beyond the initial year of commitment as leaders in training or graduates who may become counselors. Some funders have expressed concern that we are not reaching enough people at one time. Our challenge is to convince them of what we believe—that you change the world one person at a time.

In addition to the ongoing challenge of funding are programmatic concerns. One area involves how best to expose students to the religious content of the program. Some students have been conditioned by the educational experiences in their own communities to think that religion is boring or irrelevant. It is our challenge to find ways to engage and excite students, to strike a balance between information offered and the rich experiences and knowledge that they bring with them to the table. It has also been a challenge to find the best religious educators and professionals as leadership for the program. We have been variously successful in finding leaders who have experience with and appreciation for multifaith work, individuals who are rooted in their own tradition and can share their knowledge and experience in an engaging way with teenagers.

A second programmatic challenge is to build stronger and vigorous relationships with our partner organizations in other countries. Ideally it is important to make regularly scheduled visits to all countries represented. This ensures program continuity and builds relationships between home group organizations and the American organizers as well as making contacts with potential funders from these countries. Much of the ongoing interaction happens through email and occasional phone calls. It will take time, money, and focused efforts to find the right partners and to build trust. A related matter involves strengthening the year-long component of the program through more consistent and direct contact with Face to Face/Faith to Faith staff and supervision of the onsite activities. The Internet curriculum will be launched this year for the first time; it will take some experience with it and feedback from participants to assess its effectiveness.

There are many ways that the program could grow. Many of the parents of participants are curious about the experiences that their children are having because they see and report back to us about how their children have been changed. They see teenagers who will listen, who seem more mature, and who are more engaged as leaders in their religious settings and communities. Many of these parents want their own program. As one mother said: "I'm on a journey too!" Face to Face/Faith to Faith would like to explore the possibility of working with a group of parents. In this way, we will begin to expand the systemic change that we intend, affecting individuals, families, communities and, through these, the broader society.

24.

Ask Pastor Paul: Online Interfaith Pastoral Work with Youth

Paul Raushenbush

"I CAN'T BELIEVE I'M ASKING YOU THIS," read a recent email signed "Angsty Jewish Girl" sent to my advice column on Beliefnet.com. The writer was a young aspiring Rabbi who was struggling with addiction. She was surprised to be availing herself of pastoral advice outside of her own tradition, and yet her situation was so desperate and immediate that she pragmatically reached for a resource and support that was close at hand.

People outside of our own tradition asking us for advice is just one example of the relatively new kind of pastoral challenges and opportunities that are arising for all of us who find ourselves working or participating in interfaith or multi-faith settings. These settings include the military, crisis locations like the wreckage after the 9/11 tragedy, hospitals, universities, public and private high schools, or our day-to-day interactions in America's multi-faith society. While still recognizing the importance of the macro-political and sociological aspects of interfaith work, interfaith pastoral work functions at the micro, immediate level of person-to-person relationships within the multi-faith world. Ministry in the interfaith setting invites the interfaith ideals of mutual respect and co-existence into the spiritual and emotional lives of the individual.

I am using the term "pastoral" to denote spiritual and religious guidance. I do not mean to limit this role to clergy or religious leaders nor to any one religious tradition. Anyone who is in a community that is either intentionally or by coincidence interfaith should consider developing strategies that combine principles from all involved religious traditions. Interfaith cooperation, with pastoral concern for the individual's emotional and spiritual health, must be emphasized.

The case studies used in this article come from my experience working since June 2000 as an advice columnist at Beliefnet.com. My column is largely read by people aged thirteen to twenty-five. Five months earlier, I had taken a new position as the music producer at Beliefnet. As a multi-faith site dedicated to covering religion and spirituality in the broadest terms, Beliefnet aimed to be the ESPN of religion. Beliefnet has since become the most successful and widely viewed religious site on the web with over six million unique visitors a month. During my time as music producer, we interviewed Bono, Moby, Ja Rule, Mickey Hart of the Grateful Dead, Mos Def, Chuck D and many others about their spiritual and religious beliefs. We also covered religious music from many different traditions.

In June of 2000, I approached the editor-in-chief about starting a multi-faith advice column for teens and young adults called "Ask Pastor Paul." The idea behind a multi-faith advice column is to answer questions that young people are facing about the reality of living in a multi-faith world that remain unanswered within their own communities or circumstances. The connectivity of the web across geographical and communal lines makes the internet a valuable tool for interfaith dialogue and, in this case, multi-faith advice. Young people are able to be completely anonymous while seeking wisdom from what they perceive as a separate, neutral and accessible force. For a surprising amount of young people—Pastor Paul has received thousands of e-mails—Ask Pastor Paul has become a sounding board not only for questions they might have about other faiths and their relations to them, but also for their deepest questions about their own faith and existence.

Simultaneous with my work as producer and advice columnist at Beliefnet.com, I took a position as the Presbyterian chaplain at Columbia University in New York. My rationale was that I wanted to keep it real with live, interactive students. While I was hired to represent the Presbyterian denomination, none of my students were interested in the particularities of Calvinist thought. My events tended to attract students from a variety of backgrounds: Christians, of course, but also Jews, Buddhists, and agnostics. Again, I found myself in a pastoral relationship with people from a variety of backgrounds and many traditions that were not my own.

Working in two very different settings where I had pastoral interactions with individuals of many faiths allowed me to develop some general guidelines for addressing religious and/or spiritual questions in a multi-faith context. Using real questions that I received through Ask Pastor Paul as case studies, I want to illustrate five situations in which a pastoral response was specific to the multi-faith setting. This is by no means an exhaustive list, but I hope that the guidelines I have adopted can provide a springboard for further discussions around pastoral care as we move forward with our interfaith work.

My location in the virtual setting of Beliefnet on Ask Pastor Paul is as a liberal, Protestant male who is answering questions from around the world, but mostly from the United States. The questions are submitted to an explicitly multi-faith advice column. Probably 75 percent of the questions come from Christians hoping to deal with an emotional crisis, to understand their own faith better, or looking to better negotiate the multi-faith world. The rest come from young people of other faiths who are, again, dealing with an emotional or situational crisis, seeking to understand an interfaith question, or asking for guidance within their own faith. Each pastoral setting can be an opportunity for us to recognize our religious and sociological location in relation to those with whom we are in pastoral relation, and to keep those influences in mind as we provide pastoral care.

Case Study 1

The first case study addresses interfaith suspicion or misinformation held by members of our own faiths.

Question:

Dear Pastor Paul,

I'm a sophomore in high school who was very strong in Christian beliefs until about a year ago. I met a very wonderful Muslim guy who is now my best friend. Since meeting him, I've been more confused than ever. I don't feel connected to God anymore, I don't feel His love, and I certainly don't feel a need for Him in my life. I've been questioning everything—from the importance of my religion to the reality of it. Any suggestions?

—Christine

Answer:

Christine,

Frankly, I don't see the connection between meeting your wonderful Muslim guy and not feeling connected to God.

Many people go through a period of questioning and disconnection from their faith during adolescence. That may be what is going on for you right now. Are you still praying? Are you still going to church? It is important for you to have a supportive Christian community to help you through this difficult period.

Instead of blaming your Muslim friend for losing your faith—use him as a resource. Most Muslims have a very strong faith in God (Allah), and Islam locates its roots in the Patriarch Abraham, as do Jews and Christians. God does love you, and while you may not feel connected to God right now, God feels connected to you.

Hopefully, you and your best friend can both grow in each of your faiths as you grow older.

Analysis:

Within almost every tradition there exists dogma of being (if not the only) the best way to God or Enlightenment. By default, other traditions become dangerous competition that might potentially lead us away from the way prescribed by our own faith.

Multi-faith pastoral leadership has to be clear in teaching a shift from a model of competition between faiths to one of cooperative co-existence. It requires proclaiming within our own communities an approach to the world that acknowledges the legitimacy and contributions of faiths other than our own, even when this is not accepted as part of traditional dogma. We have to teach that being exposed to another person's faith is an opportunity for learning and not an essential challenge to the truth of our own religious claims.

Those of us who are brave enough to take this stance should not tolerate the accusations that this is an attempt at melding traditions together by proclaiming that we are all basically saying the same thing—in fact, we are doing just the opposite. Multi-faith pastoral leadership acknowledges difference and embraces it. Each of us should be well grounded and essentially committed to our own traditions such that we may recognize the positive in other traditions while maintaining our pastoral legitimacy in the eyes of people within our own religion.

In the case above, I begin by severing her implied connection between her exposure to another religion and her loss of faith. I then maintain my pastoral role by focusing her back to her own Christian spiritual discipline. Later in the letter, my sympathy and basic knowledge of Islam gives me the authority to introduce her to basic tenets of Islam and encourage her and her friend to grow together in co-existence within their own faiths.

Guidelines for my interfaith ministry within this case study:

1) Teach the benefits of a non-competitive, cooperative model of multi-faith co-existence.

2) Maintain a solid grounding and essential commitment to my own religious tradition so that my authority to offer guidance within my tradition is legitimate.

3) Publicly recognize the positives of other religious traditions while eschewing easy collapsing of religious traditions into one spiritual melting pot.

4) Publicly refute any attempts to demonize other religious traditions.

Case Study 2

The second case study addresses the reality of conversion—both to and from our respective religions.

As a preface I want to tell a compelling story by Lauren Winner, a doctoral student who worked with me as the books editor at Beliefnet and who recently had a popular book called *Girl Meets God*. She told me the story of a conversion experience she had from Orthodox Judaism to Christianity. She went to one of the Christian chaplains at Columbia to talk about her experience that was very real for her, only to be told that she was wrong and should go back to Judaism. Of course, the Christian chaplain was interested in interfaith work, and wanted to be respectful of his Jewish colleagues at the college, and I am sure was terrified of appearing to be evangelically "stealing" a student. But he also did not allow for the fact that people can and will change religions and we should be prepared for the pastoral challenges that come with conversion.

Question:

Dear Pastor Paul,

I'm a college freshman who has very strong feelings about converting to Judaism. But my parents are deeply Christian. They get mad when I attend synagogue or do anything connected to Judaism, even if it's for a class. My dad tends to be a bigot, he once used an anti-Semitic slur to my face! What should I do? How should I handle the holiday season? I've been given a choice—celebrate Christmas or leave the family. There's also a "no-dreidels-or-menorahs-in-the-house" rule.

—Amanda

Answer:

Dear Amanda,

It's unfortunate that your family's hostility seems to be forcing you to determine so quickly whether the Jewish tradition is right for you.

Your family sounds like it is verging on spiritual and emotional abuse. Remember you have done nothing to deserve it. It may be that all you can do right now is tell your parents how it hurts you and then walk away. In their own way, your parents are truly worried about you. They sound like the kind of Christians that believe non-Christians are going to hell. It's not an excuse, but it may help you to understand them better during this time.

Unfortunately, until you're paying the bills, you have very little say about the rules of the house. Remember, religious observances take place in the heart. You can observe Hanukkah in a very real and meaningful way without bringing dreidels or menorahs into the house. You can honor your mother and father (however hard that might be right now) by going with them to a Christmas service and appreciating it for its own sake—even if it doesn't represent your faith any more. My Jewish cousins have come to Christmas services with me and I have gone to Yom Kippur services with them because we love and honor each other, and our respective traditions.

Make sure that you take the time to hear where God is calling you, and in which faith you best understand God's will for your life. If, after a careful discernment process with the guidance of a rabbi, you feel that you want to convert to Judaism, then God's blessings upon you.

Analysis:

As leaders of particular religious traditions, many of us are actually paid to encourage people to follow the path that we are proclaiming. This is not merely a financial transaction but a calling to promote the Spiritual Good Life as our tradition has laid it out. So conversion is difficult for us to handle with objectivity. Yet it is a fact of life that because of transcendent will, intellectual pursuits, and/or any number of life's influences, people do become interested in, and desire to join, traditions other than the one they were born into. As people working in the interfaith setting, we should seek ways of handling such mobility forthrightly and with grace.

Building upon the non-competitive model above, interfaith pastoral leadership allows for fluidity of the spirit while not abdicating responsibility to ask questions and encourage self-examination within the individual. In other words, we can be flexible without being flimsy.

In the case study above, I wanted to show my immediate support for the young woman's exploration in contrast to her family's condemnation. I then gave her advice as to how she might live within the restrictions of her household, while still maintaining her spiritual integrity. This foundation of trust allows for me to advise in harder areas. I raised the question about motivation for conversion. I encouraged her to continue to seriously explore what it means to be Jewish using the spiritual tools at her disposal and to recommend she begin conversations with a Rabbi who can further guide her.

Guidelines for my interfaith ministry within this case study:

1) Acknowledge that free will conversion is a basic tenet of freedom of religion and a legitimate occurrence.

2) Protect the individual from emotional, spiritual or physical harm as a consequence of his or her religious conversion.

3) Provide a framework for deep religious reflection upon the meaning of the conversion to avoid trendy, or impulsive conversions that do not come from the Spirit (my term).

4) Get to know leaders from other traditions who will work with me in a thoughtful, cooperative way to help in the transition.

Case Study 3

Our third case study addresses the necessity of being equipped to respond to questions from people who practice religions other than our own.

Question:

Dear Pastor Paul,

I was born in Vietnam and like many South Asian families, we are Buddhist. My parents are devout and strongly encourage me to follow that path. I don't really want to because I strongly disagree with the strong emphasis that Buddhism places on family values rather than individualism. Is that true? What is the basis for which Buddhist values are built upon?

—Confused in North Carolina

Answer:

Dear Confused,

It sounds like you want to practice the same religion as your parents—but on your own terms. You feel that your parents' Buddhism stifles your individuality and they use it to support their strong belief in obedience to the family. This doesn't make them bad Buddhists or bad parents, it's simply the tradition that they know and practice. However, it may not be right for you.

Oftentimes, people look for truths in other religions when their truth may be found in their own religion. It's great to hear you asking deeper questions about Buddhism. I spoke with Mary Talbot, our Buddhism editor here at Beliefnet about your dilemma. She pointed out that while the Buddha did teach that everyone owes a great debt to their parents, his teachings almost entirely focused on the individual and his or her own path to awakening. The emphasis that your parents place on family responsibility is probably due more to their Asian heritage than to actual Buddhist teachings. Buddhism teaches that each of us has sole responsibility for cultivating our own mindfulness, wisdom and compassion.

While it's important to respect the tradition your parents practice, I hope you'll continue to explore Buddhism on your own terms. Check out some writings of contemporary Buddhist teachers such as the Vietnamese monk Thich Nhat Hanh, or visit a temple or practice center of your choosing. Remember, traditions are only as alive as each new generation makes them.

Analysis:

There will be times when the mantle of religion that we wear, whether as ordained clergy, interfaith workers, or merely open-minded friends, will invite people of traditions other than our own to ask us questions about their own faith dilemmas. Many of the situations will not require much knowledge of the religion, such as was the case with Angsty Jewish Girl who needed encouragement to deal with her addiction problem. However, others are looking for more specific assistance with their religious questioning and spiritual crises.

As people working in an interfaith setting, we view these moments as opportunities to help individuals grow within their own traditions, not as openings for conversion, except when that is explicitly requested. We have to trust each other to respect the integrity of one another's religions and maintain the aforementioned non-competitive, cooperative model.

Each of us should begin to take seriously the obligation to learn the basic tenets of other religions and cultures so that we have a framework for understanding the thought process behind some of the religious questions that will arise.

Even more important, we can serve each other in the multi-faith context by seeking each other out to provide religious authority and knowledge that we do not have. We should be prepared to ask for wisdom from a religious leader of the relevant faith when interacting pastorally with people not of our own tradition.

In the example above, the young person was chaffing against the culture of his parents and questioning his religion in the process. By first showing my approval of his search for meaning within his religion, I attempted to belay any suspicion of a conversion agenda that would have been inappropriate. I next tried to help his relationship with his parents by giving the young person an insight into their religious and cultural tradition. Finally, I turned to a religious figure in his own tradition that could potentially open doors of thought that he may choose to pass through if he truly desires to further explore his religious tradition.

Guidelines for my interfaith ministry within this case study:

1) Avoid viewing religious questioning by an individual of a faith other than my own as an invitation for conversion unless explicitly requested.

2) Learn basic tenets of religions other than my own so that I have a beginning knowledge for ways to help persons of other faiths to process questions in a familiar way.

3) Do not overstep my authority or knowledge in a religion other than my own. Consult and connect individuals of other faiths with appropriate leaders whom I trust from that tradition.

Case Study 4

Our fourth case study addresses dating and intimate relationships between people of different religions.

Question:

Dear Pastor Paul,

My boyfriend recently broke up with me because, he said, God told him he had to. My boyfriend told me he loves me too much, and it's sinful because his mind is always on me, instead of God. Also, it's against the First Commandment, because his love makes me his idol. He said he isn't ready for marriage, and that the right time to date is when a person is ready.

I'm not Christian; I grew up learning Buddhist ideas. It baffles me that he could make such a decision. Can you help me understand where he is coming from?

—Idolized

Answer:

Dear Idolized,

The First Commandment requires that we love the Lord with all our heart. If your former boyfriend was so obsessed with you that he forgot to love God, then he's right: he's not mature enough to be dating. A real boyfriend is capable of loving you, his family, his friends, his neighbor and God all at the same time. Love doesn't have to have limits. I suggest you practice the Buddhist principle of non-attachment and try to be compassionate toward him while letting him go.

By the way, when people tell you they are doing something unpleasant because God told them to do it—watch out.

Analysis:

Interfaith dating often becomes a pastoral issue in our multi-faith world and is a consistent question from readers of my column at Beliefnet. Interfaith dating combines the already potentially volatile relationship dynamic, with an added element of religious difference with its conceptual and familial implication.

We may be called upon to be the translators of traditions for one or both of the couple. If one of the individuals or families is raising up an objection based on religion, we should try to help both parties understand what the reasons behind such restrictions are, and how they are usually enforced.

We should try not to undermine one another's religious traditions and their teachings on dating and marriage outside of their faith. Instead, we should give the power of knowledge that will hopefully lead to compassion for the individuals as well as for the traditions from which they come.

In the case above, a woman was asking my help to translate the unfamiliar faith of her former boyfriend (who happens to be of my faith), to help her understand the rationale for the breakup. I tried to help her understand some of the theological basis for his argument. Although I try to maintain a level of professional objectivity, I couldn't resist giving my own opinion about how he had used that theology. I ended by drawing from her own tradition to help her let go of this fellow.

Guidelines for my interfaith ministry within this case study:

1) Learn and respect interfaith guidelines and restrictions within the various religious traditions.

2) Help to translate these guidelines to the interfaith couple involved with compassion.

3) Do not under-emphasize the difficulties of interfaith relationships.

4) If your religion permits, maintain an engaged pastoral relationship with the couple if they decide to work through the differences.

Case Study 5

The fifth case study addresses the sad fact that those of us engaged in interfaith work will come under attack from people within our own tradition.

Question:

Have you ever read the book The devine revelation of HELL? Read it. Very GOod. Just a little advice Pastor to pastor. The worstest Sin of All is doing evil and Aproving and leading other in doing evil. I don't want you togive me, the Red road theory, it's just a theory. Every person you lead to hell, their blood will be on your hands. I recomend that you get a new job or at least change you TItle. Because a Pastor is a CHristian teacher and spritual leader. You are going to hell.

Analysis:

I chose not to answer this letter or any of the other hate letters that I get. The letters are always from fundamentalist people from my own faith who feel that responding to any question without proclaiming the exclusive saving truth of Christianity is heresy or worse.

I believe that triumphal, exclusivist fundamentalism in any religion is the number one obstruction to interfaith work. While some people are gifted at debating people like the one who wrote the letter above, I know that I am not. For my own sanity and in hopes of maintaining a position of love, it is better for me to create a distance between us. I am better off sidestepping them and interacting with people who might be open to understanding that if we are to survive in this world, interfaith understanding and respect must prevail. I recommend to people of my own faith that if they can't feel the value and beauty of interfaith work in their soul, then they should think about it pragmatically for the benefit of the survival of the world.

Guidelines for my interfaith ministry within this case study:

1) Recognize that there will be severe resistance to interfaith work from fundamentalist elements within religion.

2) Find personal strength to withstand attacks.

3) Recruit sympathetic, capable liaisons to fundamentalists.

4) Teach that interfaith co-existence is the only way that we will survive as a human race.

Conclusion

My personal witness to ministering online to teenagers and young adults comes from being born into an interfaith extended family. My grandmother was Elizabeth Brandeis, the daughter of the Supreme Court Justice Louis Brandeis. My grandfather was Paul Raushenbush, son of Baptist minister Walter Rauschenbusch. They married and raised my father Unitarian. My mother is from a Swiss family and we were raised Presbyterian. My closest cousins are Jewish. It never occurred to me that either they or I were "more right" in our religion. You want to know why? Because nobody ever taught me that I was more right than they were. My parents and the religious leaders I had growing up were already employing interfaith pastoral strategies that promoted cooperation and co-existence. It is up to me to continue their work, in both real-time and cyber spaces.

Conclusion

Talking God, Sizing up Adversaries and Considering Next Steps

Eboo Patel

TOWARDS THE END OF THE FIRST National Conference on Interfaith Youth Work in 2002, Jacob Ighile, an undergraduate student at Connecticut College and a summer intern at the Interfaith Youth Core, made the following observation: "You people don't talk much about God."

The roomful of (mostly) devoutly religious people—several ordained leaders within religious communities, others active lay members in congregations—stopped in their tracks to reflect on the startling truth of Jacob's statement. Many important topics were raised during our three days together—the significance of women's leadership in what had long been the traditionally male domain of religious leadership, the effectiveness of the arts in engaging religiously diverse youth, the challenge of working around too-busy student schedules. But we had largely bypassed discussions about God.

Three questions emerge: 1) Why was God not discussed? 2) Is it important to talk about God in interfaith youth work? 3) Are there other topics that we should be considering as we build the interfaith youth movement?

The first question can only be answered by speculations. We surmise that God was not a central topic of discussion at that conference, and is, frankly, rarely talked about in interfaith youth work circles, because most of us privately decided that the dangers of opening a discussion about God outweighed the benefits.

There are certainly potential upsides to talking about God. One is the power of sharing with people from diverse religious backgrounds how God inspires us to do interfaith youth work. Another potential benefit is a mutually enriching conversation about the nature of God.

The possible dangers are deep. One is offering an idea of God that offends someone from another religion, or worse, one's own faith community. Worse still is the prospect of offering an idea of God that others find silly or naïve. Another danger, particularly in the realm of interfaith youth work, is opening a discussion that many people feel does not belong in the "public square" of interfaith programs but rather in the private space of religious communities and households.

The result was an unstated compromise—whatever idea of God, if any at all, brings you to interfaith youth work is fine by me, let's just get on with building the movement together. Until Jacob wondered aloud about the significance of the unsaid, most people seemed content with the status quo.

But once the issue was on the table, another question had to be faced: Is it important to talk about God in interfaith youth work? In private discussions with some of our colleagues in the movement, it is clear that many feel called to this work by a conviction that God wants a world of diversity and harmony. By not making such discussions public, are we robbing the movement of the opportunity of feeling the power of a collective calling?

The shadow side of that issue is the possibility of excluding those whose faith commitment turns in a different direction. People who, for example, believe that God wants the whole world to be Muslim or Christian or Bah'ai, but, given the slim chance of that reality, are committed to working for positive relations between religiously diverse communities on Earth, while still believing that only one of those groups is bound for a better life after death.

Others have pointed out that those opposed to bringing religiously diverse people together are well organized and rarely shy about proclaiming their belief that God sides with their ilk alone—others may convert or be condemned. A response that points to the importance of a diverse civil society seems positively anemic next to thunderous statements that claim to reveal the mind of God.

Facing one issue we now recognize as overlooked begs the question: What other topics should we be considering as we build the interfaith youth movement? Not surprisingly, there are many.

How should interfaith youth work engage the issue of sexual orientation, especially considering that it is polarizing religious communities? To be more specific, consider the following scenario: A member of a high school interfaith youth council confides in a meeting that he is gay. Another council member shares this information with her parents, who not only make her drop out of the interfaith youth council, but call the parents of the other members saying that the council is promoting a way of being that is against their religion.

How should interfaith youth projects engage politics? Especially in contemporary American life, religious communities are embroiled in politics, of electoral, community, racial and other varieties. Most of the leaders in the interfaith youth movement are politically progressive. Does this discourage conservatives from becoming involved? In an attempt to include all groups, should interfaith youth leaders keep their political beliefs hidden and run "apolitical" interfaith projects?

Should interfaith youth projects be a space for young Muslims and Jews to discuss the Middle East, or Hindus and Buddhists to discuss Sri Lanka? Or are such discussions too hot for us to handle and therefore best avoided? If the leader of the interfaith youth project has an opinion on these issues, should s/he offer it? Would this be viewed as siding with one group over another, and perhaps discourage the sided-against group from further involvement in interfaith youth work?

We are deliberately not offering answers to these issues. What we are doing is suggesting that such issues not only need to be considered by each of us privately, but should be given proper attention in formal spaces of our movement—at conferences and in journals, for example. Just like any other movement, interfaith youth work should be mulling the big ideas of our field as we do the practical work of it. And ideally, the thinking and the doing are in conversation with each other—improving the quality of both.

One observation, accompanied by a soft opinion, seems worth making. The two dozen projects represented in this collection offer a rich and diverse array of approaches to these questions, and others. Some projects, like Face to Face, deal with the thorniest political issues in the most direct ways. Others, like the Interfaith Youth Core's Chicago Action Program, deliberately stay away from such issues. Some projects, like Ask Pastor Paul, offer direct spiritual advice to young people with questions. Others, like the IARF's Religious Youth Project in Gujarat, keep the focus on the common endeavor of a service project.

There are different ways of doing this thing called interfaith youth work. We are a movement with multiple personalities. While we encourage vigorous conversation about effective practices and dangerous paths in interfaith youth work, we are against attempting a "one size fits all approach."

Multiple though our personalities may be, people in the interfaith youth work movement share a fundamental idea—religiously diverse young people should interact in ways that are characterized by better understanding. It is an idea that many communities do not share. Some communities are against their young being in contact with people who are from different religious backgrounds. Other communities are interested in understanding only when it is a step to converting others to their way.

Their interest in understanding sometimes extends to learning about other faith communities because it helps hone their language of proselytization.

Certain communities have made their opposition to the larger interfaith movement very clear. For example, both Christian and Muslim groups protested the Parliament of the World's Religions in Cape Town in 1999. As the interfaith youth movement grows in size and influence, it is likely that we will see resistance—mostly coming from religious quarters—directed against us as well.

Should we consider the people who offer resistance our enemies? How should we respond to their opposition?

Some movements grow by drawing clear lines in the sand and saying "we on this side are against you on that side." We think there is a different way of thinking about, and growing, the interfaith youth movement. It is best articulated in a poem by Edwin Markham:

> You called me an enemy
> A thing to flout
> You drew a circle that drew me out
> But love and I had the will to win
> You drew a circle that drew me in

There are grades of opposition, ranging from "leaning against" to "suspicious of" to "intent on destroying." Instead of facing off against all opposition, why not seek to understand where people are coming from and see if common ground can be established? Is it not natural for people to have questions, particularly when the issue at stake is the religious identity of their children or a matter of one's obligation to God? The more we talked with people suspicious of interfaith work, the more we realized their concerns are often understandable and can sometimes be allayed by establishing personal trust and offering explanations about the nature of the interfaith project.

Moreover, there is much to be learned from communities that offer respectful resistance to our work. What are we doing that makes them suspicious? If we changed the tenor of our outreach, or slightly altered the shape of our program, would they be more likely to be involved?

A second point is worth making. If the constituent parts of the interfaith youth work movement are religious young people and their communities, then we need to be in conversation with a broad range of those communities. It sounds obvious to say that interfaith youth projects should seek to engage a wide range of communities, but it is striking how often we find ourselves talking only to groups who share our general interpretive frameworks. There are wonderful examples in this book of how skilled leaders of interfaith youth projects involved communities who were initially suspicious. Annapurna Astley, in her article on Spirit into Action, emphasizes the importance of participating in the activities of faith communities as a way of showing genuine interest in their religious life, and then extending a personal invitation to be involved in an interfaith program.

So what about the groups who still, even after the interfaith project leader has seemingly exhausted creative approaches to involving them, continue to be opposed to our work. These groups come in different shades as well, ranging from "please don't bother us" to "we feel required to respectfully protest your work" to "we will do what we can to destroy you." The first two types are a protected and important part of a free society. We might wish they were acting differently, but we support their right to believe, behave, and belong on this Earth as they feel called to.

The third type, we believe, the interfaith youth movement is indeed opposed to. The third type are the enemies of not only the interfaith youth movement, but of every community other than their own (and because so many exhibit self-destructive tendencies, oftentimes they are in a perverse way hurting their own as well) and of the very fabric of the modern world. If groups like this did not exist, interfaith youth work would be a nice luxury. Because they do exist, and are so effective at involving young people in their anti-modern violence, interfaith youth work is an absolute necessity. Part of our job is to combat religious totalitarianism of every stripe and say that it is wrong for religious young people to kill each other and it is possible for us to relate in ways characterized by understanding and cooperation.

So where do we go from here? What are the next steps we should be taking as a movement? Some things seem obvious. We need more interfaith youth work projects. Every campus, neighborhood, and hometown in America with religiously diverse populations should be bringing its Christians, Muslims, Jews, and others together in positive ways. We need people in positions of power paying attention to interfaith youth work. We need professors and journalists to write about us, religious leaders to encourage their youth to get involved, foundation leaders and philanthropists to help resource our activities and political leaders to express support.

We also need to be doing the behind-the-scenes work of building a movement. This means creating the financial, intellectual, and human resources for the long term. We need to remain in touch with the high school students from our interfaith camps and youth councils, and encourage them to connect with or create interfaith projects on their college campuses. We need to be offering internships and other leadership opportunities to college students involved in interfaith work, and then helping them get jobs in related fields when they graduate. We need to be evaluating our work and constantly improving it.

Financial issues need to be front and center. Right now, the projects in our movement are largely funded out of pocket, or by a few friends, or at best, with short-term grants. We need to build a solid resource base for interfaith youth work if we want it to grow into a powerful and sustainable force. This means advocating to foundations for grants for the field, not just for a particular organization or project. It means thinking in terms of endowments and establishing partnerships with major institutions, such as universities.

And we need to be documenting, discussing and reflecting upon what we do. Other practitioner fields—social work, community development, medicine—have a strong academic dimension, and ours needs one as well. That, of course, is the reason we published, and you are reading, this book.

Finally, we need to think about the spread of this movement. Most of the people and projects in this book are North American. There are powerful religious movements and interfaith projects in Asia, Africa, Latin America and Europe. How and when should we connect with them? How should we deal with the very real challenges that inevitably characterize relationships between North American projects and our colleagues in the rest of the world—differences in power, suspicion of the South about the motives of the North, cultural differences regarding everything from leadership styles to gender relations?

Clearly, we face a long and winding road. But there are two things we do not doubt. One, the horizon is worth it. There are simply too many young people from different religions killing one another for us to ignore religious identity. And movements ranging from Civil Rights in the United States to Hind Swaraj in the Subcontinent to the Struggle in South Africa prove how powerful religiously diverse young people can be when they work together for the common good.

And we are not alone; this book proves it. There are dozens of people who have felt a personal call to bring religiously diverse young people together in positive ways, and answered that call by creating a project. And the young people came. From Puerto Rican Pentecostals in the South Bronx to Hindu graduate students at Harvard, from Muslims in the Midwest to Jews in the Holy Land, it is clear that religious young people want to be part of something that brings people together.

We will need all of them and more. And together, we will need to dream, act, reflect and connect in ways even beyond what we thought we were capable of. For our movement has as its hope nothing less than to build a new world.

Epilogue

THIS BOOK GIVES ME GREAT HOPE. For it shows that religious pluralists are waking up to the most precious resource we humans have, our young people, and beginning to invest in them.

In November 2004, I helped organize a retreat called Muslim Leaders of Tomorrow. My organization, the Cordoba Initiative, brought together over 100 young American Muslims with demonstrated leadership potential from across ethnic and intra-Islamic sectarian communities to discuss the role that this new generation could play in building a peaceful and pluralist world. I was amazed; but more important, they amazed themselves. They discovered others of equal talent and shared vision: other Muslims committed to their Muslim faith and to creating a pluralist society, and finding in Islam the resources to live as contributing citizens in America. I have seen that same talent, vision and desire amongst young Jews, Christians, Hindus, Buddhists, and members of other faith communities. The interfaith youth movement has taken as its objective uniting these religiously diverse youth in the most profound goal of all—love of God through commitment to their particular tradition, and love of neighbor as oneself.

The blueprint for a truly interfaith society is being created in the local projects highlighted in this book. America could learn a good deal from Wellesley College's Multifaith Council, the E Pluribus Unum summer camp, the efforts of the students at the University of Illinois and many of the other initiatives profiled here. Without a doubt you will be hearing much more from the interfaith youth movement in the future.

God acts through us; and Satan acts through us. Heroes are nurtured in godly and loving programs; killers shaped through hateful and demonic ones. We know for sure that the next Mother Theresa, Mahatma Gandhi, or Badshah Khan exists somewhere. That person right now may be a student in Jane Rechtman's high school World Religions class, a researcher in Harvard University's Pluralism Project or a participant in the programs of the Interfaith Youth Core.

—*Imam Feisal Abdul Rauf*

Index

A

AAR, 149, 153
Acceptance Model, 46, 48
Action Program, 259
AIDS Education Training International, 213
AIDSETI, 213, 217
Amnesty International, 55, 57, 63
Anti-Bias Project, 48
anti-Semitism, 137, 138
Appreciative Inquiry, 78–81
Auburn Theological Seminary, 233

B

Barth, Karl, 45
Beliefnet, 12, 245–247, 249, 251, 253
Bellah, Robert, 18, 20, 23, 173, 180
Berger, Peter, 16, 17, 23
Bonhoeffer, Dietrich, 234
Boston Theological Institute, 56, 60
Building Bridges for Peace, 235

C

Campbell, Joseph, 137, 139
Cantwell Smith, Wilfred, 2, 171, 172
Catholic Worker movement, 22
Chicago Action Program, 178, 179, 259
Chicago Divinity School, 5, 6
Chicago Interfaith Service House, 225
City Year, 170
Common Ground, 91, 126, 127
Cordoba Initiative, 263
Council for a Parliament of the World's Religions, 209, 226, 228, 232

Council for Spiritual and Ethical Education, 137, 139, 145, 149, 150, 154
Covenant groups, 35, 39, 40

D

Day, Dorothy, 22, 169
Diversity Digest, 117

E

E Pluribus Unum (EPU), 7, 11, 25–41, 219–226, 263
Eck, Diana, 2, 3, 6, 9, 13, 16, 18, 23, 91, 93, 96, 112, 124, 137, 144, 145, 172, 180, 186
Education in Palestinian/Israeli Coexistence, 126
Encountering God, 112, 124

F

Face to Face/Faith to Faith, 11, 233–244
Ford Foundation, 6
Forum on Religion and Ecology, 149, 150, 153

G

Ghetto Film School, 11, 199, 200, 201, 202, 203, 205, 207
Giddens, Anthony, 17, 23, 171, 180
Global Assembly, 79, 81
Global Crossroads, 129
Global Youth Cooperation Circle, 81
glocal, 2, 52, 56, 58
Griffiths, Paul, 46, 47, 48, 50
Gujarat Young Adult Project, 65–67, 69, 71, 73, 74

H

Harvard University, 6, 8, 9, 12, 51–63, 91, 93, 95, 137, 144, 149, 166, 186, 262, 263

Harvard Divinity School, 52, 53, 59, 98, 101

Heim, S. Mark, 46, 47

Hick, John, 46

I

Interfaith Center, 10, 12, 156–159, 163, 165–167, 170

Interfaith Collaboration of Emerging Leaders, 48

InterFaith Conference of Metropolitan Washington, 185–191

Interfaith in Action, 128, 129

Interfaith Service House, 11, 12, 225, 226, 229–232

Interfaith Youth Core, 4–6, 10, 12, 15, 23, 127, 128, 169–179, 209–212, 239, 257, 259, 263

Interfaith Youth Leadership Council, 181–184

Interfaith Youth Program, 208–216

Interfaith Youth Service, 127, 176–179

Interfaith Youth Work, 51, 58, 61, 257–262

International Association for Religious Freedom, 8

International Youth Committee, 51, 52, 54, 56, 61, 62

Interreligious Coordinating Council of Israel, 238

Interreligious Solidarity, 25, 35, 40

J

Jesuit Volunteer Corps, 182

K

Kashi Ashram, 209, 211, 212, 214, 216

King, Jr., Martin Luther, 1, 2, 13, 18, 169, 172, 187

Knitter, Paul F., 44–47, 50, 240

L

Leaders in Training, 243

Lindbeck, George, 46, 47, 50

Loder, James, 30, 31, 41

M

Marty, Martin, 18, 23, 155, 166

Measure of Intellectual Development, 26–30, 40

N

National Coalition Building Institute, 187, 188

National Conference for Community and Justice, 48, 50

National Conference of Christians and Jews, 48, 50, 101, 105, 107–108

National Conference on Interfaith Youth Work, 6, 257

Next Generation, 8, 83–89, 209, 211, 236

O

Oxfam, 55, 59

P

Parliament of the World's Religions, 4, 8, 11, 12, 83–89, 170, 175, 226, 228, 232, 260

Pastoral Work, 7

Perry, William, 27–31, 41

Pew Charitable Trusts, 101, 104

Pluralism Project, 6, 9, 12, 15, 18, 19, 21,

22, 23, 46, 91–99, 137, 144, 149, 153, 209

Prayer for World Peace, 59, 60, 61

Program for Religion in Secondary Education, 149

Public Allies, 170

R

Ramadan, Tariq, 16

Rawls, John, 18

Religions of New York, 157, 159, 162, 167

Religious Freedom Young Adult Network, 66, 73, 74

Religious Identity, 15, 16, 18, 22, 35, 36, 37

Religious Life Team, 120, 121

Religious Studies in Secondary Schools, 10, 137, 145–154

Religious Workers Association, 141

S

Sacks, Jonathan, 17, 20, 23

secondary schools, 147, 148, 151

Seeking Common Ground, 233, 235, 236

Seminarians Interacting, 9, 101–108

Spirit into Action, 11, 209–217, 261

T

Teach for America, 170

Ten Commandments, 138, 140

Transnational Interfaith Youth Network, 51–61

U

UN International Conferences, 55

Unitarian Universalist Church, 209

United Nations, 53, 55, 57, 59–61, 75, 79, 194–195, 214, 215

United Religions Initiative, 8, 12, 75–82, 170

University of Chicago, 5, 6, 9, 131, 134

University of Illinois, 9, 12, 125–129, 263

V

Vietnam War, 1

W

Walzer, Michael, 18

Wellesley College, 9, 109–124, 263

World Conference on Religion and Peace, 8, 12, 51–63

World War II, 18

Wuthnow, Robert, 19

Y

Youth Council, 177–182

Youth Cultural Exchange Program, 184

Youth Theology Institute, 35

About the Contributors

ZULFIKHAR AKRAM, Co-ordinator of the International Association for Religious Freedom (IARF) in South Asia, works to promote religious freedom and interfaith understanding in the region. He organizes and manages IARF activities with young adults, member groups and country chapters in India, Nepal, Pakistan and Sri Lanka. In October 2001 he was given the responsibility of administering the IARF Gujarat International Young Adult Project whose overall in-charge was RAMOLA SUNDRAM, IARF's UK-based International Young Adult Programme Coordinator. Her major role is to oversee the interfaith projects of the global Religious Freedom Young Adult Network (RFYN). For more information see www.iarf.net.

SAVVA AMUSIN received his Bachelor's of Science in Business and Psychology from the University of Illinois. During his time at the University he was the president of Bridges Dialogue Group on the Middle East and a lead organizer for the first National Day of Interfaith Youth Service. He is currently working with a team of students to put together the second annual National Day.

ANNAPURNA ASTLEY graduated from Harvard University in 1997 with a degree in the Comparative Study of Religion. She currently teaches and organizes programs for youth in Florida, and lives at Kashi Ashram, an interfaith spiritual community. She has participated in numerous interfaith events both locally and globally, and co-founded Spirit into Action, an interfaith youth program.

SARAH BIER studied Middle Eastern Conflict Resolution at the University of Illinois. There she was a leader of the Bridges Dialogue Group on the Middle East and a lead organizer for the first National Day of Interfaith Youth Service and facilitated several other intercultural and interfaith encounters.

ALISON L. BODEN is an ordained minister in the United Church of Christ and serves as Dean of Rockefeller Memorial Chapel, Senior Lecturer in the Divinity School and the College, and Co-Chair of the Board of the Human Rights Program at the University of Chicago. She received a bachelor's degree from Vassar, the M.Div. from Union Theological Seminary in New York, and a Ph.D. from the University of Bradford (UK). Her previous publications include articles and chapters on religion in higher education, religion and vocation, pediatric AIDS, and economic justice.

JOSH BORKIN received his BA from Clark University in 1996 and his MA in United States Cultural History from Clark University in 1997. Josh has worked with young people in several different capacities over the last eight years, including directing summer camps in Maryland, teaching in British Columbia, Canada and helping run student facilitator workshops in the Uptown neighborhood of Chicago. Josh served as both the Youth Director and the Education Coordinator at the Council for the Parliament for World Religions for several years. He is currently pursuing an Ed.D. at Teacher's College, Columbia University.

PATRICE BRODEUR has recently been appointed Canada Research Chair on Islam, Pluralism, and Globalization at the University of Montreal in the Faculty of Theology and the Science of Religions. Born in Canada and educated also in Israel and Jordan, he obtained his Ph.D. from Harvard University in 1999. He has published on a variety of mostly contemporary subjects in Islamic and Religious Studies, from theory to applied religion. He has been active internationally in the field of interreligious dialogue and has begun articulating theoretical implications for the interdisciplinary academic study of religion. He was a fellow at the Center for the Study of World Religions at Harvard University (1997–1998) and received a summer National Endowment for the Humanities grant to study Islam at the Center for Muslim-Christian Understanding at Georgetown University (1999).

For JULIE EBERLY, interfaith work is more than a charge, it is a lifestyle; it is a calling. As Director of Development and Outreach for Interfaith Ministries for Greater Houston (IM) it is Julie's passion to bring people of all faiths together in dialogue and in service to the community. Her commitment to furthering the strength of the shared beliefs of all faith communities has spanned more than eighteen years in the corporate world and as a participant in international volunteer work. Her work has taken her to Albania, India, Greece, Turkey, Mexico and Guatemala. She also has served on numerous school and community boards both in California and Texas. In Houston she has presided over the largest interfaith gathering of service projects in IM's history. These include IM's Interfaith Day of Service, Spiritual Gathering for Women of Faith and IM's Interfaith Youth Leadership Council.

LORI EISENBERG earned her B.A. from New College and her Ed.M. from Harvard Graduate School of Education where she studied the use of the arts in social awareness education. She currently serves as a board member of the Young Leadership Council of the International Council of Christians and Jews and works as an educator in the Boston area.

MELODYE FELDMAN is the founding executive director of the grass-roots organization Seeking Common Ground. She has over 25 years of non-profit experience primarily working with women and children. She co-directs the Face to Face/Faith to Faith program. Her religious teachings motivate her to "seek peace and pursue it" and she is committed to working with young people from diverse religious backgrounds promoting interfaith dialogue and social transformation. Melodye holds a Bachelor of Science degree in Philosophy of Education and Human Services from Northeastern University, Boston, Massachusetts, and an MSW from the University of Denver Graduate School of Social Work.

MICHAEL GOGGIN earned his BSFS degree from the Edmund A. Walsh School of Foreign Service at Georgetown University in Washington, D.C., in 1992. Mike currently serves the InterFaith Conference of Metropolitan Washington (IFC) as Director of High School & College Interfaith Programs and the Congregational Partnerships Project. Mike also serves as Secretary of the North American Interfaith Network (NAIN), an umbrella group of 65 interfaith organizations in Canada, the United States and Mexico, and he was previously Young Adult Chairperson. At Washington Theological Union, Mike is an MA Candidate in Theology (2005) with a concentration in Word and Worship.

JOE HALL is founder and President of the Ghetto Film School (GFS) an arts-based youth media organization located in the South Bronx. Joe has trained grassroots practitioners, university students and faculty, government and foundation staff on assets-based youth development practice through workshops and lectures in Latin America, Europe, India, Africa and the United States. His publishing credits include several articles and chapters in this area, as well as the appreciative inquiry organizational development model. Joe holds a Master's degree in social administration from Columbia University and an executive certificate from the Weatherhead School of Management at Case Western University. He also attended the graduate production program at the University of Southern California's (USC) School of Cinema and Television. A resident of Hunts Point/Longwood, Joe has worked the last 15 years designing and managing arts and human service programs in the community.

GROVE HARRIS is the Managing Director for the Pluralism Project. Since joining the Project in 1993, her research and writing has included the section on Paganism for the CD-ROM *On Common Ground: World Religions in America*, contributions to publications such as *Reclaiming Quarterly* and *Park Ridge Center Bulletin* and a chapter on Wicca and Healing, "Healing through Chanting and Connection," for *Religious*

Healing in America, Oxford University Press, 2004. She speaks regularly on behalf of the Pluralism Project at conferences and schools, as well as presenting her own work at academic conferences. She earned her B.A. in Women's Studies, Business, and Religion from the University of Massachusetts (1992). Her Master's in Divinity degree from Harvard Divinity School (1996) incorporated studies of organizational development and business management into the study of religion and ethics. She is an initiated Wiccan Priestess, and leads public rituals for groups ranging in size from 20 to 300.

KATHARINE HENDERSON is the Executive Vice President of Auburn Theological Seminary in New York City. She also develops and directs program initiatives, including multi-faith programs of particular interest to women. She is co-director of Face to Face/Faith to Faith, a multi-faith leadership program for teenagers from around the world. Henderson received a doctorate in higher education from Teachers College, Columbia University in 2000. A book based on her dissertation on the Public Leadership of Women of Faith is currently underway.

ARIELLE HERTZBERG is a Political Science major at the University of Illinois Urbana-Champaign. With active involvement in Model United Nations, she has strong focus towards international relations and building interfaith, multi-cultural dialogue.

ROZINA KANCHWALA is studying International Studies and Economics at the University of Illinois, focusing on human rights in development in Africa. She was the volunteer head for a year and on the executive board as the outreach coordinator for the Muslim Students Association. She worked with Bridges dialogue group and helped organize the first annual NDIYS, as well as starting Interfaith in Action.

VICTOR H. KAZANJIAN, JR. is the Dean of Religious and Spiritual Life at Wellesley College where he nurtures the religious and spiritual life of the College, building community among people of diverse religious backgrounds and working with faculty, staff and students to incorporate spirituality into the educational experience. Victor created and now oversees a new multi-faith program of religious and spiritual life which seeks to respond to the rich diversity of religious traditions and spiritual beliefs represented among community members through a vision of a multi-faith community in which all particular expressions of faith are celebrated. At Wellesley, he also serves as Co-director of the Peace & Justice Studies Program and is the Director of the Winter Session in India Program. Dean Kazanjian is also the co-founder and president of Education as Transformation, a national project engaging colleges and universities in the exploration of issues of religious pluralism and spirituality in higher education.

JAMES (JIM) P. KEEN teaches at Antioch College where he holds the title College Professor. He is co-author of *Common Fire: Leading Lives of Commitment in a Complex World*, (Beacon Press, 1996). He is co-founder of the Initiative for Authenticity and Spirituality in Higher Education and currently serves as Vice President of Education as Transformation. Jim is also active as a consultant and coach in the area of leadership development.

J. NATHAN KLINE earned a Master's from the Divinity School of the University of Chicago. For many years he served as the interreligious program specialist for the Chicago office of the National Conference for Community and Justice (NCCJ), a human relations organization dedicated to fighting bias, bigotry, and racism in America, and promotion of interfaith understanding. Nathan is currently a military chaplain stationed in Iraq.

MARIAH NEUROTH is the Program Director for the Chicago Action Program at Interfaith Youth Core. She received her Bachelor's from the University of Missouri in Interdisciplinary Studies, with emphasis on Sociology, Psychology, Women's Studies and African Studies. She worked for two years as the Youth Program Coordinator for Interfaith Refugee and Immigration Ministries in Chicago. During this time, Mariah committed herself to exposing youth to the arts as well as promoting and organizing local artists and writers. She is a founding member of *Hermit*, a local arts organization.

EBOO PATEL is the Founder and Executive Director of the Interfaith Youth Core. He earned his doctorate in the Sociology of Religion from the University of Oxford, where he studied on a Rhodes Scholarship. He serves on the Board of National Public Radio's "This I Believe" project and the Interfaith Initiative of the Points of Light Foundation and is President of the Board of *CrossCurrents* Magazine. Eboo writes regularly for international publications and has given talks at venues all over the world, including UNESCO Headquarters in Paris, Harvard University and the Nobel Peace Prize Forum, where he appeared with President Jimmy Carter. He has been profiled by the *Sunday Chicago Tribune, Conscious Choice Magazine,* and *Utne* Magazine, which named him one of "thirty social visionaries under thirty changing the world." Eboo is an Ashoka Fellow, selected as part of an elite international network of "social entrepreneurs" implementing ideas with the potential to change the pattern of our society. Eboo is currently writing a book on the interfaith youth movement with Beacon Press.

NICHOLAS PRICE studies Religion at the University of Illinois. He is currently working for the Global Crossroads Living/Learning community where he is responsible for promoting interfaith dialogue and cooperation between international students and American students.

PAUL RAUSHENBUSH is the Associate Dean of Religious Life at Princeton University where he heads up the inter-religious engagement on campus. He is a contrubuting editor for Beliefnet.com where he has an advice column: "Ask Pastor Paul." Rev. Raushenbush has recently released a book entitled *Teen Spirit: One World, Many Paths* published by Health Communications Inc. Paul studied religion at Macalester College before taking a few years off to start and run a record company in Barcelona, Spain. He attended Union Theological Seminary in New York City where he graduated with honors. An ordained American Baptist minister, Rev. Raushenbush served at Seattle First Baptist Church, the Presbyterian Chaplaincy at Columbia University and as College and Young Adult Minister at the Riverside Church in New York City before starting at Princeton.

JANE S. RECHTMAN teaches at the Masters School, an independent school in New York. Her teaching experience includes a maximum security prison, HBO, community college, and a nursery school. Jane is involved with a number of interfaith organizations and is co-author or editor of two books published by the Council for Spiritual and Ethical Education: *The Word Book: God, Sin and All That Stuff* with Barbara Jones, and *The Compendium of World Religions* with Terry Ward. Jane has a Master's in Divinity from Union Theological Seminary and is a practicing Jew with Buddhist leanings. She lives with her husband and sons in Ossining, New York.

SIDNEY SCHWARZ is the founder and president of PANIM: The Institute for Jewish Leadership and Values, an educational foundation dedicated to the renewal of American Jewish life through the integration of Judaic learning, values and social responsibility. Dr. Schwarz previously served as the executive director of the Jewish Community Council of Greater Washington, D.C. He is the founding rabbi of Adat Shalom Reconstructionist Congregation in Rockville, Md., where he now is rabbi emeritus. A Ph.D. in Jewish History, Dr. Schwarz has been on the faculties of the University of Maryland, Temple University and the Reconstructionist Rabbinical College. He is one of the co-chairs of Rabbis for Human Rights, serves on the board of the American Jewish World Service and is a member of the Religious Advisory Council of the Points of Light Foundation. Rabbi Schwarz is the co-author of *Jewish Civics: A Tikkun Olam/World Repair Manual* (1994) and *Jews, Judaism and Civic Responsibility* (1998) and *Finding a Spiritual*

Home (Jossey-Bass, Spring 2000). His new book is *Judaism and Justice: Values, Community and Identity*, to be published by Behrman House in 2004.

ALISON SIEGEL graduated from the University of Illinois at Urbana-Champaign in May 2005 with a Bachelor's Degree in Religious Studies and a Concentration in Judaica. While finishing school and job-hunting for next year, she works half-time as the religious school office manager and youth group advisor at Sinai Temple in Champaign. She is currently co-chairing the UIUC site of the National Day of Interfaith Youth Service. A former Hillel President and co-founder of Common Ground in the Holy Land, she has not only been involved with many grassroots intergroup programs at the University but has also spoken about her experiences to such groups as the Jewish Council for Public Affairs and the World Council of Jewish Communal Service.

DAVID STREIGHT is co-director of Religious Studies in Secondary Schools, a national coalition of teachers that he founded with Tom Collins in the late 1990s. Streight spent three decades as a teacher of foreign languages and religions before entering full time into the field of school psychology, where his preference was working with Spanish-speaking populations. He is the author of a book on 19th-century Provençal poetry, and the translator of a half-dozen academic texts, primarily on Islam. Streight is currently Executive Director of the Council for Spiritual and Ethical Education. He lives in Portland, Oregon.

SARAH TALCOTT: As a member of the United Religions Initiative global staff in San Francisco, Sarah Talcott has been working in the field of interfaith cooperation for more than five years. She brings to this work a passion for and understanding of diverse religious and cultural traditions through her Bachelor of Arts degree in Sociology/Cultural Anthropology at Principia College in Illinois. Sarah has served in various capacities as staff for URI—Project Coordinator, Office Manager, Grants Manager and now Youth Programs Director. In her current role, Sarah is facilitating global youth networking and interactive exchange through the URI's growing Global Youth Network, made up of more than 120 young people from more than nineteen faith traditions and twenty-six interfaith youth groups in thirty countries.

ANDREW UNGER (co-author on Ghetto Film School article with Joe Hall) is a filmmaker and author living in New York City. He graduated Phi Beta Kappa from Amherst College with distinction in English and Film Studies, starting his professional career as Program Director with the Ghetto Film School (GFS). Andrew is currently producing films and education media through his company Five Boro Productions.

MATTHEW WEINER is a graduate of Harvard Divinity School—where he studied comparative religious ethics. He is Director of Programming at the Interfaith Center of New York, and previously served as Coordinator of the Urban Program and as an academic fellow. During his work in the Urban Program, Mr. Weiner created the Religions of New York project, which now serves as the central project for the ICNY. He has served as a consultant on religion to the American Red Cross, HBO, Cornell University, New School, and the New York State Unified Court System, and has made presentations to CNN, State University of New York and the Asia Society. Previously, he was the director of Stories for Peace, a children's book and interfaith peace project in Sri Lanka. He has worked for the Office of Tibet and the Project on Religion and Human Rights. He has written about Buddhism, and interfaith dialogue.

KAREN WOOD is Associate Chaplain for Vocational Exploration at Willamette University in Oregon.

TIMUR YUSKAEV is Program Coordinator and an Academic Fellow at the Interfaith Center of New York. He is a co-coordinator of the semi-annual Rabbi Marshall T. Meyer Retreats on Social Justice. As Director of Muslims in New York Civic Life project, he also facilitates the Center's work with Muslim communities in New York City. He holds a M.A. in Comparative Religion from the University of Colorado, Boulder, and a B.A. in History from Bard College. He is an author of several articles that primarily focus on contemporary Muslim communities in the U.S., including: Redeeming the Nation: Redemption Theology in African-American Islam, Studies in Contemporary Islam, Vol. 1, No. 1 (Spring, 1999) and African-American Islam in Transformation: From Black Nationalism to Orthodox Islam, *Bard Journal of Social Sciences*, Vol. 2, No. 7–8 (April-May 1994).